This book is needed as it contains much basic information not found in other writing books. Well-written, it will be used as a reference book for years to come. *A Step in the Write Direction* could be written only by someone like Donna Clark Goodrich, who has gathered an immense amount of information over the years and wants to share it with others.

—**Jewell Johnson**
Author of *Change Your World, 365 Daily Devotions for Women,*
and *The Top 100 Christian Women*

What a resource! Answers so many questions—from taxes to copyright to the craft of writing. I don't see anything that needs to be changed or added.

—**Kathy Hardee**
Author

D1289198

A Step in the

Write

Direction

A Step in the

Write
Direction

The Complete How-to Book for Christian Writers

Donna Clark
Goodrich
Foreword by Sally Stuart

UPWRITE BOOKS

A Division of WINEPRESS PUBLISHING

UpWrite Press (a division of WinePress Publishing, PO Box 428, Enumclaw, WA 98022) functions only as book publisher. As such, the ultimate design, content, editorial accuracy, and views expressed or implied in this work are those of the author.

ISBN 13: 978-1-4141-1546-7
ISBN 10: 1-4141-1546-6
Library of Congress Catalog Card Number: 2009907195

Dedicated to:

My husband, *Gary,* who has truly been the "wind
beneath my wings," daughter *Janet,* son-in-law *Ned*
—who's more like a son, son *Robert,* daughter *Patty,*
and our two granddaughters, *Heather* and *Lindsay.*

to:
My sister, *Norma Irish,* and brothers, *Melvin* and
Orville Clark, who have been there for me my
entire life and encouraged me in my writing.

to:
My weekly critique group—Tuesday's Children—
who has endured many workshops in which
this material was taught, who has encouraged and
supported me in the writing of it, and who
has read this book one chapter at a time. Thanks to:
*Betty Arthurs, Carol Boley, Linda Carlblom,
Marsha Crockett, Marion Hocking, Andrea
Huelsenbeck, Jane Jiminez, Peggy Levesque,
Joy Moore, Judy Robertson, Pat Smith,* and *Sharon Wilkins,*
and my second critique group—*Jewell Johnson* and *Rosemarie
Malroy.* These writers have all helped shape this book—and
me—through their friendship and their prayers. Thank you!

to:
My bestest friend for over sixty years, *Kathy Taylor,*

and my greatest thanks to:
my Lord and Savior Jesus Christ
who put the desire within me to write.

I have spent my life stringing and unstringing
my instrument and the song I came to
sing remains unsung.

—Rabindranath Tagore

Contents

Foreword xiii

Writing Is a Calling xv

Frequently Asked Questions xvii

Advice for a Beginning Writer xix

Introduction xxiii

PART I: GETTING STARTED

1. Setting Up Your Office 29
   Organization . . . Supplies . . . Your Office Space.

PART II: CHOOSING YOUR FIELD OF WRITING

2. Fiction 39
   Short Stories . . . Titles . . . Length . . . Theme . . . Audience . . . Parts of a Short
   Story . . . Names . . . Dialogue . . . Developing Characters . . . Action . . . Plots . . .
   Leads . . . Setting . . . Ending . . . Differences and Similarities Between a Short Story
   and a Novel . . . Book Proposal for Novels.

3. Nonfiction. 55

Theme . . . Outline . . . Slant . . . Leads . . . Keep It Simple . . . Don't Say the Same Thing Twice . . . Use Subheads, Lists, and Sidebars . . . Check Your Facts . . . Avoid Generalities . . . Ideas for Writing Articles . . . Sources for Quotations . . . Writing for Women's Magazines . . . How Can I Get Started Writing Nonfiction?

4. Writing Devotionals and Fillers. 63

Differences Between a Devotional and a Filler . . . Similarities of a Devotional and a Filler . . . Marketing Your Devotionals and Fillers . . . Assignments . . . Twelve Steps to Writing a Devotional . . . Devotional Books . . . Do's and Don'ts For Writing Devotionals.

5. Writing and Selling Your Poetry 71

Format . . . Editing Your Poetry . . . Marketing Your Poetry . . . Marketing Chart . . . Why Poems Are Rejected . . . Change Your Style . . . Write for the Holidays . . . Writing Poetry for Children . . . Contests . . . Self-Publishing.

6. Writing for Newspapers. 87

Columns . . . Stringers . . . Letters to the Editor . . . Op-Eds.

7. Conducting An Effective Interview 91

Call for Appointment . . . Prepare Ahead . . . Getting Acquainted . . . Using a Tape Recorder . . . Stick to the Subject . . . Spin-Off Articles . . . Editor/Writer Interviews . . . After the Interview.

8. Writing Travel Articles. 97

Types of Articles . . . Where to Obtain Information . . . Photographs . . . The Grass Isn't Always Greener Somewhere Else.

9. Writing for Children 101

Ten Hints on Writing for Children . . . Write for Parents . . . Types of Children's Books . . . Query Letters . . . Illustrations . . . Writing for Take-Home Papers and Children's Magazines . . . Writing for Teens . . . Needs of Children.

10. Writing the Personal Experience Story 109

Why Personal Experience Stories Are Popular . . . The Personal Experience Article/ Book . . . Select a Theme . . . Use the Five Senses . . . Why Are You Writing This Story? . . . Be Honest . . . Idea Starters . . . God's Timing Is Always Right . . . Marketing Your Personal Experience Story . . . Family Histories.

11. Other Types of Writing 121

Bible Studies . . . Puzzles . . . Book Reviews . . . Humor . . . Things You Can Write for Christian Publications.

PART III: WRITING YOUR MANUSCRIPT

12. **Preparing a Manuscript for Publication** 135
    Article Format . . . Choosing a Title . . . Byline . . . Using Scripture in Your Writing . . . Hiring a Typist . . . Finished Manuscript.

13. **Writing and Selling Your First Book** 143
    Marketability (Personal Experience Books, How-to Books, Entertainment) . . . Permissions . . . Outlining Your Book . . . Finding An Agent . . . Finding a Publisher . . . Book Proposal for Nonfiction . . . Sample Chapters . . . e-Books.

14. **Where to Get Ideas** 163
    Newspapers and magazines . . . Children's Activities . . . Children's Quotations . . . Everyday Events . . . God's Mysterious Ways . . . The Bible . . . An Event from the Past.

15. **Editing Hints** 171
    Samples/Exercises.

16. **How to Sell What You Write** 185
    Marketing Tools . . . Periodical Analysis Sheet . . . Rights . . . Record Keeping . . . Manuscript Submission Forms . . . Marketing Books and Periodicals.

PART IV: OTHER SOURCES OF INCOME

17. **Other Sources of Income** 203
    Proofreading . . . Editing . . . Speaking . . . Teaching . . . Workshops/Conferences . . . Manuscript Reviewer.

PART V: THE CHALLENGES OF BEING A WRITER

18. **Writer's Block** 229
19. **Time Management** 235
20. **How to Handle Rejection** 247
21. **Social Networking and Online Promotion** 255

Conclusion 267

Appendix A: Using Scripture in Your Writing 271
Appendix B: Glossary of Terms 279

Appendix C: Trademarks 291

Appendix D: Creative Collaborations 299

Appendix E: Copyright Information 301

Appendix F: Microsoft Word Shortcuts 305

Appendix G: Forming a Christian Writers' Group 307

Appendix H: Ten Ways to Mentor Your Mentor 317

Appendix I: Guidelines for Devotional Periodicals 321

Appendix J: Income Taxes for Writers 339

Endnotes 347

Foreword

S O YOU WANT to be a writer! I understand that feeling. Although I'm not one of those people who grew up always wanting to write, from the time I wrote my first article in the late 1960s I've wanted to do nothing else. Writing consumes my time and my passion.

I hear from would-be writers like you all the time. People who started with a great more passion than I did, but who have no idea how to move from the manuscript phase to publication. Although my *Christian Writers' Market Guide* will lead you to appropriate markets for your writing projects—and tell you how to submit to them—there is so much more you need to know to prepare for that giant step toward publication.

Writing is like any other new business you might want to get into. It has its own rules, guidelines, and even language. If you want to enter the arena of publishing, you first need to be in the know about what preliminary steps you need to take—and what is expected of you as a writer. *A Step in the Write Direction* by Donna Clark Goodrich is a book that is going to help you fill in all those blanks and lead you more confidently and professionally toward seeing your words in print.

Many of those writers I hear from who want to know how to get published have been working sometimes for years on their writing project. They may hold in their hands a finished or nearly finished project that they want to see published as quickly as possible. They often assume that it's just a matter of writing what they want to say, sending it off to an editor, and it gets published. What they don't understand—as I didn't at the beginning—is that editors have a list of guidelines that has been prepared to help the writer come to them with a manuscript that fits their criteria—such as the right length and the right slant to fit their specific needs. And ultimately it needs to be on a topic their readers want to read about.

What this means for you as a writer is that your manuscript can be too long or too short or does not target the appropriate market for that publisher. It is critical that you see and follow those guidelines from the beginning of your writing project so you don't have to go back to square one and do a lot of rewriting. *A Step in the Write Direction* will help you take all those necessary steps to success.

Another problem I run into quite often is expressed by writers who have written something, but they don't know what category it falls into when identifying potential markets in the market guide. One of the features of this how-to guide is that it clearly identifies the different genres and will help you find your particular niche. This is a critical step in both writing with a specific audience in mind and finding those publications or book publishers open to what you have to offer.

Unfortunately I find a lot of writers who may have a great premise for their writing project, but it is written to too broad an audience—or to no identifiable audience at all. For example, writing a book or story for children probably won't sell unless you target it to children of a particular age. Or, writing an article on money management for adults may not sell unless you target it to adults in a certain stage in life. Each publication or publisher targets a specific audience, so you need to know who that audience is and write your material to reflect their specific needs.

Although I always encourage writers to attend writers' conferences—where they will learn a lot about writing in a short period of time—I know that with so many details to remember to be successful in this business, they also need a comprehensive how-to-write book that will fill in any gaps in their learning. *A Step in the Write Direction* will let you seek out those details on each aspect of the writing and selling process. I encourage you to not only read it carefully initially, but to come back to it again and again as you run across aspects of the business you don't understand. This knowledge will help you immensely as you navigate that carefully defined road to publication.

In buying and reading this book, you are taking a critical step toward finding success as a published writer. It is definitely *A Step in the **Write** Direction.*

—**Sally E. Stuart**
Christian Writers' Market Guide
Stuartcwmg@aol.com
www.stuartmarket.com
www.stuartmarket.blogspot.com

Writing Is a Calling

I, therefore . . . beseech you to walk worthy of the calling to which you were called.

—Eph. 4:1 (NKJV)

Everyone has his own specific vocation mission in life; everyone must carry out a concrete assignment that demands fulfillment. He cannot be replaced nor can his life be repeated. Thus, everyone's task is as unique as his specific opportunity to implement it.

—Victor Frankl[1]

YOU KNOW YOU'RE called to write when:

- You're tired and want to go to bed but there's something inside that must be put down on paper.
- Unexpected bills arise and you're offered a good or better job, but you feel God wants you to devote more time to writing.
- You're asked to be the neighborhood chauffeur or babysitter (because you're home all day), or the PTA public relations chairman (because you're a writer), and you have to say no because of your ache to write.
- None of your family understands why you skip a favorite TV show and sit at your computer for so long, sometimes with tears in your eyes.
- Money is tight, but you feel led to take a writing course or attend a conference.

- Your favorite "inspired" article or book proposal is sent out twelve times *and* returned twelve times with only a form letter, or no letter at all, but you send it out again because you believe in it.

Then you must know that your writing is not just a hobby but a *calling*. You'll know it's not the writing that's important, but the message you have to share. And you'll know that it's not you, but Christ who lives in you (Gal. 2:20).

Sherwood Wirt, the late editor of *Decision* magazine, spoke the following words many years ago, but they still hold true for us today:

Either we Christian writers mean business about winning souls for God, or we should go out of business . . . . If you have been ordained to write, woe to you if you put everything else first. Woe to you if you do not give to God the best part of the day when you are most alert, when . . . the juices are flowing and the mind is creative . . . .

We have the greatest subject in all history, the Man from Nazareth . . . the greatest commodity, the gospel; the greatest book, the Bible; the greatest gift to offer, eternal salvation. If that doesn't motivate us . . . we're in trouble.[2]

Frequently Asked Questions

Question   **See Page**

What advice do you have for a beginning writer? xix
What supplies do I need to get started? 30
What can I do if I don't have a separate room I can use for an office? 34
What reference books do I need to get started? 32
Do I need an agent? 149
What is a query letter? 40, 154
What should be included in a book proposal? .48, 154
How can I make my characters more real? 44
Should I include my Social Security number on my manuscript? 135
Do I need to put a copyright notice on my manuscript? 135
Do I need to register my copyright with the Library of Congress? 135
In what format should I type my poetry? 72
    Articles and short stories? 135
    Devotionals? 64
How can I obtain writers' guidelines? 73, 187
How can I obtain a sample copy of a magazine? 73, 187
Are titles important? 40, 136
When should I use a pen name? 137

Question   **See Page**

What's the difference between "showing" and "telling"? 43, 99, 111, 171

Can I use real names and places in my stories and articles? 112

When do I have to get permission for a quotation? 144

Can I quote words of a song without permission? 144

How much Scripture can I use without obtaining permission? 273

Where do I show what Bible translation I am using? 271

How can I develop a strong lead? 46, 57

What does it mean when an editor says my writing is too "preachy"? 250

What's the difference between a devotional and a filler? 63

How can I get an assignment to write devotionals? 66

Where can I get ideas? 163

Can I sell humor to the Christian market? 127

Why do my manuscripts keep getting rejected? 76, 248

How do I know if a contest is legitimate? 82

How do I get into newspaper writing? 87

How can I write travel articles without traveling? 97

Is it easier to write for children? 101

What are the age breakdowns for children's books? 103

How do I know where to send my manuscripts? 185

How can I keep track of where I send my manuscripts? 195

Can I sell an article more than once? 192

How can I find time to write? 235

How can I overcome writer's block? 229

How can I keep from getting discouraged when I receive a rejection? 247, 267

How do I show my income and expenses when I file my income taxes? 339

How can I find a good writers' group? . . . . .xx, 307

Advice for a Beginning Writer

I RECEIVED A letter from a single mother of four children who asked for tips on how to begin writing. She said that starting her writing career would lift her as a person and, hopefully, fulfill some of her financial needs. My response follows:

Dear Aspiring Writer,

I received your letter asking for tips on how to begin writing professionally. I'll try to answer your questions in this letter.

The most important thing is having a call to write. I feel a writer is called to write as much as a minister is called to preach. In fact, our influence spreads farther than a preacher's. Our ministry travels around the world and goes on even after we're gone. So make sure God is calling you to write. Without this call, you won't have anything to fall back on during the inevitable discouraging times.

Having a call to write is not enough, however. Like any other trade, writing is a learned skill. Consider the scripture in Colossians 3:23 that says, "Whatever you do, work at it with all your heart, as working for the Lord, not for men" (NIV). You may not have the money to invest in conferences, books, CDs, and tapes, but you can find many resources at your public library. Some will be on writing in general: typing format, how to submit a proposal to a publisher, writing terms, and so on. Then you can branch out into books on the specific fields of writing you enjoy, such as poetry, children's writing, fiction, and nonfiction. You may also want to pick up some books on general English—parts of speech, punctuation, and sentence structure.

If finances allow, consider taking a class or two on writing or English at night school or junior college. Scholarships and grants are often available, especially for single mothers.

You might wonder with four children where you will find the time to write. Conference instructors often suggest writing two hours every day, but this can heap guilt on those unable to find this amount in a busy day. Many writers still have children at home; perhaps they're also caring for aging parents or a sick spouse, or they're working a full-time job. In this case, I suggest setting a *workable* goal such as: "This week I'll read a book on writing," or "I'll outline an article." If that doesn't work for you, then set a goal of "This month I'll . . . "

You said you wanted writing to "fulfill" you as a person. It can, but it's more important to think how your writing can help meet the needs of others. Ask yourself: "What are my readers going through, what are they looking for, and how can I help meet their needs?" Use the challenges in your life that God has brought you through to encourage someone else.

As far as financial fulfillment, yes, there is some, but unfortunately the Christian market doesn't pay as well as secular markets. While we receive a "reward" through grateful letters from readers, I know that doesn't pay bills. Most of the income for Christian writers comes in two ways. First, after you've sold an article or story to a magazine and it is published, you can sell reprints to other denominational periodicals.

The other source of income is writing and selling books. Some conference instructors advise a new writer to begin with articles, but it's more important to write what God has laid on your heart. If God has called you to write a book, then start working on it. However, while you are writing your book, develop some of the highlights into articles. That way, you're not only earning money, but your name becomes familiar to readers and to editors.

Another help is to join a writers' group in your area. Your pastor or local librarian may know of one. If not, put a notice on the church page of your newspaper that you would like to meet with other Christian writers, and give a location and time. Being around other writers will provide encouragement and support, answers to your questions, critiques for your manuscripts, and prospective markets.

Also, if you get a chance, attend a conference. *Christian Communicator,* a magazine for Christian writers and speakers, gives upcoming conferences. The *Christian Writers' Market Guide,* edited by Sally Stuart, also lists conferences by state, or you can search for "Christian Writers Conferences" on the Internet.

The two most important things to remember as a beginning writer are 1) give yourself time, and 2) don't be discouraged. Nothing worthwhile comes easy. I recently read a good adage by George Lorimer that can be adapted for writers: "You've got to get up every morning with determination if you're going to go to bed with satisfaction."

I hope these suggestions help. God bless you.

Introduction

YOU'VE ALWAYS WANTED to write; you have a deep ache that just won't quit; or, as one woman at a writer's conference shared, "There's a writer inside me yearning to get out." So what is your excuse for *not* writing?

You don't have a college degree? Saint Francis of Assisi was a simple and uneducated man, who possessed only a basic knowledge of the alphabet, but he left behind a body of writing, including two brief handwritten texts on parchment. John Steinbeck left Stanford University without a degree, as he disliked the academia lifestyle. Ernest Hemingway did not attend college but served in the ambulance corps in World War I and worked as a journalist in Kansas City and Toronto.

You don't have time? I have written in a nine-room parsonage with three children under three. I wrote during their naps, waiting for doctors' appointments, even sitting in restrooms (hey, it was quiet!). Now I'm writing between teaching at conferences, editing and proofreading for writers and publishers, and caring for a disabled husband. Mary Higgins Clark wrote many of her books after she became a widow with five young children.

You don't have an office? Dining room tables are adaptable; friends have empty houses while they're at work; churches have empty classrooms; fast-food restaurants have empty tables. A writer in the Soviet Union, denied paper and pencil during most of her 3½ years in jail—120 days in a cell where the temperature was kept just above freezing—used what was left of a burned matchstick to carve out poems in a bar of soap. After reading a completed poem over and over, until she committed it to memory, she then washed it away. Upon her release, she had written 250 poems.[1]

You don't type? Do you have a skill a typist can use? Exchange services with him or her.

You don't have a computer? Handwrite your manuscript, then go to a library or coffee shop and use their computers.

Lack of confidence? My friend Kitty Chappell almost didn't finish her autobiography, *I Can Forgive If I Want To* (first published as *Sins of a Father: Forgiving the Unforgivable*) because she feared it would be boring. "Who cares about my experiences and how I overcame them?" she fretted. It not only sold, but now is being translated into five languages.[2]

You're too old? Cervantes was almost sixty when he began *Don Quixote*. Thomas Hardy's greatest poetry was written between the ages of seventy-five and eighty-five. Verdi was still composing at eighty-five, and, of course, the whole world knows of Grandma Moses who began painting at seventy-two and was still going strong at one hundred.

What am I saying? If you want to write, if you feel you're called to write, you will find the time and place to write. The following quotation says it best:

If you *want* to be a writer, you won't.
If you *have* to be a writer, you will.

Once an idea for a story or an article gets inside you, it will continue to nag away until you feel you will burst if you don't put it on paper.

A conference speaker tells the story of seeing a minister looking over a book table at a pastors' retreat. Finally, he turned away and said despondently, "There's nothing here to help me." The speaker asked the students gathered in the auditorium, "Did God call one of *you* to write a book that would meet the needs of that minister and you failed to do it?" Someone is waiting for what you have to write.

I cannot remember a time I didn't want to write. I wrote my first poem out of necessity when I was nine years old. It was Mother's Day and I didn't have money to buy my mother a gift so I wrote her a poem. The second one I wrote at the age of ten for Memorial Day. Our minister distributed copies to church members as they walked into the service. I wrote my third poem at the age of eleven when my dad walked out of his twenty-two-year marriage to my mother. I found even at that young age I could express my feelings on paper.

Every writer has someone to thank for helping him or her get started. I have five people:

The first is a children's librarian in Jackson, Michigan. She introduced me to *The Writer* magazine when I was nine years old and gave me a chance to read my writings at the annual talent show in the library auditorium. In 1980, I went back to my hometown and visited the library. As I climbed the circular staircase, I stopped and took a deep breath, savoring the musty odor peculiar to an old library. All the old memories came back. I walked up to the desk and, in my mind's eye, I could still see her sitting there. Thank you, *Frances Burnside*.

In the fifth and sixth grade, my brother and I were placed in a class at the old Pearl School in Jackson called the "Opportunity Room," similar to the accelerated classrooms of today. We were taught how to use the library for research, how to outline and give speeches, and how to write book reports. We were also encouraged to write poetry, short stories, and articles. Many times the teacher would rip up my writing and say, "You can do better than that." She saw something in me that others could not. Thank you, *Helen Nichols*.

At the age of twenty, I received a job offer at our denominational publishing house in Kansas City, but I didn't have the bus fare for the interview. That Sunday a friend approached me at church. "My husband and I have talked it over," she said. "We'd like to see you get that job," and she handed me enough for the ticket. I made the trip and was hired. Thank you, *Mabel Mathias*.

If ever a person had patience, it was my new boss at the publishing house—the book editor. I had a love for writing, but only one year of ninth-grade typing. However, my on-the-job training for the next two years taught me much about the field of publishing: why books are rejected and accepted; what happens to a manuscript after it is accepted; how to check quotations for accuracy; writing for permissions and copyrights; corresponding with authors. Thank you, *Norman R. Oke*, for putting up with my poor clerical skills, and accepting instead my determination to learn and my excitement of being part of the publishing scene. What a thrill it was, twenty-five years later, to have you as the guest speaker at one of my annual Arizona conferences!

And last, but not least, my mother. She instilled in me a love for reading and for writing. After I moved away from home, she often sent me little stories or personal experiences or Scripture verses in her letters, saying, "This would make a good article." After she died, we found a large box in her closet with the words written on it, "SAVE FOR DONNA." Opening it I found hundreds of articles, poems, and quotations she had clipped from newspapers, magazines, and church bulletins over the years. Truly, "[s]he still speaks, even though [s]he is dead" (Heb. 11:4 NIV). Thank you, *Freda Clark Colburn*.

There were other people who helped along the way: people who hired me for editorial positions as a columnist and reporter for a weekly newspaper; as an associate editor for a trade magazine; as a home and garden editor for a city magazine. These were employers who overlooked the fact that I had only one year of college, but who were willing to train and encourage me and nurture my desire to write.

In 1980 I attended my first Christian writers' conference. I had sold four books and around two hundred articles, but at that point in my life writing was only a hobby, something I did whenever I found the time. However, a quote by Harold Ivan Smith at that conference literally changed my writing life. He said, "We are called to write, and I feel we will be held responsible at the Judgment for the people who are hurting that we could have helped but didn't because we didn't write what God laid on our hearts to write." This statement took writing out of the "hobby" category for me and made it a calling. From that point on, I've believed that I am as called to write as a minister is called to preach.

That conference led to the formation of two local writers' clubs. Members of one of these clubs asked me to teach a writing course, which I did for six weeks, two hours a week. A trip to Michigan when my mother was sick led to teaching this same material there in a daylong workshop. Back in Arizona, I continued to teach this workshop in other cities, and in each one, I helped form a writers' support group. This culminated in the first annual Arizona Christian Writers Conference in 1982 which I led for seven years, before turning it over to Reg Forder who later founded American Christian Writers (ACW).

Now I feel the desire to share the material from my workshops with those of you who feel as I do that your writing is a calling.

By reading this book and incorporating some of the suggestions into your writing life, you have, indeed, taken *A Step in the* Write *Direction*. I would enjoy hearing from you if you have further questions, or if you would like to share what God has done in your life. May He bless you as you realize that the rewards of writing are not in the bylines nor the checks. Rather, it is when someone calls or writes you and says, "What you wrote changed my life and now I can go on."

—**Donna Clark Goodrich**
dgood648@aol.com
www.thewritersfriend.net

Part 1

Getting Started

Chapter 1

Setting Up Your Office

Organization

F. A. ROCKWELL defines an expert as "someone who knows no more than you do, but who has it better organized and uses slides." Successful writing requires organization.

For me that means at least one four-drawer file cabinet. I did give in and put all my manuscripts—sold and unsold—on a CD, with a copy in a fireproof safe, and this emptied two drawers. For my posterity, however, I printed off copies of each one and put them in notebooks divided into nonfiction, fiction, devotionals, poetry, and so on. And I still keep paper submission records, even though I include that information on the CD with each manuscript.

One writer friend subscribes to Carbonite, a software program that automatically and securely backs up the contents of your computer for an annual fee. Even if your computer is stolen, Carbonite has it all. (See www.carbonite.com/ for more information.)

I also keep idea folders. When I get more than one idea on the same subject, I give it a tentative title and a folder. Then when I find more material relating to that theme, or I have time to work on that particular manuscript, everything is in one place. You can also scan this information into a computer file.

And I keep files of quotations and articles. (See suggested list of topics in Chapter 14, "Where to Get Ideas.") I read the newspapers with a pen and scissors, and as soon as I clip something, I immediately put the source and the date at the top. These clippings can be scanned onto a CD or into a file, but I like the idea of going through the folders looking for a specific illustration. Whenever I do this, I always get ideas for other writing projects.

Quotations or illustrations I find on the Internet, or that friends send me via e-mail, I download to a "Quotations" file. The list on page 31 and 32 gives possible categories under which to file notes and articles on *writing* topics.

Supplies

After purchasing necessary equipment, such as a computer, printer, and desk, below is a list of other supplies to keep on hand:

Toner—can get refilled at some office supply stores
Paper—copy paper fine (not "Xerox" paper; "Xerox" is a trade name, not an adjective). Go in with other writers and buy a case.
Pens, pencils, paper clips
Envelopes—#10, 9 x 12", priority
Address labels
Scotch tape; scissors
Maps, travel brochures
Stapler, staples, ruler
Tape recorder—*tapes and batteries if you're not using a digital recorder*
Camera, film, batteries, memory cards
Index cards
Rubber bands
Postage, postage scale
Legal/steno/scratch pads
File folders
Telephone message pads
Business card holder
Telephone/address/Internet address book
A "Do not disturb/Writer at work" sign (unless they bring chocolate!)

Use this list to keep track of your writing expenses. (See Appendix J for more tax information, but for now, remember to *keep track of all your expenses*. As a writer, you are considered self-employed and will have to file a Schedule C. All your writing and speaking income will be taxable; however, your business expenses are deductible as well. After you deduct your expenses from your earnings, if you make over a certain amount, you'll have to pay self-employment tax.)

You may want to purchase two sets of supplies: one for the family and one for your office.

Writing Topics

Agents
Bios (well-known people)
Bios (musicians)
Bios (authors)
Book Publishing
Book Reviews
Bulletins
Business Writing
Catholic Markets
Characterization
Children's Writing
Christian Education
Collaboration
Conferences
Copyright
Curriculum
Description
Devotionals
Dialogue
Drama
Editorials
Editors
Fiction
Fillers
General
Ghostwriting
Grants
Greeting Cards
Humor
Ideas
Indexing
Interviewing
Lead
Marketing
News Releases

Newsletters
Newspaper Writing
Nonfiction
Novels
Office
Op-Ed
Permissions
Personal Experience
Photography
Poetry
Postage
Promotion
Proofreading
Pseudonyms
Query
Quotations
Radio-TV Writing
Record Keeping
Regional
Reference Material
Rejections
Reprints
Research
Retreats
Rewriting
Seasonal
Self-publishing
Singles (writing for)
Songwriting
Speaking
Sports Writing
Subsidy Publishing
Supplies
Syndicate
Taxes

Teaching Writing
Teens (writing for)
Time Management
Titles
Tracts
Trade Journals

Transitions
Travel
Typing/Word Processing
Women

Books

Roget's *Thesaurus*
Strunk/White *Elements of Style*
World Almanac/atlas
rhyming dictionary (if a poet)
Writer's Market
Christian Writers' Market Guide
Chicago Manual of Style 15th edition
Merriam-Webster's Collegiate Dictionary 11th edition

Though you can find much of this material online, I love my books of poetry and quotations. I also have a number of biographical books in which I can look up almost any famous person and find a few paragraphs about him or her, including their date of birth and/or death. Depending on your writing, you may want to purchase medical and legal dictionaries, and other books relating to your particular genre.

You'll also find it useful to get on government mailing lists. If you send to any one of the following three agencies, you can receive tons of information on various topics. Much of this information is free; the rest can be obtained for a small fee.

U.S. Government Printing Office
Superintendent of Documents
Washington, D.C. 20402
www.gpo.gov/
(on GPO Quick Links, click on Catalog of U.S. Government Publications)

Consumer Information Center
Department CA
Pueblo, CO 81009
http://pueblo.gsa.gov/
(ask to be put on mailing and e-mail list)

The Council of Better Business Bureaus
4200 Wilson Blvd., Suite 800
Arlington, VA 22203-1838
www.bbb.org/us/
(ask for list of publications)
(information also available on this Web site for Canadian Council)

You can also get on other mailing lists such as the Department of Education and Department of Health Welfare. These offices will send you fact sheets on such topics as abortion, latchkey kids, and many others, including changes in legislation.

Computer. Before you purchase a computer, talk to someone knowledgeable in that field so you don't end up buying a bigger machine than you need for your work. Start with the basics and upgrade later to a larger hard drive and other bells and whistles.

Paper. White copy paper, 8½ x 11", fifteen- to twenty-pound weight, is acceptable. You can save money typing rough drafts by using paper that has been printed on one side. If you hear of a business moving, ask if they will give you their old stationery.

Check at copy centers too. I happened to be at a store one day when a customer picked up a large order. Looking at the top sheet, she said, "Oh, no, we put the wrong date on this. We'll have to have it redone." After she left, I asked the clerk what he was going to do with the paper. When he said, "Dump it, I guess," I took the box home.

I also worked at a school at the end of the year when they were throwing away all the mimeographed sheets, and took home a large quantity.

Envelopes (for editors that don't accept e-mail). For years I sent manuscripts in a size #10 envelope, then took another size #10 envelope, folded it in thirds, and put it inside. Now if it's three pages or less, I use a size #9 envelope for my SASE. Larger manuscripts I put inside a 10 x 13" with a 9 x 12" SASE, or I use a Priority Mail envelope.

Considering the inexpensive cost of printing a new copy, it's often cheaper to tell the editor that the manuscript doesn't have to be returned, and enclose a self-addressed, stamped envelope for the reply.

You'll reap considerable savings on envelopes if you go in with other writers and buy your #9 and #10 envelopes in a box of five hundred, and manila envelopes in a box of one hundred.

Postage. A postage scale saves trips to the post office. If your manuscript weighs over thirteen ounces, however, you must take it to the post office unless you have a postage meter.

If an editor doesn't accept manuscripts by e-mail, send them First Class or Priority Mail. You can send them Fourth Class or Media rate, but First Class is faster. Also, in case the publisher has moved, First Class will forward it to the new address. (Checking the publisher's Web site will prevent this from happening.)

File folders. Many business offices toss out folders at the end of the year. Ask friends to toss them your way. A friend brought me two boxes of file folders he found in an alley behind an office complex. I needed only to stick on new labels.

Business card holders. Collect business cards. If you need an expert opinion, statistics, or a quotation, go through your cards and select someone knowledgeable on that subject. Credit her with the quotation in your manuscript. She'll love it!

Office

Although many writers aren't fortunate enough to have a separate office in their home, try to find one place you can call your own. One writer used an extra closet with sliding doors. She put a two-drawer file cabinet at each end, stretched a plain wooden door across them for a desk, and put a bulletin board and a shelf for books on the back wall. When she finished her work for the day, she closed the doors and that was it.

Remember, what works for someone else may not work for you. Another writer remodeled his attic to have a quiet place to write. A couple of days later, a member of the family caught him moving things back downstairs. He was so used to writing with the noise of the family in the background he couldn't write in the attic. It was too quiet.

Two writers were eating lunch one day and discussing their ongoing writing projects. One complained that she couldn't seem to discipline herself. The phone would ring and, while she was talking, she would see a household job that needed to be done. That job led to another and before she knew it, it was time to pick up her daughter at school. She didn't have a time problem as she was alone from 8:00 to 2:30, but she didn't have the discipline.

The other writer lamented that she didn't have a quiet place to write. Her husband had taken an early disability retirement and was home all day, her son worked nights and was up at noon, and her daughter came home from work at 2:30. She never had any time to herself.

A light bulb flashed, and the two writers agreed to meet one day a week at the quiet house. They wrote from 8:00 to 12:00, took a lunch break, and then returned to work until 2:15. Maybe you can find a writing partner who would be willing to do this.

I once felt I had to be at a keyboard to write, and I was frustrated when I couldn't be. One summer I flew to another state to help my mother after her surgery. During the flight I wrote three short stories. When I got to my mother's, I typed the stories and sent them in. Returning home eight weeks later, I found a check waiting. More exciting than the check, however, was the fact that I was no longer chained to my desk.

Years ago, when my daughter worked in a fast-food restaurant, I wrote there. In the past few years, because of my husband's health, I've written in doctors' offices and hospital rooms.

Wherever you work, one of your most important purchases will be a comfortable chair. Try different styles at an office supply store before making your decision. When you're sitting for a long period of time without a break, if your chair is uncomfortable, you will be too, and your writing will show it. Also make sure you have good lighting to prevent eyestrain.

Use whatever works for you! In the long run, having a spot to call your own will help to make you a more productive writer.

Part II

Choosing

Your Field of Writing

Chapter 2

Fiction

Short Stories

FICTION OFTEN INCORPORATES real-life, everyday events. I glean many ideas from my family, church, and neighborhood.

For example, a former neighbor had a CB radio that "bled" through our television set, tape recorder, and other electronics. One morning I slipped a music cassette into my tape player to keep me company while finishing a typing job. All I heard, however, was my neighbor's voice coming through the player telling someone about her weekend.

I fumed. Then I remembered our pastor's words the day before: "Whatever happens to you is for your blessing and God's glory." And I wondered, *What could possibly bless me and bring God glory from my neighbor's conversation?*

Then I thought about a speaker at a writers' conference who talked about playing the "what if" game. So I let my mind roam free. What if this lady has just moved here? What if her husband works long hours and the wife is home all day with two little boys? What if I hear her say on the CB that a friend has died over the weekend, and she says, "No, we can't go to the funeral. We don't have a babysitter." What if I go over and knock on the door and say, "I'm sorry about your friend dying. Your boys can come over and play with our children." She looks startled and says, "We just found out. How did you know?" I tell her that she comes through on my tape player. She apologizes, and so on.

I wrote that story, called it "Breaker, Breaker," and it's sold several times. I simply took something I was going through at the present time, wrote it in third person, and ended with a "what if" scenario. (This can also help you solve your problems because you're looking at them from a different perspective.)

The neat thing about these types of stories is that they can be "recycled" by writing them from a different point of view, then selling them to other publications. After writing the above story from my point of view, I could write it from my neighbor's point of view—how she thought religious people were all alike, then this Christian woman comes to the door and offers to do something for her, a complete stranger. If her children were teenagers, you could write it from the teen's point of view. Or you could write a nonfiction article on "How to Keep Your CB from Bleeding." The possibilities are endless.

What's going on in your neighborhood? We had a new neighbor who played very loud music in his driveway. I picked up a *Guideposts* magazine shortly after they moved in and saw an article, "How to Live With Your Wild Neighbors." I thought, *This is perfect.* (Turned out to be about birds!) This brings us to the topic of selecting a title.

Title

I've heard people say, "Don't worry about your title. The editor will change it anyway." Editors have more important things to do with their time, however, than to think of new titles. If you select a good one, they'll keep it.

I usually try to tie the title into the theme of the story as I did with "Breaker, Breaker" so the reader will have an idea what the story is about. I titled a story about a military couple "The Lord's Army," and I used a phrase from Scripture in a story titled "Such As I Have."

Length

Most short stories range from 1,000 to 2,000 words. Check writers' guidelines in marketing books or on the Internet for a publisher's specific requirements.

Theme

Write the theme of your short story in one sentence. This will keep you from wandering off on a tangent. Some magazine editors ask for a query letter for fiction. This query will include your one-sentence theme, along with length, main characters (age, sex, occupation, etc.), time story takes place (Bible times, Civil War, present-day), locale, current conflict, how your character resolves the conflict, and result of action.

Audience

What age is your story written for? If children, is it a read-to story or read-it-yourself story? If teens, is it for junior or senior high age or college? If adults, is it for singles, newlyweds, empty nesters, or retired people?

To determine if it fits the needs of that group, let someone of that age read it and give you his or her opinion. Members of writers' clubs can also help with this. (See Appendix G for information on starting or joining such a club.)

Parts of a Short Story

There are four parts to a short story: problem, struggle, barriers, and the solution.

Choose one basic problem your main character will face and carry that problem throughout the story. Don't lose it on page three, never to see it again, only to come up with a new and better problem on page five.

How does the lead character solve his problem? You can use chance to hinder resolution, but not to help. Stories where the person prays and, suddenly, everything is all right seem unbelievable. Now perhaps during this person's prayer she recalls a Scripture verse or a solution comes to her, but prayer alone shouldn't solve the problem. Show the character's willingness to listen and follow the guidance God reveals during prayer. One conference speaker said that God can perform miracles in real life but not in fiction. A reader wants to see the character's creativity dig her out of a deep mess.

Show the story's basic problem and identify the sex of the main character in the first 100 words. Have you ever gotten halfway through a story written in first person by a female author and suddenly discovered the main character is a man? When that happens, I have to go back to the beginning and read it again, because my entire perspective has changed. Somewhere near the beginning of your story, either have someone call the person by name, or make reference to a gender relationship to clarify.

Does the problem fit the character's age? I began one devotional for teens with the words, "Remember your first car?" The editor noted, "Most teens this age have only had one car."

In her article, "The Greatest Short-Short," referring to the story of the Prodigal Son, Colleen Reece says, "Stories almost invariably need three things if they are to survive and sell: an interesting *character* who faces a real *challenge* and somehow *changes* in the process. What better example," Reece asks, "than a boy who demands 'real living,' finds it isn't so hot after all, and packs his pride in his battered suitcase to go back home?"[1]

(The rest of the information in this chapter pertains to both short stories and novels.)

Names

Be careful choosing the names of your characters. Try to have them fit the time period in which you're writing. For example, popular names today are Ashley, Brynne, and Nicole, but you wouldn't want to use these names in a story that takes place in the 1800s. I've met several women named Debbie who were born the same year as our son. It was a popular name in the sixties.

The Writer's Digest book, *Character Naming Sourcebook* (Sherrilyn Kenyon, Hal Blythe, and Charlie Sweet, 1994), includes more than 25,000 first and last names and their meanings from more than forty-five countries. It also lists the top ten most popular names in the United States every year from 1880. The Internet has sites for nationality-specific names, and you can get ideas for names from newspaper stories, movies, television programs—even telephone books.

Names tend to fit characters. A high society girl may be called "Penelope" (no offense to any readers named Penelope!). An old-fashioned girl may be named Bertha or Freda.

In the original draft of *Gone with the Wind*, Margaret Mitchell called the heroine Pansy. That doesn't sound nearly as intriguing as her final choice of Scarlett.

Watch also for various spellings of the same name, depending on the country in which the story takes place. For example, John may become Sean or Juan or Ian. Mary may be Marie or Maria. Also, don't have all the characters' names begin with the same letter. Show some variety.

Dialogue

Below are two versions of part of a story titled "Weighed in the Balance" published in the *Standard* Sunday school paper in 1976. The first version shows the original draft. The second version uses the preferred "showing" rather than "telling."

"Goodbye, dear," Janet Collins bent down to kiss her husband. "I'll try not to be too late."

"Okay, honey," Jim replied. (*End of dialogue. The rest is simply telling.*)

Turning his attention back to the television program, he didn't notice how his wife's shoulders drooped as she walked out the door. But as he heard her start the car engine and back out of the driveway, the old feeling of guilt returned as it did every Sunday night. He tried to brush it away.

After all, he went to church with her every Sunday morning. Why was she always so disappointed when he wanted to stay home at night? He was tired. Lately he'd had to work on Saturdays and even some Sundays at the office to finish up a big government contract. Janet knew that. And she knew how lucky he was to still have a job when many of the other engineers had been let go.

In this version we're telling his name and her name, the fact that he used to go to church but now he doesn't and he's feeling guilty. He has a job and a big contract and sometimes he has to work on Sundays. So we know everything, but it's boring reading. Look at the difference when we add some dialogue.

"Goodbye, dear." Janet Collins bent down to kiss her husband. "I do wish you would go with me."

"I go with you every Sunday morning," her husband replied, barely looking up from the TV. "I'm tired." *(Already we see a conflict. The dialogue is telling the story, not the author.)*

"You're always tired lately." Janet picked up her Bible. "Ever since you got your promotion, you never go on Sunday nights anymore." *(We're finding out the same information as in the first opening, but this time it's through dialogue.)*

Jim turned impatiently in the swivel rocker. "You know we have that big government contract to finish." Before his wife could answer, he went on, "And you know how lucky I am to still have a job when many of the other engineers have been let go."

"I know." Janet's shoulders drooped. *(Above we wrote " . . . he didn't notice how his wife's shoulders drooped," but now we put it* after *her comments.)* "I'll try not to be late."

As Jim heard the car back out of the driveway, the old feeling of guilt returned as it did every Sunday night.

A friend who read both versions pointed out that the second version, although stronger, is not that much longer—only one line. But look at the difference. The dialogue not only moves the story along, it introduces us to Jim and Janet, it shows the conflict, it describes the work situation, and it hints at Jim's spiritual condition.

Note also that in the revised version, I primarily used action to identify the speaker. This avoids the constant use of "he said" and "she said."

"Good-bye dear." Janet bent down to kiss her husband.

Another example of this follows:

First draft: "Like my mother before me, I inherited my magic," Gwen said. She picked up the tattered parchment.

Rewritten: "Like my mother before me, I inherited my magic." Gwen picked up the tattered parchment.

You can also have the speaker call the other person by name. "Just be patient, Gwen." In this case the reader knows the speaker isn't Gwen.

I edited a manuscript in which the writer included every synonym for "said." On one page, the character "screamed," "yelled," "cried," and so on. I wrote along the side, "Didn't he ever just *say* anything?"

Keep in mind, especially in long dialogues, to identify the speakers often enough that the reader doesn't have to retrace the paragraphs to see who's speaking.

Developing Characters

Make a list of all the characters in your book. Draw a family tree. Give the ages of the characters when you begin writing and keep track so they won't age ten years in a seven-year span.

Develop character sketches. What color is their hair? Their eyes? What is their height and weight? What are some of their personality traits? Their faults? Their strengths and weaknesses? Their likes and dislikes? Get to know your characters well enough that you would recognize them if you met them walking down the street.

The following assignment was given in a fiction workshop taught by Mabeth Clem of the Nazarene Publishing House.

1. What does my character most sincerely believe in? (example: honesty)
2. Noticeable mannerism? (faltering step)
3. Music? (old gospel hymns)
4. Attitude toward person closest to him? (seventeen-year-old grandson, protective)
5. Comment made habitually or favorite saying? ("Honesty is the best policy.")
6. Favorite entertainment? (fishing)
7. Fear? (to be left alone)
8. Pet peeve? (loud music)
9. Attitude towards opposite sex? (old-fashioned)
10. Favorite foods? (meat and potatoes)
11. Greatest psychological need? (to be loved and needed)
12. How does this affect his actions? (He does what others think he should, rather than what he really wants to do.)
13. Present problem?

Using these questions, work up a synopsis of your character so you don't have him or her changing halfway through the book.

Get to know your characters—how they react to various situations. Novelist and conference instructor Bea Carlton says, "Make the reader feel emotions with the characters: fear, sadness, joy, love, anger, frustrations, etc."[2]

Katherine Paterson, in her article entitled "People I Have Known," writes, "When someone asks me about 'building characters,' I'm tempted to remind them that characters are people, not models you put together with an erector set. You don't 'build' people, you get to know them."[3]

One novelist was having trouble with her characters. During this time she was also job hunting. While filling out numerous applications, she thought how much these told about her. Then she had the idea of creating a resume for each of her characters, giving name (may show nationality), present address (locale of story), previous address (flashback), physical description, educational background, work history, personal information, hobbies, military, references (friends), and present situation. By doing this she became better acquainted with her characters.[4]

Where do you find your characters? They're everywhere: in supermarkets, doctors' offices, schools, workplaces, airports, and many other places. You just have to look for them. Keep a notebook handy and write down descriptions, conversations, gestures, and so on.

Action

Don't use action just for the sake of action. Let it move the story along, and make it logical. Following are three examples where authors had their characters doing things that were not possible:

"Levi is on his knees, sitting back on his heels, his elbows resting on his thighs." (*Try that someday and let me know how it works!*)

A girl braids her own hair the day after her broken arm is placed in a cast.

(Man in car watching girl go into apartment building.) She goes up the steps, in the front door, down the hallway, up the steps, and, from the car, he watches as she knocks at the door. (*Guess he had a periscope!*)

Plots

In a novel you will have one main plot and one or more subplots. After reading the first chapter of my novel at a conference, an editor told me, "You've shown three problems and given each of them equal prominence. You need to decide what problem will be prevalent throughout the book and make that stronger than the others."

Leads

The following are samples of different types of leads you can use for your short story or novel:

Flashback:

"I'd spent eight months in preparation for a wedding I now knew would never take place" (Sheila Boggess, "Forgiving," *Standard*, 5/29/88).

Teaser:

"The buzz of the new electric hedge trimmers cut into Martha's reverie. She slammed down the kitchen window against the irritating whine, and for the tenth time that hour implored, 'Lord, have I made a mistake?'" (Sara L. Smith, "Newlywed," *Standard*, 5/29/88).

"Just one week! Oh, why didn't I tell him sooner?" (Donna Goodrich, "The Unspoken Question," *Youth's Comrade*, 2/19/61).

Scripture or Quotation:

"A friend that sticketh closer than a brother." (Donna Clark, "No Need to be Lonely," *Youth's Comrade*, 3/8/59).

Dialogue:

"Marcia!" Judy Martin burst into the room where her friend sat sewing. "Did you see that?" (Donna Goodrich, "The Peach Pie," *Standard,* 4/19/64).

"You've got to be kidding!" June Wheatley looked at her husband in disbelief. "Invite the Camerons over to *this* house?" (Donna Goodrich, "Such As I Have," *Standard,* 5/15/77).

Setting

Where does this story take place and are you acquainted with the setting you are using? If an actual location, have you been there or researched the area?

Quoting Bea Carlton again, make the readers taste, feel, see, hear, and smell what you are describing. Use colors, scents, sounds. "Even if the setting is not exotic," Carlton says, "it should be made real to the readers. Let them feel the heat, taste the sweat and dust, see the heat waves shimmering over the cracked ground! Let them experience the agony of thirst!"

Ending

Does the main character change his viewpoint before the story's ending? What in the story caused him to change his viewpoint? This is what will make your reader say, "Oh, the person seemed so real!"

Similarities Between the Short Story and the Novel[5]

1. Both usually focus on at least one main character.
2. Both generally rely heavily on characterization.
3. Both require a plot evolving out of the needs and motivations of the main character.
4. Both require that the main character change in some way as a result of the plot action.
5. Both require clean, clear, crisp writing.
6. Both require a central theme.
7. Both require a particular point of view or slant.
8. Both require a beginning, middle, and end.
9. Both require competent use of the tools of fiction.
10. Both require the writer to feel deeply about his characters and subject.

Differences Between the Short Story and the Novel

In the novel you can:
1. Create more complex characters.
2. Change points of view with each chapter.
3. Utilize subplots.
4. Cover more ground—in time, complications, characterization, and theme.
5. Give your main character a problem that cannot be easily solved and is worthy of his wholehearted effort and concentration.

Book Proposal for Novel

A good fiction proposal should include:

1. The novel's title: Research the kinds of titles that attract readers.
2. Synopsis: This is a short (1-2 pages) summary of the novel. If you cannot describe your major plot points in this amount of space, then you do not yet have a clear enough vision of your story. If you cannot describe it in order to sell it, then you will not be able to describe it in order to promote it.
3. Details: length, delivery date.
4. Chapter-by-chapter outline: Keep them interesting—think of this as telling your story in fast-forward . . . .
5. Marketing: Who is the audience? How will you reach them? Do you have any ideas on marketing? How do you plan to publicize it? Will you be able to get some radio spots? Publicize it on your and other Web sites? Considering today's economy, publishers expect more from writers in helping to sell books. The more assistance you can give, the better chance you have of selling your book.
6. Endorsements: Who can you ask to read and review your book? Contact other authors who have written similar books and ask them for endorsements. It is more and more essential that you obtain endorsements early on in the process.
7. Competition: What similar novels are currently in print? List them, and note how they are doing. Is there room for another?
8. Author information: This is no time for modesty. What else have you published?
9. Sample chapters: Include the first three chapters of the novel.[6]

On the next few pages is a great example of a book proposal for a 'tween book by Linda McQuinn Carlblom. Notice how she aptly describes other books on the market and shows how hers differs; lists her qualifications for writing the book; gives a one-page summary of the book, then a chapter-by-chapter synopsis. Note also the marketing suggestions she includes.

(title page):

Linda Carlblom   'Tween fiction
Street address   Approx. 26,000 words
City, State, Zip
Telephone
E-mail address
Web site

A new school, a dying grandpa, and a mysterious note . . .

Meet Shelby Culpepper
By Linda Carlblom

(new page):

Meet Shelby Culpepper

Synopsis

Who could have written this note? I don't even know anyone here yet. That's what twelve-year-old Shelby Culpepper wonders when she finds an anonymous note written in green ink in her backpack on her first day at a new school. The mysterious notes keep coming and she and her two new friends, Courtney and Gunner, make it their mission to figure out who wrote them.

Is the note-writer a secret admirer or just someone trying to make a fool of Shelby because she's the new kid? And what's up with someone who always writes with green ink?

Besides all that, Shelby's favorite grandpa is in the battle of his life—fighting cancer. He now lives with her family, and helps the young sleuths from his command post, aka his bed. What will Shelby do if Grandpa loses his battle?

Join Shelby and her friends as they execute a plan to uncover the mystery note-writer and support each other through all life's ups and downs.

(new page):

Meet Shelby Culpepper

Author Qualifications

Linda Carlblom is currently contracted with Barbour Publishing to write four books in a twenty-four book fiction series for 'tween girls, due for release in June 2009. She is the author of *Interactive Children's Sermons, 52 Messages from the Psalms* (Standard, 2001), and has had several articles and devotions published. As a wife and mother of three children, ages twenty-five, twenty-two, and thirteen, she is well acquainted with the fun and foibles of 'tweens, making her an empathetic, yet humorous voice for them. Her complete resume is enclosed. (This resume included her address, e-mail address, and Web site, followed by titles and publishers of books, along with names of magazines and anthologies in which she had been published.)

The next sheet gave marketing information:

Marketing Potential

Target Audience

This fiction book is for girls eight to twelve years of age, who face challenges in their everyday lives within their families and at school. Because of the many changes they're going through physically and emotionally, they may lack self-confidence, yet want to appear they have it all together. Shelby Culpepper is someone with whom they can identify as they empathize with her struggles.

Competitive Works

Beverly Lewis' new series, Holly's Heart (Bethany, 2008), looks fantastic, but is aimed at older 'tweens—eleven to fourteen. They deal with slightly more mature topics like boyfriends, which is a subject I flirt with (no pun intended) in Shelby Culpepper, but do not allow her to indulge in, since my target audience is eight to twelve.

A strong competitor in the Christian 'tween market is still Nancy Rue's Lily series (Zonderkidz) even though it is several years old. Having read many of these books with my daughter, I feel they are very different from the Shelby Culpepper series. The Lily books are overtly spiritual, written specifically for Christian girls. Other girls may enjoy reading them, but Lily is on a much higher spiritual level than most pre-teen girls. Though Shelby Culpepper is a Christian, it isn't the focus of my books. Her faith is simply one facet of her character. Part of the conflict in the book is Shelby's embarrassment over her father being a pastor and how she can live a life of faith without being labeled weird. Spirituality is something most kids are starting to grapple with at this age, making these books not only fun reading, but thought provoking as well.

Nancy Rue followed the Lily books with the Sophie series. Sophie is a dreamer, and the stories blend her reality with her historical dream-world. Shelby is authentic and lives in the here and now, as do most 'tweens.

Though there are several historical 'tween fiction series in the CBA market, I found there are few new contemporary fiction series for girls. Shelby Culpepper could fill this gap and meet the needs of 'tween girls in a fun, yet meaningful, way.

Marketing Edge

Meet Shelby Culpepper can be formatted and marketed purely as a fiction book. Or, there are several ways to make it stand out from other fiction books on the shelf and give it a hint of nonfiction. Here are a few suggestions:

- Include a "Share It with Shelby" or "Shelby and Me" page at the end of each chapter. Each page could include one or two thought-provoking questions that help the reader think more deeply about what took place in that chapter and what she can learn about herself and God from it.
- Include a Journal Page with two sentence starters for the reader to finish. For example, the first could allow the reader to consider how she would react if she were in Shelby's shoes, and the second could let her contemplate how God would feel about her reaction.
- Include a pen with green ink with each book. Or offer a free pen to readers if they visit my Web site and answer a question or request to be on my e-mail list.
- Provide discussion questions at the end of the book for individual or small group use. This format would not interrupt the story if the reader is in "can't-put-the-book-down" mode!

Future Books Synopses

The ideas for a series of Shelby Culpepper books are as vast as there are adolescent problems, including:

- *Shelby Culpepper and Her Embarrassing Family* – Shelby is embarrassed by her father's occupation—pastor of the local church. Her parents seem to want to control her life, or do they just care so much it's hard for them to let her grow up? This book is already outlined and one-fourth completed.
- *Shelby Culpepper Reaches Out* – Shelby befriends an underprivileged, unpopular kid at school and bears the consequences of her actions.
- *Shelby Culpepper, Get to Work!* – Shelby takes on a regular after school babysitting job and finds life in the workaday world isn't all it's cracked up to be.

Marketing Strategies

Speaking

- I have been a faculty member at Glorieta Christian Writers Conference from 2006-2008.
- I am a 2004 CLASS (Christian Leaders And Speaker Services) graduate and will use this association to broaden my speaking opportunities.
- I speak at churches, conferences, women's luncheons, and meetings.
- I speak at schools regarding my writing profession and will use my contacts to set up speaking engagements and book signings to promote my Shelby series.

- I will contact local bookstores to set up book signings.
- I will send out promotional fliers and/or press kits announcing my book release and my willingness to speak to schools and youth groups.

Internet

- My Web site, www.lindacarlblom.com, is newly operational, and will be undergoing updates and changes to target ministering to the needs of 'tween girls. Features could include an Ask Shelby column where readers' questions would be answered; free green pen or book giveaways; games; stationery pages; devotions; a suggestion box for future plotlines or character types; and a message board or chat room where readers can connect with each other. My Web site address in the back of the book will allow readers to e-mail me, building a loyal reader base.

Interviews

- I am willing to do radio and TV interviews.
- I will provide suggested questions prior to the interviews.

Newsletter

- I will do a Shelby e-newsletter to keep in touch with readers and inform them of upcoming book releases.

Manuscript Status

Book one, *Meet Shelby Culpepper,* is complete at sixteen chapters and approximately 26,000 words. Book two, *Shelby Culpepper and her Embarrassing Family,* is one-fourth complete at four chapters.
(new page)

Meet Shelby Culpepper
Book One of Four

Outline

Chapter 1 – The Note

An anonymous note written in green ink falls from Shelby's backpack at lunch on her first day at a new school. Shelby, Courtney, and Gunner (the only friends she has so far) look for clues within the note to try to figure out who it's from. Popular Shane Hawkins, the student body president, and his cheerleader girlfriend, Misty Piper, tease Shelby at lunch. Shelby and friends spot a green pen left on a neighboring lunch table.

Chapter 2 – The Fainthearted

Shelby faints in math class and is humiliated in front of her classmates. The nurse makes her ride to her office in a wheelchair, just as a precaution, embarrassing her even further. Jimmy Thompson shows an interest in her. Could he be the note-writer?

Chapter 3 – Stranded

Shelby and her friends go back to the lunch area to see if the green pen is still there. It's gone, but a new note awaits them. In their excitement, Shelby misses her bus. At home, she confides to her sick grandpa about her miserable first day of school and the mysterious notes.

Chapter 4 – The Plan

Shelby and friends determine to launch a full-scale investigation. They devise a plan to uncover the owner of the green pen. Grandpa offers to help by commandeering from his bedside.

Chapter 5 – Dissection

Dissection of frogs begins in science. Shelby, Courtney, and Gunner play practical jokes on their lab partner, prissy Misty Piper, who is also Shane Hawkins' girlfriend. The group discovers Shane has pens in all colors.

Chapter 6 – The Invitation

Misty wants to join in on the investigation, but the friends don't trust her and don't want her hanging around. Jimmy Thompson invites Shelby to the football game that night. Shelby receives note number three.

Chapter 7 – The Game

Shelby and friends go to the football game, hoping to avoid Jimmy and discover the note-writer. Chaos ensues.

Chapter 8 – Rally Cap

Grandpa's health takes a turn for the worse. Shelby is scared and worried.

Chapter 9 – Hunger

Note number four arrives. Hospital visits occupy much of the Culpeppers' family time. Shelby wants things to be the way they used to be.

Chapter 10 – Lying

Grandpa and Shelby spend lots of time together, though he tires easily. He's the one person who she feels really listens and understands her. Investigation continues.

Chapter 11 – Grandpa

Grandpa dies. Shelby is devastated. Gunner and Courtney come to visit her.

Chapter 12 – The Breakup

Disappointed at life's cruel twists, Shelby determines to press on with her investigation regarding the notes, which gives her a sense of purpose. Misty and Shane break up.

Chapter 13 – The Envelope

The hunt for the author of the note intensifies. Jimmy Thompson asks Shelby to the school dance. Note number five arrives.

Chapter 14 – The Sampling

Shelby and friends think they have the mystery figured out, but discover they had the wrong conclusion.

Chapter 15 – The Dance

The mystery is solved at the school dance. Shelby and friends are surprised, but happy at the outcome.

Chapter 3

Nonfiction

(**Note:** While much of the material in this chapter relates to writing nonfiction articles, it can be helpful in nonfiction books as well.)

WHEN I FIRST considered writing nonfiction, I found that someone had already covered every topic I wanted to write about. I had a lot of ideas, but wondered how they differed from those already written.

Then while sitting in a nonfiction workshop, I realized, *It's in the slant that I alone can give it.* We can interview experts and collect information from reference books and the Internet, but we're also adding our particular slant. God has given each of us a distinctive personality, and He has allowed you and me to go through circumstances in a way no one else has experienced.

You are a unique individual—a mother or father, brother or sister, aunt or uncle. You're part of a married couple, a single parent, or never married. You're a student, you're employed, you're retired.

If married, what have you experienced? First-year adjustment, in-law problems, financial struggles? As a parent: infertility, adoption, preschool children, challenges with teens, adult children still living at home? Whatever you've gone through, you're the only one who can write an article or book in your own voice.

The emotion you share in your story will make your article stand out from the other manuscripts the editor receives. They may have facts—the skeleton, so to speak— but yours can have "flesh." You may have added research and statistics, quotations from other books, and even a friend's story, but you're also showing how this experience has affected your life. Then you can wrap it all up in a solution that can help your reader.

Years ago I could have written an article on suicide. I could give statistics on how it's the third leading cause of death for teens.[1] I could give warning signs for parents and friends to look for. I could even list places where a teen could go for help. But the article would end there—facts only, no emotion.

After my great-nephew committed suicide, however, leaving behind an eight-month-old son, I could describe in detail the horrific emotion each family member experienced that day: my sister who found him hanging on his bedroom door, my brother-in-law who attempted CPR, my niece who didn't get to the hospital in time to see her son take his last breath, his girlfriend who sobbed, "Didn't he know how much we all loved him?"

This is what will grab your reader. It's more than statistics. It's *writing!* And this is what will set your article apart from all the others.

Theme

As in all writing, nonfiction articles need a theme. What is your takeaway? While writing my first nonfiction book for John Wiley & Sons, *How to Set Up & Run a Typing Service*, the publisher sent me a fifteen-page questionnaire to complete for advertising purposes.

One section of the questionnaire asked for a description of the book in three paragraphs, then in one paragraph, then in one sentence. It was difficult to do.

Not so with the second how-to book for the same company, *How to Set Up & Run An Income Tax Service*. I wrote the descriptions *first*. Posting the theme sentence near my desk helped me keep on track as I outlined and wrote the book.

Each Sunday our pastor includes a sermon outline in the bulletin so we can fill in the blanks as he preaches. This not only helps us follow along, but it also helps him stick to his theme. It's the same way with our writing. If we don't know where we're going, the editor won't know either, and the reader will never get a chance to know.

Outline

When I first began writing, I wrote mostly short stories and devotionals so I didn't feel I needed an outline. Then I was hired at a local magazine as a home and garden editor. For two articles each month, I interviewed three business owners, sending them a list of questions ahead of time and recording the interviews for more accurate quotations. When I transcribed the tape, I found the article almost wrote itself. In preparing these questions before the interview, in essence I was outlining my article. I knew where I was going, which made the article easier to write.

In my typing service book, I outlined the book as far as the chapter headings, but I got bogged down in writing the chapters. Then I realized I could outline the chapters just as I outline an article. Later, when I wrote the tax book, I outlined it so thoroughly ahead of time with headings and subheadings, that when I sat down to write it, it took only thirty days to complete the entire book. I knew where I was going.

Slant

How do you know where to send your manuscript? This will be covered more thoroughly in Chapter 16 on marketing, but consider your audience and their desires and interests. Think of a friend who fits the magazine's typical reader, and write as you would talk to that person.

Lead

Capture the editor's attention in your very first paragraph. It takes only five seconds for a reader to turn the page and go to another article. If an editor doesn't like your first page, it won't take him long to return your manuscript in your SASE, or send you an e-mail rejection, and go on to the next manuscript in his pile.

The next time you read an article, stop after the first paragraph or two and ask yourself why you want to continue with that article. Or what is the reason you *don't* want to read further? I like the saying, "The lead brings your reader from the front porch into the living room and invites him to sit down and have a chat with you."

Following is one of the best leads I've ever read:

We brought her home from the hospital. We had awaited the moment with excitement for almost nine months. We brought her into the newly remodeled room that had been a sewing room. It was freshly painted a pastel pink, and the flower print curtains just matched.

We gently laid her in her new bed and raised the sides to keep her from falling out. We looked at her pink and wrinkled face. She looked like a prune, but she was ours and we loved her.

We changed her diapers. It was no fun, but we knew it would be necessary for awhile. We fed her slowly, being careful not to spill food on her bib.

She was crying herself to sleep as we tiptoed out of the room. We looked at each other, put our arms around each other, and held each other close. It was a loving moment: Grandma was home from the hospital.[2]

Or how about some of these leads?

"Where's Papa going with that ax?" said Fern to her mother as they were setting the table for breakfast (E. B. White, *Charlotte's Web*).

"Nancy, you're kidding, no statue can whisper!" (Carolyn Keene, *Nancy Drew: The Whispering Statue*).

The Herdmans were absolutely the worst kids in the history of the world (Barbara Robinson, *The Best Christmas Pageant Ever*).

One of the things I've noticed while editing manuscripts is that I often can delete the first two or three paragraphs without hurting the article. Sometimes it helps to move the lead paragraph to the middle and then flash back as seen in the following example:

A friend wrote an article that several publishers had rejected. The story told of a girl in a wheelchair who was admitted to the hospital. While there, her fiancé didn't visit her for several days, and when he finally did, he announced that he wanted to break the engagement because he had fallen in love with her roommate.

After he left, she wheeled down to the hospital chapel, sat in front of the statue of Christ, and said, "Why, Lord? Why did you take Jim away from me?"

Up to this point my friend had written the story chronologically. I suggested that she move the paragraph about the chapel to the beginning of the article. Right away the reader will wonder, Why is the girl in a wheelchair? Why is she in the hospital? Who is Jim? And how was he taken from her?

Making that one change, my friend sold the article the next time out to a singles' magazine.

Keep It Simple

Jesus gave us the most profound truths in simple language, for example, John 3:16 and John 11:35. Short and easy to understand. I'll never forget the first Sunday I attended church after my mother's funeral. The preacher spoke on John 11:35, relating how Jesus wept after the death of His good friend Lazarus. The strength and power of those two words enveloped me and I knew that, in my hour of sorrow, Jesus was weeping with me.

As a teen I worked for a local variety store. Each day, walking to the employees' lounge, I passed by nine paper sacks on the wall—ranging from the largest the store used to the smallest. Each sack had a word on it, and together they spelled out: DON'T USE THIS SIZE IF THIS SIZE WILL DO.

That's what we need to remember as writers. Don't use a five-syllable word if a one- or two-syllable word will do.

Charlie Shedd speaks of using "gobbledygook" and "Protestant Latin." We may know theological terms, but we need to consider our audience. If we're writing for a preacher's magazine, that's one thing, but most of us aren't.

I love the following story shared by Larry Mowrey in the *Come Ye Apart* devotional booklet:

> People tend to get all phony when the preacher is around. There's a story about a little boy who came home in the middle of a pastoral call. He didn't realize that the pastor was there. He just saw his mother, and he came running into the house, holding a dead rat by the tail, exclaiming, "Look, Mom! Look at this rat I caught out behind the barn! I smashed its head in with a baseball bat! I threw rocks at it! I stomped on it! I spit on it, and I . . . I . . . " He looked up, saw the preacher, cleared his throat, and said, "and . . . and . . . and then the dear Lord called it home!"

"Jesus doesn't require us to be eloquent in speech," Mowrey reminds us. "If He has done anything in your life, all you have to do is share that with other people. You'll always find a way to get the story told. Let's allow God to use us to touch the lives of others."[3]

Someone has given this good advice: "Write it quickly, then go back and make it half as long and twice as readable."

Don't Say the Same Thing Twice

It's often possible to cut large chunks of material from your article or book because you've repeated the same thought in several paragraphs. Combine these into one strong paragraph. Repeating the same thought over and over says to your reader, "If you didn't get it that way, maybe you'll get it this way."

Use Subheads, Lists, and Sidebars

Break up your article by inserting subheads at appropriate places. Or place facts in a bulleted list instead of in a long paragraph. This will make it easier for your reader to remember what you have written. You can also use sidebars; for example, "Ten Ways to Break the Plastic Habit." Sometimes if an editor can't use the entire article, he or she may purchase the sidebars.

Check Your Facts

If you're including statistics, dates, and various spellings of names, always double-check your facts. When I worked for a book editor, we placed a red check on the rough draft after we double-checked Scripture verses, numbers, or names. Now if I have facts to double-check, I place three XXXs so the spell-checker will bring them to my attention.

Avoid Generalities

Give your readers specific numbers and sizes. Create a picture for them. Don't leave a question in their minds. Instead of saying, "It was a large house," describe the five bedrooms, wraparound porch, kitchen big enough to hold twenty people.

Ideas for Writing Articles

- Use the five senses.
- Be a people watcher.
- Tell stories your readers can relate to.
- Think back to the "good ol' days."
- Go through your photo album.
- Share an experience that makes your readers laugh or cry.
- Look for anniversaries of local businesses and churches. Go through old newspapers and see what happened twenty-five or fifty years ago.
- Walk through cemeteries.
- Look up old city or state laws.
- Visit landmarks

Sources for Quotations

- A number of articles I found listed the Web site Profnet at www.profnet.com—a service provided by Business Newswire—as a good source for information. Sign in as a "journalist," then post your query and e-mail address so experts can respond.
- Jot down names of organizations in the Yellow Pages that can be sources of articles or quotations.
- Check the *Encyclopedia of Associations.*
- Get on mailing lists of various state and federal departments, such as health, education, and so on, or check www.govspot.
- Talk to professors at local colleges and universities.

- Write to authors who write on the same subject as your article or book.
- Talk to friends and relatives.

Writing for Women's Magazines

It's helpful to study and compare women's magazines to find the best fit for your article. I studied two—*Woman's Day* and *Today's Christian Woman* (the latter no longer published). I found the most popular topics in *Woman's Day* were weight, finances, looking younger, love, organization, traditions, things for free, travel hints, health. Key words in titles were "easy," "new," and "best." Many of these titles contained numbers: "6 Weeks to Slim"; "20 Ways to Get Things for Nothing"; "11 Common Drug Mistakes."

Articles in *Today's Christian Woman* included weight, child-raising, preemie stories, anorexia, sisters, "8 Dates for $10 or Less," humor, book reviews, letters from readers dealing with various problems, an advice column, profiles of recording artists, and an article on an Olympic gymnast entitled "Running Ragged in the Fast Lane." This last article included a sidebar entitled "12 questions on how to tell if you're too busy."

Besides studying the types of articles these magazines publish, it also helps to check their advertisements. For example, *Today's Christian Woman* included ads for books, colleges, videos, Christian agencies, fund-raising, an anorexia ranch, fat fighter, albums, World Relief, cruises, adoption, and music club.

A third woman's magazine included articles on travel bargains, recipes, gardening, garage sales, hairdos, home health tests, boredom and fatigue, nostalgia, and fillers on home protection, retired singles, stocks/taxes, birds, hearing, board games, retail outlets, savings, and grandparenting ideas.

How to Get Started Writing Nonfiction

First jot down five things you'd like to write about, perhaps something you're now going through or have gone through:

- Job
  Like/don't like . . . Relationships . . . Looking for job (discrimination because of age or gender)
- Family
  Marriage (Joys, problems)
  Children (New baby . . . Discipline/setting boundaries . . . School problems . . . Friend problems . . . Teens . . . Adult children . . . Foster children . . . Adoption)

- Something you're interested in
  Hobby . . . Favorite subjects at school . . . Your favorite topic of conversation—cars, sports, children, redecorating, cooking, etc.
- What are you skilled in?
  How-to articles are popular. If someone has asked you how to do something, you have the makings of an article or book. Do you type term papers for students, cater luncheons, run a day-care service, repair automobiles? Perhaps others would like to know how to start a similar business, and by sharing what you've learned through trial and error, you can help them reach their dream.
- Social issues
  What upsets you? What can you do about it? Do you really believe you can change something or help others see something from a different point of view through your writing?

Out of the five possible articles you jotted down, select *one* you feel strongly about. Give it a tentative title, three main points, then two sub points under each main point. Write a lead and closing paragraph.

Before you start the actual writing, go through the *Christian Writers' Market Guide* or the *Writer's Market* and find at least five possible markets. You don't want to go to the work of writing an article or book that no one wants to buy. Determine the required length—whether an article or a book—and if the editors will look at a complete manuscript or if they require a query or book proposal.

Now decide what you have to do to complete this project. Will you need to interview an expert on this subject? Talk to a friend or relative who can share their story? Do some research at the library or on the Internet?

When your article is finished, or you've completed at least one chapter of your book, take it to a local writers' club to be critiqued. If you have none in your town, ask a friend who is skilled in the English language to give it a look. Catching these weaknesses early on will help you in writing the remainder of your book.

Write a query letter for your article or a book proposal (see Chapter 16), put it in an envelope with a self-addressed stamped envelope or, if acceptable, send it via e-mail, and then begin your next project.

Chapter 4

Writing Devotionals and Fillers

Introduction

W E LIVE IN an instant gratification world. We pop a waffle into our toaster or a frozen dinner in our microwave and voila! instant meal. By the same token, we want to pick up our Bible and devotional book in the morning, read a few verses, and shazam! instant religion.

Just as the commercials spell "relief" with the name of a popular antacid, so some Christians spell it with the letters "d-e-v-o-t-i-o-n-a-l." Take one in the morning for relief of spiritual heartburn all day.

Because devotionals are short, you may feel they're easy to write when, in fact, this very brevity makes it harder. You have to get an important truth across to your readers in three hundred words or less. As you gain experience, the writing will become easier and the struggle less. But don't allow yourself to get to the point where you just "dash one off." Go to your knees before you go to your keyboard.

A good definition of a devotional comes from a *Daily Guideposts* reader who wrote, "The best devotional is something I can read in five minutes and remember for a lifetime."

Differences Between a Devotional and a Filler

There are several differences between a devotional and a filler.

Length

A devotional may range from one hundred to three hundred words, depending on the specific periodical and guidelines. Your devotional may be shorter than the given length, but should never be longer.

On the other hand, a devotional filler is just what the word implies: a short piece of inspiration to fill a column or page in a newspaper, magazine, or weekly take-home paper. It can be as short as fifty words or as long as 750 words. Markets for these are numerous.

Don't worry, however, about the length or editing when writing your first draft. Concentrate more on simply getting your thoughts on paper. Correcting grammar, sentence structure, and punctuation can come later.

Format

Devotional format. For an individual devotional, place your name, address, phone, and e-mail in the upper left-hand corner of the page. If it's an assignment, type your name, address, phone, e-mail, and dates of assignment on a cover page, along with a brief bio sketch. (The editor may also request a photo. This is a good time to put in a supply of 3 x 5" or 5 x 7" black and white or color glossies.) For a multiday assignment, begin each day on a new page.

A devotional format will depend upon the publisher's guidelines. One editor may ask for a single Scripture verse with the devotional; another will request related scriptures. Others may ask for a prayer, a quotation, or a verse of a song. An assignment packet will include these guidelines and usually a sample devotional.

Body of devotional. A devotional includes three parts:

1. Scripture verse
2. Illustration or anecdote
3. Spiritual application

The illustration is what makes this devotional uniquely yours. Nothing happens to anyone else exactly the same way it happens to you. Sharing a specific experience helps your reader identify with the thought you're trying to get across.

Ask yourself: If an editor could select only one devotional out of several written on the same passage of Scripture, what would stand out in your brief piece of writing to grab his or her attention? Often it's the illustration, so make it strong.

This illustration or anecdote doesn't have to be personal. It can be an event in the life of a friend or family member, a biblical or historical illustration, or an item in the news. (See Chapter 14 for "Where to Get Ideas.")

Type the text of the devotional, share your story, and then wrap it up with a spiritual application.

Filler format. The format for a devotional filler is the same as that of a short story or article (see Chapter 12).

Similarities of a Devotional and Filler

Devotionals and fillers are alike in three ways.

Takeaway

Write the theme of your devotional or filler in one sentence. This is the thought you want your readers to take with them throughout their busy day. A devotional or filler is not a sermon with three points and sub points. They both should have *one* main premise.

Universalism

Because many religious periodicals are published worldwide, do not use words or phrases, or refer to movies, television programs, or news events that only readers in your country can understand. Also, if you are writing for nondenominational publications, or periodicals other than your own denomination, don't use theological terms specific to your own belief.

Emotion

One conference speaker suggested that we recall something in our life in which emotion played a strong part. "You don't have to use the actual event in your writing," he says. "Just inject that emotion into your writing." This emotion can be happy or sad. Someone did something that either hurt you or made you happy. Let your reader feel that same emotion.

Dina Donohue, late editor of *Guideposts* magazine, said if your writing doesn't touch you, it won't touch your readers. Her thoughts are echoed by S. T. Coleridge, who wrote: "What comes from the heart goes to the heart." And Cyrano de Bergerac penned these words: "I have but to lay my soul beside my paper and copy."

This thought is best summed up by an unknown writer who wrote: "The writer's task is to make men *see* things, then *feel* them, and then *act* upon them. If the first result is not gained, then the others, of course, will fail."

Marketing Your Devotionals and Fillers

Devotional Assignments

There are two ways to sell devotionals. Some periodicals, such as *The Upper Room*, accept unsolicited individual devotionals because they do not have a theme. Other publishers work by assignment only, often for seven days, concluding with that week's Sunday school lesson. Or they may assign a devotional for one day only—first, to see if the writer can follow the periodical's specifications, and second, to see if he or she is punctual in meeting deadlines.

If you would like to be considered for an assignment, request a sample copy of the magazine and guidelines. If you are already acquainted with the magazine, send a query letter giving your writing background, along with one or two devotionals using their format. This gives the editor a sample of your writing ability.

Sample Devotional Assignment

Below is a letter I received on July 6, 2007, from a devotional booklet entitled *Devotions*.

Re: writing invitation for *Devotions*, the daily devotional magazine of Standard Publishing.

This is your official invitation to write seven devotionals for the SUMMER 2009 issue of *Devotions*. The due date for the assignment would be **August 4, 2007**, and total payment would be Standard's rate for all devotional writers: $140 for the project. (You have almost a month to write these, but ask for more time, if you really need it.)

You will receive a Work-for-Hire contract (all rights sold to Standard Publishing).

Please indicate your response *within three days* by replying to me with an e-mail that includes your home address and phone number. (And ask questions, too, if you like . . .)

If you agree to accept this assignment, our Administrative Services Department will send you a contract by snail-mail (within two weeks). I will also quickly send out the Writer's Packet so you can get started on the assignment. The Packet will include all the necessary information and Writer's Guidelines you'll need. And, of course, it will indicate the Bible passages for the devotionals you will write.

Thank you so much for considering this invitation . . . and I hope you'll say "Yes"!

Sincerely,

Devotions editor

P.S. The devotional pieces are short, the body containing about 180-200 words. To show you what *Devotions* looks like, go to www.standardpub.com on the Internet and click on the "Daily Devotions" link of the homepage. Thanks again for considering this offer to write for us!

The above letter contained the following Scriptures (editors also usually specify their preferred version of the Bible):

June 1 M Exodus 2:1-10
June 2 T Exodus 2:11-22
June 3 W Acts 7:23-29
June 4 T Acts 7:30-34
June 5 F Deuteronomy 32:48-52
June 6 S Deuteronomy 34
June 7 S Exodus 3:1-12

For June 1, I selected Exodus 2:4 as my text, and wrote the devotional as follows:

The Freedom of Letting Go

Today's Verse: His sister stood at a distance to see what would happen.
—Ex. 2:4 NIV

Today's Scripture: Exodus 2:1-10

Song: "Have Thine Own Way, Lord (Adelaide A. Pollard, *Worship in Song*, p. 276. Copyright 1907. Renewal 1935 by G. C. Stebbins. Assigned to Hope Publishing Co.)

In his late thirties our son-in-law felt a call to preach, and went back to school to obtain his degree. Thrilled with this turn of events in his life, I prayed for God's will, adding a P.S. to my prayer that God would open up a church nearby.

Shortly before his graduation, he received an invitation to submit his resume—to a church in Oklahoma, over 1,000 miles away. "No, Lord," I prayed tearfully. "I can't bear for them to move that far away and take our two granddaughters."

I prayed many agonizing prayers that week, and was finally able to put the family in God's hands. Then I wrote my daughter a poem, closing by saying that just as I gave her to the Lord when she was born, I was giving her back to Him, and would rejoice with them, no matter where God led.

The result? Just as Moses' mother gave up her son for a time and then was allowed to raise him for a time, so God called someone else to pastor the Oklahoma church, allowing our daughter and family to stay in our area—for a time.

Prayer: Lord, help me today to let go of all those in my family. I pray for Your perfect will for each one—no matter what the sacrifice may be for me. Then let me stand at a distance to see what will happen.

Twelve Steps to Writing a Devotional Assignment

1. Copy Scripture passage in required version—either in longhand or computer printout—and take it with you when you leave the house to read while waiting in a doctor's office or elsewhere.
2. Use this passage each day for your private devotions.
3. Read verses in different versions.
4. Look in a Bible commentary or dictionary, or a Web site for background of verses: who's involved, where does the story take place, what else is going on at the time?
5. Select one verse from the Scripture passage to use as a text for your devotional—not just the easiest one to illustrate, but one that's meaningful to you.
6. Write a one-sentence theme for your reader's takeaway.
7. Choose an illustration—personal, friend, church, neighborhood, historical, biblical.
8. Choose a title (unless editor gives you one).
9. Write a rough draft. Don't worry about length or editing; just get your thoughts on paper.
10. Begin to edit, first for length, then for clarity.
11. Final typing—in publisher's specific format.
12. Proofread carefully (especially Scripture), then take to critique group if you belong to one.

Devotional Books

Visit your local Christian bookstore and notice the assortment of devotional books, then scan the devotionals you have written. Can you divide them into specific groups—women, teens, children; singles, retirees, writers, Sunday school teachers; seasons of the year; spiritual topics—faith, trials, thanksgiving; seasons of life—empty nest, illness, unemployment? The possibilities are endless.

I mention in Chapter 6 about my newspaper devotional columns selling as a book. God's timing is always right. I sent a few of these to a publishing house, asking if they were interested in a devotional book for women. The editor quickly replied that this book would fit perfectly into a new series they had in the works. Then he asked if I could also do one for children and one for teens. I was glad to comply.

Conclusion

Recently I visited a friend's house. She had just hung up the phone. "I called for a doctor's appointment," she said, "and they put me on hold. First I heard a singer saying how she 'needed someone,' how she 'just had to have him.' Then they switched to a commercial for a new subdivision. 'Move up to the good times,' they said. 'You've worked for it, you deserve it.' After that," she continued, "the news told about a man who hung his four-year-old nephew by his heels and used him for a punching bag because he had wet his pants."

She looked at her watch and shook her head. "In five minutes," she said, "I heard lust, greed, and violence."

I couldn't help but think: Five minutes. About the time it takes to read a devotional. This is what Satan offers the world today. With God's help, we can offer them so much more.

Do's and Don'ts for Writing Devotionals

1. Do make certain your idea is new and fresh. Editors say a major problem with the devotions they receive (and the reason for rejection) is sameness. Familiar thoughts on familiar biblical themes and passages do not sell well. That's not to say you cannot or must not write on a familiar theme (i.e., God's love), but bring fresh insights and illustrations or anecdotes (normally space restricts you to one). "Show, don't tell" applies here.

2. Do consider whether your idea is universal. Will readers be able to identify with what you have written?

3. Is your idea memorable—something that will stick with the reader throughout the day?

4. Do develop only one idea. Was the writing tight? Confined to *one* idea? Devotional writing leaves no room for tangents. Your title, scripture, thought for the day, body, and prayer must be developed around one main idea. Everything needs to go together. Think of it in terms of choosing an outfit for an important occasion. Casual and formal don't mix. Everything needs to be appropriate to the occasion and complementary to each other. So, too, the various devotional parts need to be part of the whole—that one single thought you want to communicate to your reader.

5. Do make it your very best writing. Editors have no time to rewrite awkward sentences, clarify confusing statements, restructure thoughts, correct grammar, punctuation, spelling, or do biblical research for a passage better suited to your devotional. It is your responsibility to do these things as unto the Lord. Write to give God your best work.

6. Don't sermonize. Your writing should be devotional, not preachy.

7. Do follow the guidelines carefully. If an editor states "250 words or less," don't go over this amount. [Author's note: Determine if these 250 words refer only to the devotional itself, or if they include the prayer and thought for the day.] Your devotion won't fit on his page and he hasn't time to cut it. If he requires a scripture reference, thought for the day, and a sentence prayer, then include *all* those things.

8. Do avoid the taboos. Shirley Pope Waite notes, "Most devotional markets ask the writer to avoid controversial subjects, poetry, the topic of death, and quotes from copyrighted sources."

9. Do know what Scripture translation the editor prefers and quote exactly down to the commas and capitalization. Note translation used.

10. Do know the editor's stand on "sexist" language.

11. Do be familiar with the doctrine of the magazine.[1]

Chapter 5

Writing and Selling Your Poetry

Introduction

PETER FINCH, IN his book, *How to Publish Your Poetry*, asked some people why they wrote poetry. Their response: "It's an urge." "It's a disease." "I don't try to write poetry, but there are times when I just have to say something."[1] If you enjoy expressing your feelings through this medium, then this chapter is for you.

Format

As you will see on page 72, the format for typing a poem is different from that of fiction and nonfiction. The information in the left- and right-hand corner is the same; however, you can omit the word count. Whether you choose to put a copyright notice on your poetry you submit to editors or not, for your protection place one on the poems you give to friends or have printed in your church bulletin.

Editing Your Poetry

Poets seem to feel more than other writers that their work is inspired. They say, "I couldn't write fast enough. The words just poured out." Because these writers believe God gave the poem to them word for word, they often refuse to change anything. Dave Clark, an award-winning songwriter, says, "God gives us ideas but He doesn't always give us the edited version."

One way to edit your own poetry is for you or a friend to read it aloud. If you find yourself or the reader stumbling over a word, it probably needs replacing.

Format for Poetry

Name

Street address

City, state, zip

Telephone

E-mail address

(a poem written for a friend who had
lost his first wife and was remarrying
an old friend of the family)

We both have known love; this is not new.
Another person held our trust before,
But that was in another day and time,
And we have gently, firmly, closed that door.

I needed someone, yes, for I was lonely,
But I knew that not just anyone would do.
I asked the Lord to help me in my searching
And, in His love, He guided me to you.

For many, many years we've shared a friendship.
You've been there through a large part of my life,
But now we'll share in even greater measure
Since I have asked you to become my wife.

This is a new beginning for us both.
God's love allowed our paths once more to cross,
And I love you just because you're you,
Not a replacement for the one I lost.

My prayer is, "God, please guide our lives together.
Help with decisions that shall come our way.
And let us always feel the deep contentment
That we are feeling on this special day."

Following are a few hints on editing your poetry.

- Be careful using vague pronouns like "it" and "they." Make it clear to what or whom you are referring.
- Watch your punctuation. Some poems do not require any; however, if you do use punctuation, be consistent.
- Be careful of repeating the same word close together unless you're doing it for emphasis.

Marketing Your Poetry

On page 74, Elaine Hardt gives an A-to-Z list of where to market your poetry.

Sunday school take-home papers are a good market. They often use two or three poems an issue, and cover ages from preschool to adult. Denominational magazines also buy poetry, along with devotional magazines, Sunday school quarterlies, and children, teen, and family magazines. Check the general interest magazines as well.

Sally Stuart's annual *Christian Writers' Market Guide* gives a wealth of information on each magazine: name, address, phone, e-mail and Web site, editor, denomination, circulation, what rights they buy, how much they pay, and so on. But it is just a guide. There isn't room to include everything. Go through this book and jot down the markets that buy poetry, then send for sample copies and guidelines, or find that information online.

On page 75 is a marketing chart which can be completed using information from marketing guides. Include on this chart:

- Name and address of periodical and editor
- Denomination (needed for sending reprints)
- Type of poetry magazine buys—free verse, traditional, haiku
- Length
- Maximum number of poems you can submit at a time
- Amount of payment and when
- How to obtain a sample copy
- Rights

Keeping this chart up to date will show you at a glance where to send a finished poem.

Remember, you're a salesman. You have a product to sell and the editor is your customer. Do your homework.

ABCs for Poetry, Plus!

by Elaine Hardt*

A - adult Sunday school periodicals
B - brochures
C - contests
D - decoupage
E - emotional release
F - frame to hang
G - greeting cards
H - holidays
I - inside insulated mugs
J - journals and magazines
K - keep copies for yourself
L - letters to friends and family
M - meetings and conventions
N - newspaper features
O - occasions calendar/birth/death
P - personalized greetings
Q - quotes for speakers
R - radio personalities
S - songs
T - tape recorded
U - undertake new forms
V - vanity press
W - worship services at church
X - extra copies to hand out
Y - young children's publications
Z - zany parodies

* Used by permission.

Poetry Markets

Periodical	Denom.	Type	Length	Max Pay	When	Sample	Rights

Why Poems are Rejected

They're Too Long

Most poems range from one to four verses so you have to get your thought across in four to sixteen lines. It's important to make every word count.

As in other writing genres, it helps to write a *one-sentence theme* describing your poem, or a "takeaway." After the reader has read your poem, what one thought is he or she going to take away? If your poetry tends to be long, ask yourself, "Do I have just *one* theme in this poem?" If you have more than one, divide it up. Now you have two poems to submit. Remember, it's not the length of the poem that counts; it's the message.

Forced Rhyme

Another reason a poem may not sell is because of what I call the "moon/June" rhyme. How often in a hymn can you anticipate the last word of the next line because it's always the same rhyme? Forgiven/heaven. Cross/loss. Bear/care.

It's exciting to find a poem with words that you may not find in a rhyming dictionary, but they fit. Dave Clark, quoted earlier, has a unique way of ending sentences as shown in the following words:

But now I'm more dependent on his will instead of mine,
While learning how to live in God's own time.[2]

You won't find "mine" and "time" in a rhyming dictionary, but the two words fit his theme and they don't grate on your ears. The mark of a good writer is to ask yourself, "What word will fit here?" This is where *rewriting* is important.

Forced Rhythm

The third weakness is what I call forced rhythm—inserting a word *just to make the rhythm fit*. These include filler words such as "oh," "so," "ah," "very." They don't add anything to your poem; you use them just because you need another syllable.

If you find yourself struggling with rhyme and meter in your poetry, you may prefer to write free verse where you're not bound by these. This type of poetry still requires a form of rhythm and smoothness, however.

Following are two of my favorite poems that I like to share in poetry workshops, showing excellent rhyme, meter, and message.

Heavenly Production

A humble barn became a rude theater,
The empty stage—a rough and simple stall;
The props—a milking stool, a sheaf of barley,
And halters draped in garlands on the wall;
In shadowed wings the bovine extras waited,
As bleating sheep the orchestration played;
The grandstands filled with ruminating oxen,
And heaven's searchlight lit the little stage.

The overture was sung by angel choirs,
On heavenly balconies the scene to view;
And when they placed the Infant in the manger,
Life's greatest drama opened, right on cue.[3]

Handyman

God surely honors the handyman
Who builds for his wife the best he can.
Like searching for parts when her courage is gone,
And mounting a hook for her faith to hang on.
Fixing the leak in her weepy spout,
And restoring her strength when the bottom drops out.
Rummaging through words of every size,
He rewires the hope that once lit her eyes.
Scrapes up her confidence from sawdust remains,
And shingles her dreams before it rains.
With overalls soiled and worn at the knees,
The man labors at love the world rarely sees.
Please bless him, dear Lord, for his wife understands
That he works with Your heart and the skill of Your hands.[4]

Dealing with Rejection

Don't be discouraged if your poem is rejected. At a songwriting workshop, one of the students sang a song she had written. "I like the song," the instructor said, "but I'm not sure it will sell."

The writer replied, "Every time I sing it in church, someone comes up afterwards and says, 'You wrote that song just for me,'" to which the instructor said, "One thing you need to remember is this: Everything you write isn't always meant to be published. If it gets you through a rough time, if it gets someone else through a rough time, perhaps that's the only reason God gave it to you."

The same is true with a poem!

Change Your Style

For years I wrote only traditional rhyming poetry. I worked hard at my craft and tried to make the rhyme and meter fit. But one day while looking for a card to give to my daughter's mother-in-law on Mother's Day, I couldn't find anything on the rack that fit, so I wrote the poem below for her—my first free verse.

**To My Daughter's Other Mother
on Mother's Day**

Thank you for accepting our daughter into your family.

Thank you for helping to make her transition into married life easier by your patience and understanding.

Thank you for listening when she wants to share.

Thank you for introducing her to a new world previously unknown to her—new songs, new hobbies, new places, new people, new foods.

Thank you for loving her.

Above all, thank you for raising, nurturing, and then letting go of a wonderful son we're proud to call our daughter's husband.

And thank you for being the kind of person we're happy to introduce to our friends not as our daughter's mother-in-law, but as her mother-in-love.

(Copyright 1993 by Donna Clark Goodrich)

A short time later a friend told me that a mutual friend's husband had died. "He's better off," she added. "It was a blessing."

After she left, I thought of all the things people say when a loved one passes away. Later when a friend lost her mother, remembering friends' comments when my mother died, I wrote the following poem. It's never been published, but I've sent out about 40 copies, including one to President Clinton when he lost his mother.

On the Loss of Your Mother

People say you wouldn't wish her back . . .
>But you would.

People say her going is a blessing . . .
>But you can't see any good in it.

People say she's in a better place . . .
>But she's there—and you're here—and you feel so alone.

People say she's now free from pain . . .
>But now you're aching.

People say it will get better with time . . .
>But it's today . . . and it's hard to think of tomorrow without her—
>>. . . the letters
>>. . . the phone calls
>>. . . the visits

Have faith . . .

The day will come . . .

>When—you wouldn't wish her back;
>When—you realize her going *was* a blessing;
>When—you're aware she's in a better place;
>When—you're thankful she's now free from pain.

But until that day comes . . .
Know that you're in my thoughts and prayers.

I've been where you now are;
I've gone through what you're now going through;
I've felt the pain you're now feeling.

And I understand.

(Copyright 1985 by Donna Clark Goodrich)

Light Verse

One source of ideas for humorous verses is a book of quotations from which you can do a takeoff or change words around as shown by the following poems.

Rear View Mirror

I was walking past the dress shop,
When the "Sale" sign caught my eye.
"I'll just go in to look around;
I won't go in to buy."

Alas, I found the perfect dress,
But no, I'd better wait.
Then I heard Satan say to me,
"It really does look great."

"Get thee behind me, Satan.
I'll pay no mind to you."
He left, and then I heard him say,
"Looks good from back here, too."

Evolution

"If man descended from the ape,"
The primate asked his mother,
"Could it be true, I ask of you,
Am I my keeper's brother?"

We've all heard the quotation about the "saddest words of tongue or pen." Here's a takeoff on that:

> Of all sad words which I abhor,
> The saddest are these, "I've gained five more."

You can also use a play on words, or use words that sound alike but are spelled different. For example, I wrote one based on slogans of fast-food restaurants, ending with the lines:

> But at all these fast food restaurants,
> All the food just went to *waist*.

Many magazines and newspapers buy light verse: *Wall Street Journal* has a section called "Salt and Pepper"; *Good Housekeeping*'s page is called "Light Housekeeping"; *Saturday Evening Post* has a page called "PostScripts." Some Christian periodicals also buy humorous poetry.

Try a new style of poem. You may surprise yourself at how well you do.

Write for the Holidays

Keep your calendar open eight months in advance—the typical lead-in time for submitting holiday material. If it's January, open your calendar to August and think: end of summer and vacation, fall, kids starting school, or Thanksgiving.

Or write a poem during a holiday season when you're in the mood. Then lay it aside for a month or so, pick it up when it's cold, take it to your writers' group, do any necessary editing, and you're ready to send it out eight months before the holiday when the editors are buying.

And don't forget the lesser holidays. Editors are deluged with Christmas, Easter, and Thanksgiving poems, but how about the Fourth of July, Arbor Day, Flag Day, Veteran's Day, and so on. A book entitled *Chase's Calendar of Events* (New York: McGraw-Hill, updated annually) lists little-known holidays, such as "National Pickle Week."

Writing Poetry for Children

In a *Writer's Digest* article on writing poetry for children, Barbara Steiner asks,

"Do you remember how your grandmother's lap felt?

"Do you remember how it felt lying on your stomach in the grass watching ants, watching frogs?

"Do you remember the pain when your best friend moved away?"

If you do, she says, then you can write poetry that children can enjoy. "Children spend time wondering about things that adults take for granted," Steiner reminds us. She suggests using playful words and color words: "pumpkin moon," "lemon-bright sun," or putting your poem in shapes such as a Christmas tree.[5]

Contests

Legitimate poetry contests can be found in such magazines as *Writer's Journal* and *Byline*. However, be careful of publishers' ads saying they want your poem for an anthology. Unfortunately, no matter how good or how bad your poems are, they are almost always accepted. The publisher then offers you the book for an outrageous price (usually beginning at $49.95, with a biographical sketch included for another $20)—relying on your ego to order several copies for yourself and your family members and friends.

An elderly friend won an "award" for her poem. To receive this award, she was required to attend an out-of-state convention which would have set her back about $900. Her age and health made this impossible.

Another friend—who wrote and sold beautiful poetry—supposedly won a $500 "second prize" in an anthology contest. After waiting several months for the check, she wrote them and received a letter in reply saying, "We're sorry. That letter was sent in error. However, you'll be happy to know your poem received an Honorable Mention. Enclosed please find a certificate which we know you'll be proud to frame and show to your friends."

If entering contests excites you, stick to those offered by well-known publishers. You may have to pay a small entry fee to enter, but you should *never* pay to have your poems published or be required to purchase books in which your poems appear. Know also that you will never find these anthologies in libraries or in bookstores.

Self-Publishing

Unless you're a well-known writer such as the late Helen Steiner Rice, it is difficult to sell a *book* of poetry. This is when I definitely recommend self-publishing. While attending poetry conventions, I have seen people leave at the end of the day with fifteen or twenty books. Poets support each other.

If you want to self-publish a book of poetry, consider the following hints:

Choosing a Publisher

As most local printers require a minimum order of 250 books or more, you will do better to select a POD publisher.

Print-on-Demand or POD is a process in which new copies of a book are not printed until an order has been received. Some publishers will give you a fixed cost per copy, no matter the size of the order. However, most require that authors buy at least 500 to 1,000 copies to get a decent discount. Many university presses use POD to maintain a large backlist. Larger publishers may use POD in special circumstances, such as reprinting older titles that had been out of print or doing test marketing. Advantages to POD are:

- Technical set-up is usually quicker than for offset printing.
- Large inventories of a book or print material do not need to be kept in stock, reducing storage, handling costs, and inventory accounting costs.
- There is little or no waste from unsold products.[6]

Check out printers in your hometown as they can provide references from satisfied local customers, as well as show you copies of books they have published. However, there are also a number of excellent Christian publishers around the country—including WinePress Group—who will give you a fair price and a professional product. Check the *Christian Writers' Market Guide* and *Christian Communicator* for names of others.

Get Estimates

Before selecting a printer, visit or write to several and tell them exactly what you want: How many pages are in your book? What type of binding do you prefer? Will you include artwork or photographs? Will your material be camera ready or will it need to be typeset? Will the cover be two-color or four-color?

Obtain several estimates and when you have made your decision, get everything in writing, and don't be afraid to ask questions. Will they merely give you the finished books or will they assist with marketing? Will the price be reduced if the book isn't finished by the deadline? Will they drop ship orders? Do they have a Web site to advertise your book?

Prepublication Orders

After you give the printer your manuscript, send prepublication advertisements and order blanks to everyone on your mailing list, offering a discounted price if they order before your book comes off the press. That way, you'll have enough to pay for the printing up front, and the income from that point on will be yours.

Proofreading

Whether your book is camera ready (already typed when you take it to the printer) or the company typesets it, have someone else proofread it carefully. You are so familiar with what you wrote that you will skip over a typo, seeing instead what you know *should* be there. And although spell-checkers are great, you can't depend on them as shown by the following poem:

> Eye halve a spelling chequer
> It came with my pea sea
> It plainly marques four my revue
> Miss steaks eye kin knot sea.
>
> Eye strike a key and type a word
> And weight four it two say
> Weather eye am wrong oar write
> It shows me strait a weigh.
>
> As soon as a mist ache is maid
> It nose bee fore two long
> And eye can put the error rite
> Its rare lea ever wrong.
>
> Eye have run this poem threw it
> I am shore your pleased two no
> Its letter perfect in it's weigh
> My chequer tolled me sew.

—Sauce unknown[7]

Conclusion

There are two things to remember about writing poetry (or any type of writing):

Your Writing Can Go Where You Can't

The first month after my friend Pearl Burnside McKinney retired, she sold thirty-seven poems. One Saturday she shared with club members that she had received a phone call that morning from her sister who lived across country. "I had a nice visit with you last night," the sister said, adding that she had taken her husband to the hospital in the middle of the night and he had undergone emergency surgery.

"I didn't know if he was going to make it or not," she told Pearl, "but while I was sitting there alone at 2:30 in the morning reading a magazine, I found a poem you wrote about Christ riding through the storm with us."

"Only the Lord knew two years ago when I wrote that poem about *my* trial," Pearl said, "that two years later my sister would pick up that same poem 2,000 miles away in a hospital emergency room, and it got her through the night until she knew her husband would be okay."

She was right. Only the Lord *does* know. We write the poem and then we give it back to Him and let Him use it however He sees fit.

Your Writing Goes On After You're Gone

The second thing about your writing is that it continues to bless people even after you're gone.

Pearl's daughter called me one afternoon and said her mother had had a stroke. Later, doctors diagnosed it instead as a brain tumor. Fifteen minutes after completing her first radiation treatment, she suffered cardiac arrest and was gone.

Besides poetry, Pearl also wrote devotionals. In God's timing, her latest published ones—written for a specific week—coincided with the time of her passing and her pastor read the one for that day at her funeral. Thus, even though she was gone, her words still touched our hearts.

Summary

- Develop a one-sentence theme for your poem
- Make every word count
- Don't be afraid to rewrite
- Take it to a critique group if you belong to one
- Study sample magazines and select a market
- Submit your poem and then,
- *Let go of it and give it to God to use for His glory!*

Chapter 6

Writing for Newspapers

THE LOCAL NEWSPAPER is a great market for both beginning and advanced writers. Consider the following opportunities.

Columns

Columns can be written on almost any subject, including inspiration. While living in a small Michigan town, I wrote a column entitled "Bits and Pieces" for the weekly newspaper—a few thoughts of encouragement to brighten the readers' day.

When we moved to Arizona, I offered these same devotionals to the religion (note: "religion," not "religious") editor of the daily newspaper. She accepted them and printed them in the Saturday church section under the title "Faith at Home." (As mentioned earlier in this book, these eventually ended up in a woman's devotional book for Standard Publishing.)

Perhaps you'd like to write a column on a hobby or another topic you feel knowledge-able about—household or car repair hints, financial tips, couponing, or gardening.

Could you write a column based on your occupation? A pediatric nurse wrote a question-and-answer column concerning children's health problems.

Maybe your interest lies in history, especially of your city or state. A column on what happened ten, twenty, or even fifty years ago on this date will catch the eye of old-timers, as well as newcomers to your area.

How about profiles on celebrities or other interesting people in your area? At the same time my "Faith at Home" column ran, I wrote a second column entitled "The Parsonage Queen," in which I interviewed local pastors' wives.

While teaching a daylong workshop in New Mexico, I described various genres of writing, such as fiction, nonfiction, and so on. When I mentioned newspaper writing, one attendee's eyes lit up. The next year when I returned to that town, she proudly showed me a selection of columns entitled "View from the Pew" she had written for her local newspaper.

Do you like to read? How about a book review column?

Or humor? Do you always see the weird side of things? You may be an Erma Bombeck in the making, but you'll never know unless you try.

Other columns could include: advice for senior citizens, hobbies, computer tips, marriage relationships, and parenting.

If you're interested in writing a column for your local newspaper, call the appropriate editor and make an appointment to take him to lunch. Give him a bio sheet stating your experience, along with five or six sample columns. This serves several purposes. First, it shows your writing ability, and second, if he accepts the idea, you have extra columns on hand in case of a medical emergency or you go on vacation.

If the editor expresses interest but says the paper can't pay, offer to write the column for free for a period of time. Then, during that time, ask friends to call or write the newspaper, saying how much they enjoy the column. After an agreed-upon period, talk to the editor again and say you'd like to continue writing at their regular rate.

Chapter 16, Marketing Your Manuscript, describes the various rights you offer to editors. For these columns you will use one-time rights, which gives this particular editor the right to use your column one time, and you are free to sell it to other newspapers with a different reading audience. If the story has nationwide interest, you can conceivably send it to hundreds of newspapers across the United States at the same time or a denominational magazine. Or, as I did with my devotional columns, you can compile them in a book.

Stringer

Many newspapers cannot afford a full-time staff to cover all the local news so they hire a "stringer"—someone they can send out to cover a human interest story. These stories can be on any subject. For example, if you're interested in writing church news, not just from your church but other churches in the area, let the editor know you're available.

I received a call one day saying, "We have a fellow who does chalk drawings and illustrates the pastor's sermons. Would you like to interview him?" The newspaper provided the photographer.

I recall one conference workshop I attended entitled "Getting the Gospel Message to the Secular World." A young man in the class brought a scrapbook of stories he had sold to a St. Petersburg, Florida, newspaper. These were human interest stories with a Christian slant. The one I remember most was about how a teen's faith in God brought him through his father's murder.

One year four couples in our church celebrated their wedding anniversaries the week of Valentine's Day. The length of their marriages ranged from fifty-six to sixty-four years. I called the religion editor and asked if she was interested in a story on these couples. She said, "Great, and we'll send out a photographer."

The story appeared as a full-page spread in the Sunday newspaper. I had asked each couple, "To what do you attribute your long marriage?" Each answer included something about their faith in God, church activities, praying, and reading the Bible together. I heard comments on that article from people I knew would not pick up a religious magazine.

In writing these stories, remember to use the inverted pyramid structure you learned in your English or journalism class in which you give all the important facts first in case material is cut due to space limitations. In the above story, the editor deleted the last paragraph giving the names of the fourth couple's children and the number of their grandchildren.

Many church activities never make it into the local paper because either the editor doesn't have anyone to cover the story, or the church has no one qualified to write it. This includes such things as Christmas or Easter cantatas, concerts, a new pastor or staff member, vacation Bible school, missionary speakers, and so on.

You can also cover other community events. What about school activities, such as concerts and programs, or stories about special students or teachers? Or, if you're a sports fan, you can send in reports on school games and local adult softball and basketball leagues.

Organizations also like publicity, especially for fund-raisers.

As you can see, possibilities abound. Editors look for qualified people to write these stories. Why not you?

Letters to the Editor

How often does conversation among family members and friends turn to current events? You complain about what is happening in the world, each of you offering your opinion of what should be done, or you praise someone in the community or in politics for doing a positive deed. Then you go home, and what happens? Probably nothing.

Organize your thoughts in a Letter to the Editor. State how you feel about an elected official, a law that's been passed, or a school event you attended. The tone can be laudatory or critical, but the letters usually have to be within a certain length. *You do the editing.* If you send it in longer than acceptable, the editor may delete a paragraph that contains the crux of your letter. By following the rules, you maintain control.

These letters are a great way not only to share your faith, but also to get your name in front of readers and the editor. After a few well-written missives, he may call you with assignments.

Op-Ed Columns

Op-ed columns are like a Letter to the Editor, except longer—usually between 600 and 850 words, focusing on a local issue or a current event happening nationwide or worldwide, and something you feel passionate about. These columns are stronger if you include more than just your opinion; it helps to include statistics.

Give your column a catchy title, use a strong lead, present your facts in order, and wrap up the column with a strong ending—perhaps tying it in with your title or lead paragraph. Include your name, address, phone number, e-mail address, word count, and photograph—if requested—and send it out.

Who knows? In a few days when you open up your newspaper to the editorial page, you may see your op-ed column—for everyone to read!

Note: If your column is published in a secular newspaper or periodical and you quote at least one Scripture verse, after publication you can submit it to the Amy Foundation for its annual awards, ranging from $10,000 to three prizes of $1,000 each. (See www. amyfound.org/amy_writing_awards/amy_writing_awards.html for more information.)

Chapter 7

Conducting
An Effective Interview

I LOVE INTERVIEWING people and getting their story. At one time I wrote biographies for a local mortuary. After a person passed away, the funeral home sent the family a questionnaire, asking them to fill in such things as date and place of birth, name of parents and siblings, education, jobs held, and date and place of death.

I then made an appointment with the surviving spouse, children, or parents and, using the questionnaire as a guide, I interviewed them and gleaned more information: what the deceased and their family did for fun in childhood, where they went on vacations, their favorite or least favorite subjects in school, how they met their spouse, parenting experiences, their favorite song or poem, and so on. Then I wove this information into the biography, trying to put enough of the person's character into it that when family members read it, it brought back pleasant memories.

When the mortuary owner asked if I knew other people who would like to write these biographies, I recommended some friends and jotted down the following hints to help them. These suggestions can be used for any type of interview.

Call for An Appointment

Tell the subject approximately how long the interview will take and try to stick to it. You may find, however, that the subject will be so interested in talking about himself he won't want the interview to end. Older people will welcome your visit simply for the company.

Give Reason for the Interview

Let him or her know why you're calling. Do you have an assignment and, if so, for what magazine or newspaper? What specific topics will you cover?

Confirm Appointment

Call or e-mail the day before to confirm the appointment. I once knocked on the door of a pastor's wife for a newspaper assignment and caught her coming out of the shower. She thought the appointment was an hour later. When you call, also repeat the directions to the person's home or office. You may even want to make a dry run to the location.

Prepare Ahead

Find out as much as you can about this person, especially if you are going to be interviewing a celebrity.

I have three folders of biographies in my file cabinet: one of writers, one of singers, and one of people well-known in the Christian field. If one of these people came to town and I wanted to interview her, I can go to my files, or to the Internet, and find material to use as a springboard to develop my own questions for the interview.

You can also send for a press kit for singers, authors, or other celebrities. Don't waste precious time asking questions you can obtain the answers to ahead of time.

And prepare *yourself*. Dr. Dennis E. Hensley says, "When preparing for the interview, always work with Murphy's Law ('If it can go wrong, it will go wrong') and be prepared in advance in case your pen goes dry, your mike cord develops a short, or your cassette tape gets tangled and breaks."[1] (Note: You won't have the tape problem if you use a digital recorder, more popular today.)

Dress neatly, but don't overdress. Hensley says, "People will not talk openly to someone in blue jeans and tennis shoes, so *look* like you mean business."

Send List of Questions Ahead of Time

You will get a better interview if the interviewee is also prepared. For this reason, you might want to send a list of your questions in advance. This is especially helpful with what I call "thought" questions: Who had the greatest influence on your life? Who do you consider to be your spiritual mentor? How would you like to be remembered when you're gone? If your article is for a magazine, the editor may suggest topics that would interest its specific readership.

However, don't be limited by your list. If your subject makes a comment that brings another question to mind, jot that down and come back to it later.

Take Time to Get Acquainted

This pre-interview conversation can include comments about the person's house, the furniture, a painting, and so on. When I interviewed families for the mortuary biographies, I often asked to see pictures of the deceased person.

One widow showed me a picture of her husband's tractor. "It was almost like a member of the family," she said. "He even gave it a name." In the biography I compared some of the qualities of the tractor with those of her husband: dependable, hardworking, and so on. "When did I mention the tractor?" she asked, when reading the finished copy, and I reminded her of the pictures she had shown me. I had turned on the recorder as she shared memories from the photos.

Use Recorder Wisely

I prefer face-to-face interviews as they offer an opportunity to more accurately portray the subject—dress, gestures, and so on—and his surroundings. Also, people tend to feel more at ease in their own home or office where they have access to photographs and other information. Others may feel more comfortable in a neutral environment, such as a coffee shop. But whether the interview is in person or over the phone, I record it to avoid any later disputes regarding quotations.

If you are taping an interview over the telephone, by federal law you have to inform the subject that this is being done and get his or her approval on tape before asking your questions.

Test the recorder ahead of time. If you're not using a digital recorder, take along an extra tape. The interview may turn out to be longer than expected. It's a good idea to also take written notes during the interview in the event of a recorder failure.

In a face-to-face interview, it's important that you conduct your taped interview in a quiet environment. I once interviewed a friend who, as Miss Michigan, participated in the Miss America pageant. The interview took place in a crowded restaurant and we were seated near the kitchen. This made transcribing the tape very difficult, with the banging of pots and pans and the noisy chatter of the workers. Other friends have shared horror stories about airport interviews.

C. Hope Clark, editor of several Internet writers' newsletters[2], notes that if you're interviewing from your home, "Make sure the kids are gone, the television is off, and the dogs are outside . . . . Taped telephone interviews reveal all kinds of background noise," she warns. "Even pay attention to the acoustics. High ceilings and tile floors are prone to echo."

Ask the subject to spell out names of people, places of employment, exact job title, and any unusual words that will appear in the final story. Also, make sure you quote statistics accurately.

If you have a laptop or if the subject comes to your office, then you can just enter the information as the person answers your questions. Leave out the "chatter" and capture only the important information. In this case, however, you won't have a taped record if the subject later disputes a quotation.

Stick to the Subject

It's often difficult for writers to not respond to the subject's comments with some of their own. Be careful that you're not talking more than the interviewee. I became more aware of this when I began to tape my interviews and later transcribed them.

Kelly Ettenborough, former religion editor for the *Mesa* (Arizona) *Tribune*, says, "A good interviewer is a good listener. People want to talk; they're excited. Ask a leading question, then shut up." You can let them know you understand, she suggests, by nodding your head or saying an occasional "Yes" or "I understand."

Dennis Hensley agrees. "Observe common courtesy. Don't talk along with them. Don't cut them off. Don't finish their sentences."

Writing Spin-Off Articles

Also determine if the subject has any religious, fraternal, or educational affiliations, and if this organization has a publication you could submit related stories to.

Editor/Writer Interviews

If you're interviewing a writer or editor for a trade magazine, the following are some questions you might ask.

Writer:

- Briefly tell about your childhood: where born, a Christian home, conversion.
- Briefly describe your education: college attended, degrees, etc.
- How did you meet your spouse? Occupation? Number of children?
- When did you first become interested in writing? Your first sale? Genre of writing?

Editor:

- How did you get into the editorial field? Previous jobs?
- Describe the needs of your periodical.
- Biggest reasons you reject manuscripts.
- Advice you would give a new writer.

After the Interview

Write your article as soon as possible after the interview so details are still fresh in your mind.

I often send a rough draft to the interviewee if the editor allows it. This isn't a hard and fast rule, but it is a courteous gesture if you have the time, and especially if you've included quotations and statistics you want to verify.

Send the subject a thank-you note and a copy of the published article.

One thing to remember in interviewing is that "You're a Christian first, a writer second." If you've had the experience of being interviewed and misquoted, you know that the best rule to follow is the Golden Rule. One author in a book on interviewing says that you get your best interview when you've turned off your recorder. This is the same person who says you get your best quotes when the subject says, "This is off the record."

I do not agree. When the subject tells me it's off the record, it's off the record; we shouldn't even have to be told that. We should have an inner sense that tells us when the subject is sharing something not for publication.

Treat your subject as you'd like to be treated, and you'll be welcomed back for a second interview.

Chapter 8

Writing Travel Articles

YOU HAVE HAD the good fortune to travel to many exotic places and would like to explore this genre. If so, the hints in this chapter will help.

The most important thing to remember is that most editors don't want a "diary" type of travel article. Rather, they want a theme: unusual places to visit in the United States or foreign countries; ethnic restaurants; comparing sports facilities—food, prices, souvenirs; out-of-the-way tourist attractions; inexpensive family destinations.

Types of Travel Articles

In his article on "Travel Article Types," Bob Brooke lists the following twelve types of travel articles:

1. Advice—basically a service piece that helps the reader make a decision. Example: "Should You Book Air Travel Online?"
2. Here and now—a topical article with limited life. Example: "Christmas in Williamsburg"
3. Flavor—an article using the five senses. Example: "Savor Mexico"
4. Roundup—a collection of information on the same topic. Example: "The Top 10 Romantic Inns"
5. How—an article about how to get there. Example: "Traveling Across America"
6. What—an article about an activity—what to do? Example: "Kayaking the Coast of Oregon"
7. Historical—an article featuring the historical aspects of travel. Example: "The Grand Tour Revisited"

8. Humor—exaggerated adventures. Example: "Wild and Wooly Nights in Las Vegas"
9. Destination—also called Definitive—the last word on a place. Example: "Yellowstone, the Granddaddy of National Parks"
10. Gimmick—an idea in very sharp focus. Example: "All About Suitcases"
11. Who—an article that centers around a particular group of people. Example: "Honeymooning in Paradise"
12. Personal experience—sharing a personal experience with the reader.[1]

Where to Obtain Information

If you haven't had the chance to travel, it's possible to still write this type of article without leaving the comfort of your armchair. Look for coupons in your auto club travel magazine or the travel section of your Sunday newspapers that read, "Visit North Carolina," or some other destination. Fill out the coupon, put it in the mail, and before long you'll receive brochures, city maps, a list of places to visit, and things to do. And, of course, much of this information is also available on the Internet.[2]

Set up a folder for each state, and begin filing this information—or store the Internet data on a CD. One word of warning, however. If you're recommending a particular restaurant, hotel, or place of entertainment, make sure it's still in business before including the information in your article.

(Note: You can use this same information to check statistics for a nonfiction manuscript or as a background for a novel. By using actual names of streets and tourist attractions, your reader will say, "She must have been there." You haven't; you've just done your homework.)

Photographs

In travel writing, it's very true that a picture is worth a thousand words, so it's worth investing in a dependable camera. If photography isn't one of your talents, sign up for a class at your local community college or a camera store.

You can also order stock photos at www.istockphoto.com/index.php. Chambers of Commerce will supply you with requested photos of local tourist attractions as well.

The Grass Isn't Always Greener Somewhere Else

Too many writers look to other states and countries for ideas, failing to look in their own backyards. As Dorothy said in *The Wizard of Oz*, "There's no place like home." Are there landmarks in your hometown, annual festivals, and seasonal activities that others would be interested in reading about?

Kayleen J. Reusser, in her article, "Travel That Pays," reminds us that "A travel article can be about a person, as long as there's a travel tie-in." She wrote an article about Gene Stratton-Porter, a novelist who lived in Indiana during the early twentieth century. Because both of Stratton-Porter's homes—one in Geneva and one in Rome City—were state historic sites, Reusser included directions, cost of admittance, and hours of operation. She sold this article to a woman's magazine.

Reusser also reminds writers to be alert to anniversaries for tourist-related events. Find out who died on a specific day in your area and then check to see if your town is planning a celebration, or the anniversary of a landmark opening or an entertainment venue.[3]

Show, Don't Tell

It is especially important to remember to "show, don't tell" in travel writing. How do you do this? By using the five senses. Through your words, let readers taste the dish being served in the ethnic restaurant, let them hear the clop-clop of the horses on Mackinac Island where no automobiles are allowed, let them see the sun setting over Waikiki Beach, allow them to feel the ivory tusks of an elephant on your African safari, and enable them to smell the scones in a Scottish bakery.

Following is a quote from the *New York Times* describing a trip to Norway:

There were little white candles flickering everywhere in Oslo—even in the breakfast room of the hotel, where we guests all lingered over our lavish Scandinavian smorgasbord. According to our preferences, we fortified ourselves with three kinds of herring, with soft-boiled eggs or shrimp salad, with mackerel in tomato sauce or muesli. We refilled our plates and sipped our tea and coffee, reluctant to go out into the winter cold. Little white candles in silver-stemmed goblets, in smoked-glass boxes, in pewter saucers were burning on every table in every café and restaurant, like a promise to hold onto the light right through the winter darkness.[4]

Doesn't that make you want to pick up the phone and make a reservation to visit Norway? Your travel articles can do the same thing for your readers. They'll want to dig out their suitcases and start packing right away!

. . . .

Chapter 9

Writing for Children

IN ITS GUIDELINES for children's book writers, one publisher states, "All manuscripts are selected to accomplish three purposes:

- To help draw children into a lasting relationship with Jesus;
- To help children develop insight about what the Bible teaches;
- To make reading an appealing and pleasurable activity."

10 Hints on Writing for Children

Many writers have the false impression that because their writing is for children, it's easier, but the truth is that it's more difficult. If this field of writing appeals to you, the following ten hints might help. Pat Egan Dexter, a contributing editor to *Guideposts*, suggested these while looking over a picture book written by a teenaged friend of my daughter's and gave me permission to include them here. I've added some notes of explanation dealing with this particular book.

1. Don't present more than one universal truth in each story. It's too much for children to handle, especially younger children.
2. The truth the main character learned from the story should be the same learned by the reader.
3. Things shouldn't happen by accident. The main character has to do something to help himself.

4. In writing for younger children, short sentences work better. This goes along with the following hint:

5. Children love repetition.

    For example, this book included the following sentences: "He picked up the hammer. He picked up the nails. He pounded the hammer." If I were editing that for adults, I would warn about starting three sentences in a row with the same word. I would also suggest combining two of the sentences with an "and" to avoid choppiness, but children like the shorter sentences and repetition.

6. Write from the viewpoint of the main character.

    You can't get into any other character's head and know what he's thinking except through his conversation and facial expression. In this book, the author wrote, "Mother could hear the noise Timmy was making." But how did Timmy know that? He was upstairs in his bedroom; his mother was downstairs. The sentence should read, "Timmy *wondered* if his mother could hear the noise he was making."

7. Unless the book is illustrated, every sentence should paint a picture the child can visualize. Instead of, "The piece of wood was twelve inches long," write, "The piece of wood was as long as Timmy's arm."

8. Determine the age of the child you are writing for.

9. Ask yourself if it is a "read-to" book or a "read-it-yourself" one.

    I edited one children's book in which I couldn't identify the target age. Some words were too hard for younger children; others were too simple for older children. I asked the author about this and she replied that she used it in junior church with children from three to twelve years old. That is a wide range as the vocabulary and interests are too varied. I explained to her that in writing for children, the approach needs to be narrowed down to specific ages such as three to four years old, five to six, seven to nine, and ten to twelve.

    I also noted that it was different if she was *reading* the story to children and could explain things as she went along, which she said she was doing. Then she added, "And I use flannel graph." That brought out an even different slant. You can get away with a little more if you use visuals.

10. Read your book to the specific age group. Are you keeping their interest? Watch their facial expressions. Are they bored? Ask them what they liked or disliked about the book.

One children's author and former assistant children's editor sits on the floor—on the level of her audience—and reads her material to them. Afterwards, she asks for their opinion and records their answers, paying attention to the sentence structure and vocabulary of that age group.

I read my granddaughter a mystery book I had written for nine- to twelve-year-olds. "Grandma," she protested, "kids my age don't talk like that!"

You can buy books that contain word lists for various age groups. One of the best is entitled *Children's Writer's Word Book* by Alijandra Mogilner (Writer's Digest Books, 2006). You can also purchase dictionaries for individual grades. It doesn't hurt, however, to introduce a few new words, perhaps including a glossary at the beginning of the book and putting these words in boldface type throughout the book.

Write for the Parents

Children's books must also appeal to parents! They buy the books, as well as read them to their children.

An instructor in one writing workshop asked students their favorite children's book and why. I thought of the one I enjoyed most: *The Little Engine That Could*. Thinking over why I liked it, I realized it carried a lesson that even adults can relate to: Something impossible became possible because someone thought he could do it. How many times do we come up against an obstacle and say to ourselves, in so many words, "I think I can. I think I can. I think I can."

Types of Children's Books

Concept books. two to four years old, twelve to thirty-two pages, up to 350 words but most under a hundred words. Full-color illustrations on every page.

Picture books. three to seven years old, twenty-four to forty-eight pages, 250 to 2,500 words, usually full-color illustrations every page.

Story books. five to nine years old, thirty to forty-eight pages, 1,500 to 4,000 words, usually full-color illustrations on every other page.

Easy readers. six to eight years old, 350 to 2,000 words, thirty-two to sixty-four pages, full-color illustration every page or two.

Chapter books. seven to ten years, fifty-six to eighty pages, black-and-white pictures spaced throughout book.

Middle grade(MG)/'tweens. eight to twelve years, 112 to 144 pages, black-and-white pictures spaced throughout, or none at all.

Young adult (YA). twelve and up, 144 to 232 pages, no illustrations.

Remember, regardless of the age of the child, use lots of dialogue in your books. The rule of "show, don't tell" is especially important in this genre.

Query Letter

One instructor stated at a writers' conference that editors want the following information:

1. Subject and purpose of book
2. Market or age range. Who is going to read it? Who will the book be read to?
3. Number of words
4. Why are you the one to write this story? Are you a teacher? Do you interact with children in other ways?

The editor doesn't need to know that you've never written before, or that you've told this story to your kids and they loved it, or that you've quit your job and you plan to support yourself writing children's books. It is acceptable, however, to let the editor know that you've tested this material at a school or Sunday school class or children's church and received a positive response. You might even include some of the children's comments.

Illustrations

Most of the children's editors I've heard speak at conferences say that unless you're a professional, don't submit illustrations. They all seem to agree with one editor who said, "A terrific illustrator will help; a mediocre one will hurt."

Also, using your own illustrator results in two contracts. Thus, you receive only half of the royalties, whereas the majority of publishers have a salaried artist on staff.

Remember that in a picture book, the text on a page is limited to what can be illustrated in one picture.

Writing for Take-Home Papers and Children's Magazines

Sunday school take-home papers and children's magazines use a variety of material including fiction, fillers, puzzles, games, quizzes, and poetry. Most of them also accept nonfiction—science, nature, animals, and so on. The typical length for preschool is 500 to 800 words; first grade through third grade, 800 to 1,000 words; for older readers, up to 1,500 words.

Marjorie Miller, former editor at Standard Publishing, gives the following pitfalls to avoid when writing for children:

- Insertion of your (adult) personal opinion

- Dual (or triple) viewpoints
- Needless details
- Perfect characters
- Conflicting moods
- Coincidental happenings
- Unrealistic dialogue
- Impossible feats
- Forced humor
- Unnecessary adverbs
- Mixed tenses
- Stale characters and situations—lack of imagination

Writing for Teens

Many of the rules in this chapter will easily adapt to writing for teens. Besides fiction, editors look for nonfiction articles concerning issues that teens struggle with today. They also accept such things as Bible studies, puzzles, devotionals, and curriculum.

Hannah Gomez, a sixteen-year-old writer from Arizona, gives this warning: "Articles that tell you what teens like to read are usually written by middle-aged adults who don't have children."

Gomez suggests that, besides doing extensive research, check out teen online hangouts. "If you want to know anything about current events or even if you are planning just one chapter where your character talks to a friend online, you must go to at least one online message board to see how it works." She adds, "In the hundreds of books I've read, I have not seen one book that correctly describes the way we use online lingo."[1]

Joëlle Anthony, in her article, "Red Hair Is Not As Uncommon As You Think," made the following observations after reading approximately four hundred young-adult and middle-grade novels over a period of thirty-six months and keeping a record of everything she read.

"Before I was very far into the program," Joëlle states, "I began to notice similarities in many YA and MG novels. At first it just made me laugh, but after a while I began to take notes. There may not be any original stories, and nothing may be new, but some things are way overused. Here's a countdown, based on my reading, of the twenty-five things that show up repeatedly in young-adult fiction:

25. Vegetarian teens with unsympathetic, meat-eating parents.
24. Shy or withdrawn characters who take refuge in the art room, where they find a compassionate art teacher.

23. A token black friend among a group of white friends. Usually it's a girl, and she's always gorgeous.
22. A tiny scar by an eyebrow, sometimes linked to an embarrassing story.
21. Using the word 'rents for parents, but not using any other slang.
20. A beautiful best friend who gets all the guys but doesn't want them.
19. The wicked stepmother who turns out to be simply misunderstood, and it's all cleared up in the climax.
18. Authors showing *their* age by naming character names *they* grew up with (e.g., Debbie, Lisa, Alice, Linda, etc.).
17. Parents who are professional writers or book illustrators.
16. Using *coffee, cappuccino,* and *caffe latte* to describe someone's skin color.
15. Main characters named Hannah, and noting the name is a palindrome.
14. Younger siblings, who are geniuses and adored by everyone and who usually run away during the book's climax, causing dramatic tension.
13. The mean-spirited cheerleader (and her gang) as the story's antagonist.
12. A dead mother.
11. Heroines who can't carry a tune, even if it were in a bucket.
10. Guys with extremely long eyelashes.
 9. The popular boy dating the dorky heroine to make his ex-girlfriend jealous, then breaking the heroine's heart.
 8. The diary, either as the book's entire format or an occasional entry.
 7. Fingernail biting.
 6. Characters who chew on their lips or tongues in times of stress and usually until they taste blood.
 5. Raising one eyebrow.
 4. Characters who want to be writers.
 3. Calling parents by their first names.
 2. Best friends with red hair.
    And the number one thing found in YA novels, Joëlle notes . . .
 1. Lists.

Note: Red-haired best friends are amazingly predominant in both MG and YA fiction, and certainly gave "lists" a run for its money. Red hair might be an easy way to quickly identify a secondary character, but it's a lot more common in books than in humans.

Joëlle states that her reading was not a scientific study, but adds, "If you've used any of these things in your manuscripts, think long and hard about how important they are to the story. Stretch your imagination, make your characters' career choices different than those you know, find new ways to show emotion—and read, read, read."[2]

Needs of Children

Author Jean Conder Soule states that basics in writing Christian juvenile material include these fundamental needs of children:

1. The need to be loved;
2. The need to belong;
3. The need to achieve;
4. The need for security (material, emotional, spiritual); and
5. The need to know—to learn new facts, explore the world, try new things.

"Know your children," Soule says. "Learn to communicate with them; discover their likes and dislikes, fears, hopes, and dreams. Remember that you must please a child reader—or he'll put down your story and go watch TV."[3]

A father wondered why it took his six-year-old son an hour to get home from school. Finally, he decided to make the trip with his son to see why it took so long.

After the trip he said, "The twenty minutes I thought reasonable was right, but I failed to consider such important things as a side trip to track down a trail of ants, or an educational stop to watch a man fix a flat, or the time it took to swing around a half dozen telephone poles, or how much time it took for a boy to get acquainted with two stray dogs and a brown cat. In short," said the father, "I had forgotten what it is really like to be six years old."

And that, writers, is what you need to remember if you want to write stories children and teens will read and remember long after they put down your book.

Chapter 10

Writing the Personal Experience Story

EVERYONE HAS A story just waiting to be written. The great thing about writing the personal experience story is that you have done the research. You've lived through the crisis, thus *no one* can say it like you because no one else has gone through it exactly like you.

Why Personal Experience Stories Are Popular

Author and conference speaker Jewell Johnson gives the following reasons personal experience stories are so popular:

- *People like to read personal experiences.* These are usually short (up to 1,500 words), easy-to-read articles that provide a few minutes of relaxation.
- *They help people solve problems.* How you coped with the death of a parent or spouse, or how you went through a valley experience, will give support to a reader facing a similar problem.
- *There is a wide range of markets.* Personal experiences are in constant demand by Sunday school take-home papers, denominational magazines, and women's magazines, as well as other markets. Some periodicals like *Guideposts* are totally devoted to the personal experience story.
- *Personal experiences do not go out-of-date.* These are timeless stories and can be sold over and over again.

When you're looking for an idea for a personal experience story, Johnson says, think *PROBLEM!* You must have a problem you have grappled with *and* resolved. If you're in the middle of the problem, keep notes, but don't write the story until it's resolved to some degree.

The Personal Experience Article/Book

The difference between writing a personal experience article and a book is that in the article you're not covering a long period of time; rather, you are lifting *one* experience out of your life and writing about it. Following are examples of personal experience stories:

- life-changing crisis, trauma, or joyous event
- experiences that give you a new understanding of spiritual truth
- a significant experience that has helped you to grow in your faith
- articles written as therapy
- conversion testimonies
- as-told-to articles

One of the main thrusts of the personal experience article or book is to help readers feel that they're not alone in the struggle they're going through. However, be careful that this doesn't develop into simply a "poor me" narration. Jeanette Littleton suggests several ways to avoid this.

- Check the emotions. Do you spend too much time describing your anger or pain? An article laden with heavy, uncontrolled, unresolved emotion scares readers off!
- Is your experience an "I guess you had to be there" scenario? Some personal experiences just don't translate to an audience through the written page.
- How big are your "I's"? If your article is filled with "I," "me," "my," you might need to soften it.
- Do you really have a point, or are you just venting? Evaluate and ask yourself, "What do I want my reader to glean from this?"
- If your article has a "therapy" feel, broaden it by including not just your experiences, but others' experiences that support your point.[1]

Select a Theme

Whether you're writing a personal experience story or a book, you must have a theme, or a "takeaway." It's boring for the reader to muddle through a chronological biography: I was born, I started first grade, and so on. Select a theme and weave that theme throughout your manuscript.

One of the best examples of this was a talk a minister's wife gave at a ladies' luncheon. Using the theme, "God Is Enough," she shared how God was enough when she grew up in a poor family and how He supplied their needs. God was enough when she felt led to go to Bible college. He was enough when she met her husband and they married while still in college. God was enough when her husband was killed in an accident a year later. She went on to tell how she married an evangelist and how God was enough as they traveled around the country. God was enough the day their teenaged daughter came down the stairs and said, "I no longer believe in God. I'm an atheist." She had us hanging onto every word as she told her life story using this theme.

Use the Five Senses

Whether you're writing a personal experience article or a book, remember to *use the five senses*. When I was younger, I enjoyed reading *Reader's Digest Condensed Books*. Forget the description. I wanted to get right to the dialogue. Let's get this show on the road! The condensed books were great. They were compact and I could finish them in a short time.

Then I read the book, *Exodus*. What impressed me about this book was how the author used the five senses. I could see the people walking naked up to the crematoriums. I could hear the cries. I could smell the flesh burning. From that point on, I began to try to use this method more in my writing.

After you have finished writing your story, go back and underline each word that describes one of the five senses. How many did you find? What can your readers see? What can they smell? If you're telling a story about your grandmother, don't tell her whole life story. Pick out one event, such as baking day. Can your readers see her as she peels the apples, wearing her ever-present apron? Can they smell the aroma when the pies come out of the oven? Can they hear the oohs and aahs as family members take their first juicy bite?

My grandmother was a total nonconformist. Even after all her neighbors had modernized their houses, she and my grandpa had an outside pump and an outhouse. To this day when I see a *Farm Journal* magazine or Sears catalog, I think of it as Charmin tissue. When I hear the buzz of bumblebees, I can see them flying around the chicken coop. When I see hollyhocks, I'm sitting on the workbench on my grandparents' back porch, listening to WCKY Cincinnati on their old Philco radio.

In my classes, I ask my students what a particular smell reminds them of. Some respond with a specific perfume or powder that reminds them of their mother or grandmother. While popcorn reminds some of early dates at the movies, that aroma takes me back to when my mother was in the cancer ward at the hospital and the nurses brought popcorn to the room every night. I could smell it as soon as I walked off the elevator. When I went to the mall after returning home from her funeral, the buttery smell sent me running to my car in tears.

Incorporate the five senses into your writing. It will make your story come alive.

Why Are You Writing This Story?

In a personal experiences workshop, Dina Donohue suggested asking yourself these questions before writing any story:

1. Will it interest the reader?
2. Will it be of help to others?
3. Will it move the readers? Sway emotions?
4. Am I writing in a fresh, intriguing style; offering something new?

When I submitted an article on how inheriting my grandma's antique pump organ changed my life, the editor asked: 1) What were you like before? 2) How did you change? 3) What initiated the change? and 4) What is your life like now?

Other questions to ask yourself before sitting down to write your story are:

Why am I writing this story? Writing can be very therapeutic. This type of writing may not be in publishable form to begin with, however. First sit down and write the events as you remember them, getting any feelings of anger, bitterness, and resentment off your chest. Then lay those sheets aside, and rewrite the manuscript in a format that will show your readers how God gave you victory over those negative feelings.

Yes, God can speak through my words and touch someone's life. Yes, God might be pleased by my efforts. But if my goal is in any way to gain recognition for myself rather than pleasing him and focusing on *his* priorities, then this project is a failure in his eyes . . . . God . . . isn't constructing a bookshelf in my heavenly mansion to display my publications. My name will not light up celestial storefront windows. There will be no book signings in eternity. (Erin Keeley Marshall, *Navigating Route 20-Something*)

Are people still alive this story can hurt? Be careful if your story identifies relatives, friends, neighbors—or families of these people—who are still alive. There are several ways of dealing with this.

1. Write under a pen name. A friend wrote a book about her half-sister who was molested by their father. She not only wrote the book under a pen name, but when she speaks on the subject, she is introduced by her pen name.
2. Use composites of people involved. Instead of describing a brunette secretary who lived next door with two boys and two girls, make her a red-haired schoolteacher with two girls and a boy who lived in another city. How you describe this person isn't as important as the lessons learned.
3. Write the events as a short story or a novel. Fiction doesn't always have to be solely entertainment; you can also use this medium to get a message across.

Tim Riter, a pastor and author, commenting on this subject on the Writers' View Web site, says, "I confess my sins, not those of others. We need to either obtain the permission of others, or change at least three significant details." He adds, "Write for impact, not therapy. Our transparency should help the reader, not ourselves. If we write for personal catharsis, keep it in a journal."

"I write when I'm at least part of the way down the path," Riter adds. "If we merely share our pains and troubles without offering some hope, we just increase despondency. We don't have to have it all together, but we should at least know what the parts are and how they should fit. Otherwise, we give little benefit to the reader."[2]

The third question to ask yourself is, *Have I dealt with this situation in my own life?* If your story involves someone who mistreated you at some time in your life, have you forgiven this person? Unless you have, the bitterness and resentment you feel toward this person will bleed through your story. While reading a story at a conference appointment, I asked the writer, "You haven't forgiven this person, have you?" "No," he replied. "He never asked me to." The unforgiveness showed in the writing.

We may have to go through a process of letting go before we can write. As mentioned above, we can write for therapy, and this can bring us to a point where we can give it up to God. Then we can write the story as *victors*, not *victims*.

Let me share a personal experience. During a difficult period in my life, I spent a week with a friend at a Benedictine monastery. We went to do some writing; however, I also had some feelings in my life toward a particular person who had hurt me.

The first day, while walking around the grounds, I came across the twelve Stations of the Cross. Each station was made up of sticks and other desert materials, with a typewritten Bible verse attached. Passing the last station, I found a large cross made from mesquite and twigs. Then I saw two concrete benches facing each other.

I decided that the next morning I would come to these benches, mentally put this person across from me, and let him have it! Then, when I was done, I would go back to the cross and ask forgiveness for my feelings. (Deeply spiritual, right?)

That night I made a list of all the things this person had done and said to me in the past to make sure I wouldn't forget any slight or any hurt—real or imagined. The next morning I got up, determined to carry out my resolution.

But something happened on the way to my destination. I got lost! Instead of the benches, when I rounded the bend I saw . . . the cross! And God whispered, "Go to the cross first." I literally fell at the foot of that old rugged cross and poured out my heart, asking God to heal my broken emotions. When I rose to my feet, I found I no longer needed the benches! I told this story in an article entitled, "I Found Peace at the Cross."

What am I saying? Only after you allow God to release you from the chains that trap you in pain or bitterness and resentment can you lead the way for someone else. It might not be easy, but the freedom is worth the cost.

Be Honest

For a long time, I didn't allow much room in fellow Christians' lives—or my own for that matter—for humanness. For this reason, I took all my weaknesses and gave them to my characters in short stories. But once I accepted myself as God accepts me—just as I am—I allowed myself to be more vulnerable and began sharing in personal experience stories of how God can use us not *in spite of* these weaknesses, but *because* of them.

Honest emotions allow readers a peek inside our hearts. A friend who had lost two daughters wrote a book about their lives and deaths. Filled only with praises to the Lord, its pages contained no spiritual struggles or family problems during all those years.

After reading it, I asked the author, "Didn't you ever get mad at God? Didn't all that tension trigger arguments between you and your husband? And what about your son, with your daughters getting all this attention? Didn't you have any problems with him?"

She replied, "Oh, my, yes. My husband and I separated twice, and our son got in trouble at school. He even set fires in the neighborhood. Night after night I shook my fist at God. But," she protested, "I can't put that in the book. *I'm a Christian!*"

"Then you won't help anyone," I told her. "A mother reading your book who's lost a child will say, 'What's wrong with me? Why do I feel such desperation and depression when she's praising the Lord all the time?' And Satan will say to her, 'That's because you don't truly believe. If you did, you wouldn't feel the anger and the pain.'"

She rewrote the book, including not only the struggles the family faced, but also how God brought them through victoriously. The end product has helped many families.

Idea Starters

I'll never forget the day . . .

When I threw this question out to a class, one lady replied, " . . . when I got arrested in Russia." A good lead for a story!

Draw a map

If you're trying to remember something that happened years ago, sit down and draw a picture of the house you lived in when this event took place. Make a sketch of the kitchen, the living room, the bedroom. Put in some furniture. You probably won't get through one room before ideas start coming to you.

I recall one house we lived in. My brothers bought a little movie projector and some cartoons and charged the neighbor kids a nickel to watch them in our basement. I also remember the dining room table as the center of all our activities. My dad left when I was eleven, leaving my mother to raise three children alone. Although she worked during the day, she provided a variety of activities to keep us entertained. The dining room table was where my brothers built erector set structures and we put jigsaw puzzles together.

My mother had a system for puzzles. We didn't just dump out the pieces and start. First, we turned over all the pieces, then we put the frame together. Sometimes the puzzles had a shape that went in the middle of the puzzle, such as a ball or star, and one of us would put that in the center and begin working out from it.

During this activity, my mother taught us that in life, we also have a frame, a base, certain principles that never change. She taught us about turning over all the pieces (getting all the facts) before making a decision, and she taught us to put Christ in the center of our lives. Thus, as she taught us to form a perfect picture from a jumble of puzzle pieces, she also taught us how to live.

So as you think back about your house and the activities that went on there, you will find many memory-joggers to develop into articles, short stories, and books.

Then branch out. Draw a map of your neighborhood. Who lived in what house? One day, after I was married and we moved back to our hometown, I walked home from work, traveling the route my brothers and friends and I took home from "intermediate" school. I crossed what used to be called Catholic Hill (why I don't know), went by the little grocery store where we all congregated each afternoon after school, drinking Nehi soda and playing "Twenty Questions." While walking through the alley filled with cans and trash, then on past our old house where we lived, writing ideas overwhelmed me.

Maps of your home and neighborhood, your school, your church, places you worked, and so on, will help you recall family activities, school successes and failures, classmates and teachers, your first date, going off to college, your first job, and other highlights of your life.

Ideas from Photographs

Go through your photograph albums (or boxes) and jot down the story behind each picture. What did your family do on vacation? On holidays? On birthdays? Compare the customs, dress, furniture, and style of houses between your childhood days and today. What comes to your mind about kindergarten, first grade, your senior year, the day you moved out of your parents' house? How did you meet your spouse? Describe some of your dating experiences. How did your mate propose? And how about the stories behind all the people in those photographs: best friends, siblings, grandparents, neighbors, teachers, church friends?

Divide Your Life into Segments

Divide your life into five-year segments. Where did your family live from the time you were born up to your fifth birthday? Describe your immediate family and other relatives. Who were your playmates?

First grade: You lived where? Your house was (recall what it was like). Your family consisted of who? Your best friend was an adult, another child, a pet? You liked doing what? going where? You were afraid of what? Your biggest wish was for what?

Ages five to ten: What did you do for fun? Where did your family go for vacations? Favorite subjects? Favorite teachers? Favorite foods?

You can write these as personal experiences; you can write them as fiction; you can include them as parts of a book. You can add statistics and write them as nonfiction.

God's Timing Is Always Right

A friend wrote a book for wives married to unbelieving husbands. It was a well-written book but she had no success marketing it. One day the Lord said to her, "Don't send it out again. Put it aside for awhile." She was very frustrated, feeling He had directed her to write the book. Why hadn't it sold? And why did God want her to lay it aside? She didn't understand, but she put it in her desk drawer and began work on another project.

Two years later her husband had a heart attack which resulted in bypass surgery. Before he went into the operating room, he shared with her that while reading the Gideon Bible in his hospital nightstand, he had accepted Christ as his savior. My friend was then able to add another chapter to the book.

Another friend wrote a book in the late 1970s about her nephew, a youth minister, who left his wife and daughter for the homosexual lifestyle. Again, this book was well-written, but the timing wasn't right. Now the market is open to such books.

You may not be able to write about an event while you're going through it, but do remember to take notes during this time. During the last eighteen months of my mother's final illness, I knew I wanted to write a book about her. I couldn't do it then, but I kept a journal, and several years later I wrote the book.

Someone once asked me, "But what if I didn't take notes during that time?" I shared with her my belief that God would bring to her mind what He wanted her to write. If she couldn't remember something, perhaps He wanted her to forget it and leave it in the past.

If you do write your story while going through a crisis experience, it's a good idea to lay it aside for awhile after you finish it, and then come back to it after the crisis has passed. At that time, you can look back on the experience from a perspective of victory, better equipped to share what God has taught you in this situation. Often we don't appreciate the lessons we learn until the trial is over and we look back in retrospect.

Marketing Your Personal Experience Stories

The field is wide open for personal experience stories. Almost every denominational magazine accepts them. Start with your own church magazine and take-home papers.

Perhaps your personal experience is along the how-to line. Share your expertise in arts and crafts, household or auto repair hints, or opening a business. These articles can be sold to general markets as well as religious periodicals.

Have you been a Sunday school teacher? Write your experiences for religious education magazines.

Study family and marriage magazines. What have you experienced in your family that you could share with others?

Things that happened to you as a youth can be written as fiction or nonfiction and submitted to teen magazines and take-home papers. Dating problems. Homework struggles. Studying for tests. A favorite class or teacher. Witnessing to friends.

Hobbies? There's a magazine for almost every leisure activity.

Family Histories

Earlier I mentioned writing biographies for a local mortuary. Following is the questionnaire the family filled out before I conducted an interview. This can give you many jumping off places in writing your own and others' personal experiences.

Personal Information

Name; nickname; maiden name, etc.

Birthplace; date; area; how long family resided there; any unusual events surrounding birth.

Parents: father, full name; mother, full name including maiden name.

Brothers and sisters: names; dates and places of birth; anything unique about them you want to include. Occupations; residences.

Childhood: location (including family moves); friends; hobbies; summer activities; vacations; houses you remember.

Marital status: name of spouse (maiden name, if woman).

Courtship: how you met; places you went on dates; how he proposed; wedding day (any unusual or humorous events); church; wedding party; favorite gifts; honeymoon.

First house: where located; neighbors; furniture.

Children: names and dates of birth; special information at time of birth; their childhoods; discipline; vacations; games played; friends.

Education

Elementary school: where; when; activities; honors; events; friends; favorite teachers and subjects.

High school: where; when; activities; honors; events; friends; favorite subjects and teachers; graduation; social events; clubs; sports; music; drama.

College: where; major; degrees or certifications; clubs; awards; honors; activities.

Other education: training; apprenticeships; seminars.

Organizations

Memberships in civic, social, fraternal, business or religious organizations: offices held; special contributions; honors, stories, and anecdotes.

Employment

Chronological record from first job (include part-time during school); places and dates; description of job and responsibilities; titles; promotions; incidents; friends; job-hunting experiences; layoffs or firings; retirement.

Religious

Denomination; date of membership; conversion; baptism; activities; offices held; additional information on growth in Christ.

Military

Branch of service; date of entering and discharge; rank; war or peacetime; war stories; experiences recalled; medals; honors.

Personality Profile

Description of yourself and family members; family traditions; favorite foods, clothes, entertainment; talents and skills; hobbies; favorite sayings (songs, poems, quotations, Bible verses); favorite authors; collections; vacation spots; pets; volunteer activities; friends; nicknames.

Special Heritage

Values; philosophy of life; reflections on family and friends.

The Old Testament tells the story of a man named Job, who went through more than any person should have to endure. He lost his cattle; he lost his children; he lost almost everything he possessed. But what did he say in chapter 19, verse 23: "Oh, that my words were now written in a book" (KJV). Why did he say this? Because he wanted to share with others what he had gone through.

What are you going through today? Do you feel it will never end? Are you experiencing heartache? Do you feel there is no answer? Has the Lord given and then taken away? Are you lonely?

Put your words on paper. Share with others what you have gone through, but don't forget to also share the conclusion you—like Job—hopefully have reached: "I know that my Redeemer lives" (Job 19:25 NIV). You don't necessarily have to give your readers a solution to their problems, but you can point them to the One who *is* the Answer.

Chapter 11

Other Types of Writing

Bible Studies

P RAY FOR ME," I requested fellow staff members as I prepared for a fifteen-minute appointment with a conferee. I had looked at her material the night before and didn't know what to tell her. It was mostly Scripture, with comments in between. What advice could I give her concerning publication?

She came to my table and, as was my custom, I asked if we could pray first. During that prayer, God gave me the answer.

"You have such a keen insight into Scripture," I told her. "Have you ever considered writing Bible studies?"

Her face lit up. She hadn't considered that possibility. I gave her suggestions on how to obtain information (conference workshops, online groups, etc.), and a few months later she wrote me that she had made her first sale.

If you enjoy studying the Bible (and shouldn't we all?), this may be a genre for you. Many publishers are looking for curriculum writers, although to receive an assignment, you may have to be a member of their denomination and know their beliefs. Magazines—for all ages—often include a Bible study in each issue, or you can compile entire books on biblical themes (i.e., faith, money, relationships), as well as individual books of the Bible.

You can also write a small group Bible study for a specific amount of time—thirteen weekly lessons for a three-month period, or twelve monthly lessons for a year. Again, these can be on particular themes or a book of the Bible.

Another option is to write Bible studies for specific groups—children, teens, singles, newlyweds, women, men, retirees, and so on.

Sometimes a publisher may not accept your whole manuscript but will purchase the concept. This happened to a writer friend who submitted a Bible study on marriage. The publisher turned down the study, but paid her a flat fee to use the concept in a book written by another author.

Writing Bible studies can be rewarding—not only in the checks received, but in a more intimate walk with the Lord because you have gone deeper into His Word.

Puzzles

Almost every newspaper and magazine—whether directed toward adults or children— contains some type of puzzle. Someone has to write these; why can't that someone be you?

Obviously, it helps if you're a puzzle lover yourself, and it's easier to construct the type of puzzle you enjoy solving. The choices are many. (Note: If you're creating puzzles for Christian periodicals, be sure to indicate which version of the Bible you're using.)

For help in building crossword puzzles, go to http://www.puzzle-maker.com/CW/. If this isn't easy enough for you to use, search further under "Make a crossword puzzle."

I enjoy cryptograms in which one letter represents another. The code is the same throughout the puzzle. For example:

Disciples of Jesus[1]

In the following puzzle, one letter represents another in the alphabet. The same code is used throughout the puzzle. When you decipher the code, you will have the name of the twelve disciples. (Hint: The letter "F" represents "E.") (See Matthew 10:2-4.)

1. T J N P O Q F U F S   _____

2. B O E S F X   _____

3. K B N F T   _____

4. K P I O   _____

5. Q I J M J Q   _____

6. C B S U I P M P N F X   _____

7. U I P N B T _____

8. N B U U I F X _____

9. K B N F T _____

10. T J N P O _____

11. U I B E E B F V T _____

12. K V E B T J T D B S J P U _____

Another popular type found in magazines and entire books is the Seek and Find as shown below:

Seek and Find

Read the following Bible verses from James 1:23-24, then look for the words shown in capital letters in the puzzle below. The words can go from right to left, left to right, or diagonal.

For IF ANY BE a HEARER OF the WORD, and NOT a DOER, HE is LIKE unto a man BEHOLDING his NATURAL FACE IN a GLASS; FOR he BEHOLDETH HIMSELF, and goeth his WAY, and straightway forgetteth WHAT manner of MAN he WAS.

B	E	H	O	L	D	I	N	G
E	H	E	F	I	O	N	A	L
H	E	A	S	K	E	D	T	A
O	C	R	Y	E	R	A	U	S
L	A	E	A	O	T	N	R	S
D	F	R	W	Q	A	Y	A	Z
E	B	N	O	T	H	R	L	O
T	E	A	S	A	W	O	P	I
H	I	M	S	E	L	F	X	F

Other puzzle forms are:

Fill in the Blanks

Fill in the missing words to complete the Ten Commandments. (These are found in Exodus, chapter 20.)

1. Thou shalt have no other _____ before me.

2. Thou shalt not make unto thee any _____.

Bible Occupations

1. He was a shepherd boy (1 Sam. 16:19) _____.

2. He was a tentmaker (Acts 18:1, 3) _____.

Questions about the Bible

1. How many books in the Bible? _____

2. Into how many parts is the Bible divided?_____

3. What are they? _____

Bible Spelldowns

Below is a list of Bible women whose names are misspelled. In the blank space, spell the names correctly. The reference shows where you can find the correct answer.

1. Ester _____ seventeenth book of the Old Testament

2. Marry _____ Matthew 1:20

4. Noami _____ Ruth 1:21

Bible Numbers

Fill in the missing numbers

Other Types of Writing

1. While Noah was in the ark, it rained _____ days and _____ nights (Gen. 7:12).

2. The children of Israel marched around Jericho _____ times on the seventh day (Josh. 6:4).

3. God created the earth in _____ days (Gen. 1:31).

Bible Children

Can you identify these children in the Bible?

1. He was placed in a basket in the bulrushes _____ (Ex. 2:3-10).

2. His mother left him with Eli, the priest, to be raised in the Temple (1 Sam. 3:1).
   _____

3. His father could not speak until he named this baby _____ (Luke 1:63-64).

Acrostics

Jesus, Our Savior

His Father's name   J _ _ _ _ _ (Luke 2:16).

His parents fled with Him to
this country   E _ _ _ _ (Matt. 2:14).

Jesus met a woman at a well
from this city   S _ _ _ _ _ _ (John 4:7).

Jesus died for the   U _ _ _ _ _ _ (Rom. 5:6)

Jesus is the Good   S _ _ _ _ _ _ _ (John 10:14)

Strange Events

Identify these people by the strange events that happened to them.

1. She was turned into a pillar of salt _____ (Gen. 19:15, 26).

2. They were driven from the Garden of Eden for eating forbidden fruit _____
   and _____ (Gen. 3:20, 24).

3. He was swallowed by a big fish _____ (Jonah 1:17).

Don't limit your submissions to religious publications, however. Make a list of holidays and design your puzzles around them, perhaps in various shapes as a pumpkin for Halloween or a flag for the Fourth of July. A puzzle in the shape of a tree would be appropriate for Christmas or Arbor Day, or in the shape of a heart for Valentine's Day.

As you can see, the possibilities are endless. Begin today looking through the magazines you receive, or those you find at the library, in bookstores, or at garage sales. The pay ranges from $10 to as high as $75 per puzzle, and once editors see your work, they may begin sending assignments. It's a fun way to bring in extra income.

Book Reviews

If you like to read, this is the perfect job for you. The first thing to do is to look in the market guides and see which periodicals publish book reviews (Sally Stuart's *Christian Writers' Market Guide* lists almost two hundred magazines that accept these), then obtain copies of those magazines to study their format. Are the reviews written in a theological style? Technical? Formal/informal? Chatty?

Also obtain writers' guidelines to see what type of book reviews they publish, the length, and lead time for holiday books. (These guidelines, along with recent issues, may often be found online.) After studying several issues, send a sample review in the format and length of that particular magazine, along with a short cover letter and a resume.

For book reviews, you'll want to sell one-time rights or simultaneous rights, but again, not to competing magazines. First rights don't work well with this genre because if you sell a review to one magazine, then wait until they publish it so you can send out reprints, the book would have been on the market too long, and editors like reviews of newly published books.

Because each magazine may use a different length, compile a list of names and addresses, beginning with the longest length. After you send it out to a magazine that prefers 2,000 words, cut it down and send it to the next one on the list that wants 1,800 words, then 1,500 words, and so on—down to those who publish fifty-word reviews.

If the editor sends you a book to review, ask for permission to submit the review to other magazines. More than likely he or she will give permission as long as it isn't a competing market or the same reading audience.

The pay isn't exceptionally high on book reviews; it usually runs from $15 to $50, plus the book. However, it's a great way to get your name in front of readers—and build an extensive library at the same time.

Humor

What makes you laugh? Whatever it is—jokes, family stories, comic greeting cards, cartoons—will probably make others laugh too. And, contrary to what you may think, it *is* possible to sell humor pieces to Christian publications. You can find ideas for humorous fillers in many places: signs on marquees, stores, panel trucks, billboards; actions and reactions of people; unusual hobbies; window displays; and family or college reunions. Other sources include:

Newspapers

I enjoy looking for typos in newspaper ads such as the ones I saw in a real estate column. One house had a "lonely bedroom," the other had a "stained glass widow." And our local community college catalog advertised a new class in "Pubic Relations."

Following are some other newspaper ads that tickle the funny bone:

- Illiterate? Write today for free help.
- Experienced mom will care for your child. Fenced yard, meals, and smacks included.
- Dog for sale; eats anything and is especially fond of children.
- Man wanted to work in dynamite factory. Must be willing to travel.
- Stock up and save. Limit: one.
- Three-year-old teacher needed for preschool. Experience preferred.
- For sale: antique desk suitable for lady with thick legs and large drawers.
- Wanted: man to take care of cow that does not smoke or drink.[2]

Children:

You can get many ideas for humorous fillers from listening to children. Just remember to write these things down when you hear them, or they'll be lost forever. Following are some remarks children made about the Bible:

- Adam and Eve were created from an apple tree.
- Noah's wife was called Joan of Ark.
- Lot's wife was a pillar of salt by day, but a ball of fire by night.
- Samson slayed the Philistines with the axe of the apostles.
- The Egyptians were all drowned in the dessert. Afterwards, Moses went up on Mt. Cyanide to get the ten amendments.
- Moses died before he ever reached Canada.
- Joshua led the Hebrews in the battle of Geritol.
- Solomon had 300 wives and 700 porcupines.[3]

Family Experiences

Family trips can often lead to humorous articles. When writing about a trip to New York City with family members, I could simply have listed the places we visited. Instead I described our trip into the Big Apple on the train as follows:

> The seven of us—including three young children in shorts and sleeveless tops, my mother with her usual flowered dress and tie belt, and my six-foot-tall stepdad with his crop of white hair and suspenders—boarded the 7:20 elevated train, filled with businessmen in suits and carrying briefcases. Glancing at the cameras hanging around our necks, I asked my husband, "Do you think anyone will know we're tourists?"

Even the most serious situation can have a humorous side. My husband fell one day while dressing, and fractured a vertebrae, coming within one inch of being paralyzed from the neck down. Later, listening to the Arizona Diamondback announcer talk rapturously about the team's two ace pitchers—Randy Johnson and Curt Schilling—my husband (who is a Dodgers fan) said, "They're not God. They put on their pants one leg at a time just like I do." "Yes," I replied, "but they don't fracture a vertebrae doing it."

A hungry lion was roaming through the jungle looking for something to eat. He came across two men. One was sitting under a tree reading a book; the other was typing away on his typewriter. The lion quickly pounced on the man reading the book and devoured him. Even the king of the jungle knows that readers digest and writers cramp. (www.worldwidefreelance.com/writing-jokes.htm)

Other Types of Writing

Internet

Humor is everywhere. You just have to look for it, write it down, and then keep an eye out for magazines and newspapers who accept these fillers. Always give the source, if you know it. Unfortunately, too many things arrive in e-mails with no source included. That was the case with the following obituary I received in an e-mail and later found online:

It is with a sad heart that I pass on the following. Please join me in remembering a truly great icon.

The Pillsbury Doughboy died yesterday of a yeast infection and complications from repeated pokes in the tummy. He was seventy-one. Doughboy was buried in a lightly greased coffin.

Dozens of celebrities turned out to pay their respects, including Mrs. Butterworth, Hungry Jack, Betty Crocker, the California Raisins, the Hostess Twinkies, and Captain Crunch.

The gravesite was piled with flours, as longtime friend, Aunt Jemima, delivered the eulogy. She described Doughboy as a man who never knew he was kneaded.

Doughboy rose quickly in show business, but his later life was filled with turnovers. He was not considered a very smart cookie, wasting much of his dough on half-baked schemes. Despite being a little flaky at times, still, as a crusty old man, he was considered a roll model for millions.

Doughboy is survived by his father, Pop Tart, and his wife, Play Dough, two children—John Dough and Jane Dough, plus they had one in the oven.

The funeral was held at 3:50 for twenty minutes.[4]

We need to let the world know that Christians can laugh at themselves. We shouldn't be like the grandma whose grandson, while looking at a mule, said, "He must have religion, because my grandma has religion and she looks like that all the time."

Even in embarrassing situations, we can pick ourselves up and go on as one pastor did during his first sermon at a newly organized church. While issuing a challenge to the congregation—"We need to reach out to the community. We need to show love to those around us"—a cell phone rang and, without missing a beat, he continued, "We need to answer the call."

Let's answer the call today to add some joy to the world. If you have a talent for writing humor, put your fingers to the keyboard, open your mouth, and laugh!

Things You Can Write for Christian Publishers
(compiled by Faye Frost)

Fillers
Press releases
Devotionals/prayers
Poetry/greeting card verse
Columns
Letters to the editor
Book reviews
Articles:
    Reportorial
    Narrative:
        Adventure
        Personal experience
        Conversion
        Nostalgia
    Personality profile
    Problem/solution
    How-to articles
    Informative
    Survey articles
    Photo stories
    Travel articles
Curriculum
    Lessons
    Puzzles/quizzes
    Projects
Short stories:
    Purpose story:
        Purpose achieved
        Purpose failed
        Purpose abandoned
    Decision story:
        Decision affirmed
        Decision faced
        Decision reversed
    Theme story:
        Theme exposure
        Come-to-understand
        The parable

Compilations for anthologies
Church/Sunday school plays
Songs/music
Encyclopedias
Bible atlas
Nonfiction books:
    Biographies
    Devotional
    Educational
    Historical
    Issue/problem
    Missionary
    Theological
Novels:
    Concept and theme story
    Problem/solution story
    Allegory/fantasy
    Science fiction
    Biblical
    Mystery
    Romance
    Historical
Family/marriage
Adventure
Children's books:
Devotionals/prayers
    Bible stories
    Bible-based books
    Seasonal books
How-to/activity books
Pre-school picture books
Kindergarten/primary-5-7)
'Tweens (8-12)
Teens (13-19)
Tapes/CDs
Bible-based children's stories
Films/Documentaries:
    Expose, educational,
    audio-visual

Part III

Writing Your Manuscript

. . . .

Chapter 12

Preparing a Manuscript
for Publication

THERE ARE SPECIFIC rules for preparing a manuscript that are common to the majority of publishers (see page 136). Print out your manuscript, double-spaced, on 8½ x 11", twenty-pound, white paper, allowing at least a one-inch margin on all four sides. Do not justify the right margin, leave only one space after periods, and do not leave an extra space between paragraphs, but indent each one. If you've signed a contract, follow the publisher's style guide.

Article Format

In the upper left-hand corner, type your actual name (the name you want on the check), address, telephone number, and e-mail address. Do not send your Social Security number until an editor asks for it.

In the upper right-hand corner, type "First Rights" (see Chapter 16 on "Marketing Your Manuscript" for further explanation on Rights). Underneath the rights offered, put the word count. Then (optional) type a copyright notice, i.e., Copyright 2009 by Donna Clark Goodrich. This protects you if your article is published in an uncopyrighted periodical.

Writers often ask if they should send their manuscript to the Library of Congress to register the copyright. This isn't necessary. Whenever you write something down under your name, or record it in another way, it's automatically copyrighted. The difference between having a simple copyright notice and a registered copyright is that registering your work allows you to collect statutory damages and attorneys' fees if you went to court.

Sample Page

Name (real name)   Rights offered
Street address   Word count
City, state, zip   Copyright notice
Telephone   (optional)
E-mail address

(1/3 of page down)   Title

by Real Name or Pseudonym

Skip two or three lines, then begin first paragraph.

If your article goes beyond one page, at the top of the second and succeeding pages, type your last name and short title in the upper left corner as shown below. (Word processing headers can do this for you.) The page number can be centered or placed in upper right corner.

Last name, short title   page number

* *

To save money, if you want to register individual items such as poetry or short stories, rather than registering each one individually, compile them in a book and register them under a collective title.

(For more information on copyrights, go to http://www.copyright.gov/. See also Appendix E, Copyright Information.)

To help remember what to place in each corner, the *personal* information goes in the upper left-hand corner; *manuscript* information in the upper right-hand corner.

Choosing a Title

After typing your personal and manuscript information, skip a few spaces and center your title. Make it catchy enough to hook the editor and then the reader.

For several years I said I had never had a title changed, but one publisher changed that in a short story for teens. Its title, "Tank the Terrible," was far more intriguing than my blasé title, "A Gift for Danny."

I do put a lot of thought into titles, however, and sometimes they even come before the article. Let me give you a few examples:

I entitled an article on upholstery "The Great Cover-Up."

For an article on water beds I used the quotation, "Water, Water Everywhere, but Not a Drop to Drink."

And as mentioned in the fiction chapter, I titled the story about our neighbor's CB radio that bled into my tape recorder "Breaker, Breaker."

In choosing a title, you can use part of a Scripture verse or another quotation, the title of a song, or a thought relating to the story's theme.

I've also found that numbers work well in titles. An article on gift-buying found no market under the title, "Gifts That Make a Difference," but changed to "100-Plus Gifts That Make a Difference," it has found several homes.

While waiting in a doctor's office or at a grocery checkout line, glance over the titles in current magazines. Do they tempt you to read the rest of the article? A friend recently sold an article entitled "My Father Never Told Me He Loved Me." Wouldn't you love to read on to see how this affected the writer? Did it leave her bitter or determined to show more love to *her* children?

Attract readers with your titles, but don't promise them more than you can deliver. Your writing should live up to the title. There's nothing wrong with being clever as long it isn't overdone. (For example, a splashing headline in a tabloid inviting the reader to a story concerning the health problem a popular singer was ashamed to admit, turned out to be only a weight problem.)

Another hint is to tie your title in with the opening or closing paragraph of your article, or both. A travel article on Yuma, Arizona, entitled "Yuma, the Swinging Gate," begins with the thought that Yuma is the gateway into Arizona for those coming from California and into California for those coming from Arizona. After describing the town's history and then bringing the reader up to date on its present-day commerce and economy, in the final paragraph I repeated the opening thought by saying, "Yuma is not only a gateway swinging into California and Arizona, it also swings into the past with pride and into the future with confidence."

What's in a title? Plenty, if it catches the eye of an editor and leads to a sale.

Byline

Under the title you'll place your byline—either your real name or a pseudonym. I wouldn't recommend using a pen name on a regular basis because you want your name to become familiar to readers and editors. However, there are times this is a wise choice.

If you're writing something personal about a family member, you may want to use a pseudonym. In my article, "Living with a Disabled Husband," I used a pen name, even though my husband was okay with the story. An article about a young relative who committed suicide also carried a pen name because of the close relatives involved.

I also get ideas from events happening to people in my church. If I sell a short story to our denominational take-home paper based on one of these friends, people from our church who read it may see my byline, recognize the character involved, and not know what is fact and what is fiction. In this case, I'll also use a pen name.

Some women use a pseudonym if they want to write for a male-oriented magazine, and vice versa. Others may use initials instead of a first and middle name.

One other time you may use a pseudonym is at the request of an editor who wants to use two of your articles in the same issue.

Style Sheet

For the sake of consistency, whenever you look up a word, place it on an ABC style sheet (see page 140). This helps you remember if you capitalized a word; if it's one word, two, or hyphenated; if you used an "e" or an "a" when both are accepted (as in descendant/descendent); comma in series; and the rule you followed for numbers.

Using Scripture in Your Writing

The biggest weakness I find in manuscripts I edit is that authors do not know what format to use when quoting Scripture. (See Appendix A for fourteen hints covering most of the basics you will need to know.)

Hiring a Typist

"I make changes up to the final period," you may say. But for those of you who don't have the time, or who use the biblical system of keyboarding ("seek, and ye shall find"), here are some hints on working with a typist.

First, offer the job to members of your writers' group as they are familiar with manuscript formats. The graduate office of your local college may have a list of typists, or check the ads in a college newspaper. Secretarial services in town can be your next step, or check listings in *The Writer* and *Writer's Digest*. For simpler jobs, such as rough drafts, contact "Jobs for Youth" in your community.

Payment for typists varies in different parts of the country. At present, rates run from $1.50 to $2 for a double-spaced page, but may be higher for tape transcription or handwritten copy. Some typists work by the hour instead of by the page. Establish the rates *before* you take the work to the typist, not when you get there. Be honest, however.

Don't tell her it's one hundred pages and omit the fact that twenty of those pages are tables. Or don't tell her it's two hundred pages that need retyping, and neglect to mention that it's now typed single-spaced. Unless you have made previous arrangements, pay for the typing when it's finished. In fact, it's not uncommon for typists to ask for a deposit when doing a lengthy job. Establish up front that you will pay for any retyping because of your changes, but she (or he) will retype, or correct and reprint, without charge pages in which she made errors.

Publishers prefer manuscripts typed in twelve point Courier or Times New Roman. Avoid using various typefaces. I edited one manuscript in which the writer had used short, fat typestyles; tall, thin ones; words stretched out with spaces between the letters; myriad words and phrases with underlines and boldface; and an inordinate amount of exclamation points. I told him the whole manuscript shouted out "SEE ME!" instead of the gospel message he wanted to share. Editors say, "You write; we'll do the typesetting." It is acceptable, however, to use italics when you want to stress a point.

Keep track of all your expenses—paper (if you provide), typing costs, and mileage back and forth to the typist's office as it will all be deductible on your income tax. When the manuscript is finished, get an itemized receipt with the date and amount.

If you're just beginning your book and know you'll need a typist, begin your search *now* and give her a tentative date. This is especially important if the one you select types for a living, as she will need to adjust her schedule accordingly.

If you have a long manuscript, you may want to give her one chapter at a time and let her store it in the computer. This will be easier than dumping a three hundred-page manuscript on her all at once. If you find you won't be done when you thought you would, let her know so she can take another job.

Following are some hints to make the job easier both for you and your typist:

- *If you handwrite your manuscript, write on every other line and on one side of the paper only.* This makes reading easier, especially if you have to add material.
- *Don't write over words.* If you want to change a word or a figure, cross it out and put the new word above or beside the old.
- *Print all foreign and proper names.* Or spell out the words if your typist is transcribing tapes.
- *Use common sense with insertions.* Rather than adding a long insertion between lines or up the side of the page, say, "See insert A" and attach a separate sheet.
- *Avoid writing in all caps.* This makes it difficult for the typist to know what words should be capitalized, especially in a technical manuscript.

Style Sheet for *A Step in the* **Write** *Direction*

AB	CD	EF	GH
all clear babysitter backyard	coffee shop daylong double-check day-care double-space	every day (n.) everyday (adj.) endnotes e-mail empty-nest (adj.) first time freelance fund-raiser fast-food (adj.) full-time (adj.) full time (n.)	GH hometown homeschool head-on hairdos hardworking
IJ in-depth	KL lightbulb long-range lead-in	MN multiday nonfiction noncompeting nonexistent nonwriter	OP on-the-job (adj.) out-of-date (adj.) online old-timer preschool prepublication preinterview
QR record keeping rearrange	ST spell-check staff written self-defense self-publish single-space teenaged(ager) take-home takeoff (n.) thank-you (adj.)	UV up front	WXYZ weekend Web site wraparound well-known
MISC. no comma before final too comma in series Scripture—Bible scripture—verse abbreviate Bible refer- ences in parentheses.	MISC. "A" headings—no underline "B" headings—underline "C" headings—indent, italics	DATES	NUMBERS Spell out numbers one through one hundred and round numbers. Comma in four digit numbers.

- *Unless you pay extra, don't expect your typist to be your editor.* Most typists will correct spelling, but don't expect her to catch inconsistencies such as a person's name spelled two different ways or changing your heroine's hair from black in the first chapter to blonde in the fourth. If your typist does have editing skills, be willing to pay the extra fee. This will save you from eventually having to have the manuscript retyped and will help you find a publisher that much sooner.

The last page is typed and—unless you've obtained the services of an agent—you're now ready to submit the book to a publisher. Look it over one last time, however, for any typos or missing material. Remember, you only get one chance to make a first impression. A neatly typed manuscript with a well-chosen title will go a long way toward finding its way to the top of an editor's pile, and hopefully lead to a letter of acceptance and a check or contract for your article or book.

. . . .

Chapter 13

Writing and Selling
Your First Book

WRITING A BOOK may sound scary to you, but it doesn't have to send you into a panic. The hints in this chapter can reduce this anxiety.

Marketability

Is there a need for your book? Have you checked *Books in Print* or publishers' catalogs to see how many books similar to yours are already on the market? How will yours differ? Is the slant different? Will yours fill an existing void?

Your book probably will fit into one of three categories:

Personal Experience

"You can't believe the things I've gone through in my life," people often tell me. "Everyone says I should write a book."

Your experiences alone won't sell your book to an editor, however. It's a question of whether readers can relate to what you've gone through. Can you offer hope to those going through the same dark tunnel?

If you want to write your personal experience, read Chapter 10 for more helpful information.

How-to Books

Have you started a business, remodeled your house on a budget, adopted a child, taken an elderly parent into your home, or completed a project where you learned by trial and error? These types of books allow others to learn by your experience. My how-to books published by John Wiley & Sons came from two businesses I began in my home: secretarial and tax preparation.

Any time someone asks you how to do something, you have the possibility of, first, an article on the subject, and then, a book. The advantage of these books is that most of your research has already been done—through your own experience.

Entertainment

The novel or humorous personal experience book fits here. That's not to say that your reader can't learn something through your book, however. G. K. Chesterton is a classic example of a writer who uses great wit to reveal life-changing principles in his novels.

Permissions

As you do your research, keep a record of all quotations, poems, and music lyrics, along with the name and address of the source. In writing for permission, include your book title, length, title and author of the book or magazine article in which you found the quotation, date of publication, and material you wish to use. You can give the page number and beginning and ending words, or photocopy the page on which the quotation appears to show the context in which it will be used.

Be sure, however, that you need to obtain permission. Once you've requested it and used the material, you must pay the stated fee. I once wrote for permission for every quotation, regardless of the length or the source. However, after I was billed $275 for material I later found in a government publication (for which you must give a credit line but do not have to obtain permission), I became more careful.

Anything published before 1978 had a maximum of fifty-six years. Thus, anything published before 1922 is in the public domain. (See chart on page 145.)

If your quotation is under a hundred words, you need to give credit but you don't have to get permission. The definition of "fair use" refers to how much of the original material you want to use compared to the length of your manuscript. For example, it's not fair use to use two hundred words of someone else's material in your 250-word devotional. One conference speaker suggested that you can use one hundred words from a one-hundred-page book without obtaining permission, two hundred words from a two hundred-page book, and so on.

Fair use doesn't relate to music, however. If you use more than *one line* of music in an article or a book, you need permission. And quoting secular music may entail a hefty charge.

There are two ways of getting around asking for permission: Either paraphrase the words, or give only the title, which cannot be copyrighted. Even if you paraphrase a quotation, however, if the phrase is one with which a particular author is associated, give him or her credit. For example, if you wrote "Big Brother is watching you," credit should be given to George Orwell and his book *1984*.

Be sure to check all quotations for accuracy. I find reference books to be more accurate than the Internet. Don't use "Anonymous" or "Author Unknown" after a poem or quotation *until* you've made *every* effort to locate the source.

Quoting words of old hymns and documents usually is not a problem as these songs are in what's called "public domain," meaning that the copyright has expired.

WHEN U.S. WORKS PASS INTO THE PUBLIC DOMAIN

DATE OF WORK	PROTECTED FROM	TERM
Created 1-1-78 or after	When work is fixed in tangible medium of expression	Life + 70 years[1] (or if work of corporate authorship, the shorter of 95 years from publication, or 120 years from creation[2]
Published before 1923	In public domain	None
Published from 1923 – 63	When published with notice[3]	28 years + could be renewed for 47 years, now extended by 20 years for a total renewal of 67 years. If not so renewed, now in public domain
Published from 1964 – 77	When published with notice	28 years for first term; now automatic extension of 67 years for second term
Created before 1-1-78 but not published	1-1-78, the effective date of the 1976 Act, which eliminated common law copyright	Life + 70 years or 12-31-2002, whichever is greater
Created before 1-1-78 but published between then and 12-31-2002	1-1-78, the effective date of the 1976 Act, which eliminated common law copyright	Life + 70 years or 12-31-2047, whichever is greater

Definition: A public domain work is a creative work that is not protected by copyright and may be freely used by everyone. The reasons that the work is not protected include: (1) the term of copyright for the work has expired; (2) the author failed to satisfy statutory formalities to perfect the copyright; or (3) the work is a work of the U.S. government.

1. Term of joint works is measured by life of the longest-lived author.
2. Works for hire, anonymous and pseudonymous works also have this term. 17 U.S.C. § 302(c).
3. Under the 1909 Act, works published without notice went into the public domain upon publication. Works published without notice between 1-1-78 and 3-1-89, effective date of the Berne Convention Implementation Act, retained copyright only if efforts to correct the accidental omission of notice were made within five years, such as by placing notice on unsold copies. 17 U.S.C. § 405. (Notes courtesy of Professor Tom Field, Franklin Pierce Law Center and Lolly Gasaway)[1]

Below is a sample letter you can use to request permission. When the publisher returns this letter giving the permission and the credit line to use, make a copy for your file and send the original to the publisher of your book.

Sample Letter to Request Permission[2]

Your name
Address
City, state, zip
Phone
E-mail address

Name of publisher
Address
City, state, zip

Dear _____:

In my book called _____, which will be published by _____, I wish to quote the following material from your book [name of book/author's name, date of printing]. I wish to quote from page _____ to _____, beginning with line _____.

If this is acceptable to you, I will use the following credit line and copyright note:

If you are agreeable, please sign and date the request below and return one copy to me.

I/we hereby grant permission as outlined above.

Date_____

Signature _____

Page 148 contains a form to keep track of your citations. Give each one a number (endnotes usually are numbered consecutively, beginning with number 1 in each chapter), write down the page number on which the quotation appears in your manuscript, and then note the source, including the address. Put the date you write for permission on this form, along with the date you received the permission. Also note the date you paid a required fee for using the quotation, or if you sent only a requested copy of the book. Keep this information in your file in the event the book goes out of print and another publisher picks it up for reprint.

Research

Don't over-research. For my typing book, I read related material for over a year and ended up with over a hundred pages of notes. I felt the numerous quotations, which were properly cited, gave a greater air of authority to the book.

The editor disagreed, however, reminding me that I was writing the book from my background of running a secretarial service. Also, she said, she had purchased the book based on my style of writing, believing that the informality suited the subject and would appeal to their readers.

With the tax book, I wrote the entire manuscript from my own experience and knowledge. Further research resulted in the addition of only two quotations.

The Internet offers information on almost every conceivable subject. However, some of this information may not be up-to-date. For more accurate information, check such places as state and federal offices, local Chambers of Commerce and Better Business Bureaus, and associations related to your research, as well as recently published books written on your particular subject.

Don't forget the Yellow Pages, and for overseas material, contact travel agencies and consulates.

Internet sources include:

- www.lexisnexis.com—contains court cases; requires paid subscription.
- www.questia.com—contains more than 60,000 books and 1,000,000 journal, magazine, and newspaper articles. Free trial period, then paid subscription.
- www.gutenberg.org—contains texts of more than 18,000 older books.
- www.pubmed.com—searches over sixteen million citations from medical journals.
- www.bartleby.com—includes *Complete Works of William Shakespeare, Roget's Thesaurus, Simpson's Contemporary Quotations, Bartlett's Familiar Quotations,* and more.

Permission Summary Form for:

Title: _____

Page _____ of _____

Perm. #	Page #	Source	Date Req'd.	Date Rec'd.	Fee	Date Paid	Comp. Copies

- www.chicagomanualofstyle.org—style guide. Free registration.
- www.biblegateway.com—Scripture words and verses in multiple versions.
- www.freebiblesoftware.com—sign up to receive a free CD containing Bible study tools, sermons, classic Christian books, and more.
- www.howstuffworks.com—if you need to know how anything works, visit this site.
- www.profnet.com—offers access to more than 16,000 professionals looking for journalists and writers to interview them.
- www.fedstats.gov—locate statistics from more than one hundred government offices.[3]

Outlining Your Book

Outlining forces you to plan. It's difficult to convince an editor in a query letter that you know where you're going if you don't know yourself. At one time I typed and edited a novel for a writer who hadn't prepared an outline. The book ended up over 500 pages—and then he ended it before he felt he was done. Because this was longer than most published novels, we both ended up re-editing the book. It was difficult at that point to decide what to leave out to reduce its length. A well-planned outline would have avoided this.

If your book is a novel, your outlining will consist of making a list of your characters with a description of each. This includes personal appearance, strengths, weaknesses, likes and dislikes, and so on, along with notes of the location and time the story takes place. A brief synopsis of what happens in each chapter also helps as you write your book.

Expenses

While working on your book, keep a record of all expenses for tax purposes. (For more information on this subject, see Appendix J, "Income Tax for Writers.") Basically, whenever you get into your car or make a purchase, ask yourself if it's for business and, if so, write it down. Because your writing income is taxable as self-employment, you will have to pay your own Social Security tax. You'll want to bring the taxable total down as low as possible, so subtract every legal deduction.

Do I Need An Agent?

You've established a need for your book. You have it outlined and two or three chapters written. This is the time to decide whether or not to seek out an agent. The following hints may help in this decision.

First, let's consider some *disadvantages* of having an agent.

- *You lose sight of the markets.* Studying marketing guides and submitting your own manuscripts puts you in touch with editors' needs. You write *for the markets,* instead of finishing a project and *then* looking for a market. Eventually, you will write for a specific market, or complete a manuscript knowing from experience that it meets a need. If you have an agent, this limits your knowledge of what editors are buying.
- *You lose enthusiasm.* It is exciting to look through marketing books and publishers' guidelines and realize, "I have an article or outline in my files that meets those requirements." I am convinced one cause of writers' block is that writers do not take the time to study these resources. Doing so will give you more ideas for articles, stories, and books than you'll have time to write.
- *You lose money.* Why pay 15 percent of your income to another person when, with a little work on your own part, you can bank the entire check? An agent—unless he or she has been an editor or a bookstore owner who knows the market—is simply a person who has done the marketing research for you.

Following are several reasons writers tell me they need an agent. Decide your own responses to these reasons.

"I don't know where to send my manuscript."

"I can't afford the postage."

"I don't have time to research markets. I'd rather spend my time writing."

"I don't want to bother with addressing envelopes or sending out e-mails."

Now, if you have a legitimate reason for wanting an agent: 1) you are a full-time published author and do *not* have the time for the numerous details involved in submitting manuscripts, 2) you want to submit to a publisher who accepts manuscripts only through agents, or 3) you feel an agent can broker a better contract, then the following hints may help.

Working with an Agent

- *Present a well-written manuscript.* Writers often expect an agent to sell manuscripts that are poorly written and stand little chance of publication. When *they* don't have to buy postage, pay phone bills, or go through the work of studying the market guides, they often are not willing to produce well-written manuscripts. They think agents can sell their work simply because they're agents. Learn to outline before you write. Study basic writing skills. Use correct grammar and type it in the correct format. Give your agent a manuscript ready to submit to a publisher.

- *Be willing to make recommended changes.* Sometimes writers aren't willing to rewrite. When I was an agent, a friend asked me to handle a mystery book for young teens. It was a confusing melee of myriad plots and subplots. I suggested she reduce the number of characters and plots, but she insisted that I send it out and if it received more than one rejection, she'd rewrite it. I realized this would not only cost me time and money, but it would hurt my reputation with editors, so I refused. Before you turn your manuscript over to an agent, let a writer friend or members of a critique group read it, or hire a professional editor. Then rewrite it, incorporating any worthwhile suggestions.

- *Know your audience.* Whether you are writing for children or adults, go to a bookstore or library, study the books for your target market, and use appropriate vocabulary. Writers of children's material, especially, often fail to aim their book toward a specific age or determine if the book is a read-to book or read-it-yourself.

- *Produce a clean manuscript.* One writer sent me a manuscript with five typos *on the first page!* She wrote, "I know there are a lot of typing mistakes, but tell the editor that if he accepts it, I'll make the corrections. I just want to get the manuscript in circulation." An agent's job is to sell the manuscript, not make excuses for it.

- *Use an agent for book manuscripts only.* Sometimes the cost of being an agent is more than the 15 percent commission. Writers sent me batches of poetry and short stories, usually for the Christian market, which, if sold, might garner checks of $5 to $75 for weekly take-home papers—perhaps more for monthly magazines. I turned these down, knowing if they didn't sell the first time, I would be spending considerable time and money for a $1-$5 commission.

- *Choose a non-writer for an agent.* Writer/agents may dispute this advice, but I find it can prevent problems. The fact that an agent is a writer doesn't ensure a sale. If we knew the perfect market and timing, we would sell 100 percent of our own manuscripts. As an agent, I submitted several well-written books I felt certain would sell the first time out. They didn't, nor did they sell the second, third, or fourth time out. Agents do know markets better than others, because that's their job, but if they're also writers, they probably have received their share of rejections.

  Having a writer for an agent can also lead to another problem. Suppose you send me a manuscript similar to one I am writing. Later I sell my book. You read it, see something that sounds familiar, and think I stole some of your material.

My nephew used to critique tapes sent to him by aspiring songwriters. Eventually his publisher discouraged him for this very reason. My nephew told me, "There are only so many ideas for songs, and it is logical these ideas are used over and over, but try telling that to someone who sent you a song and later hears one similar that you've written. He won't believe you wrote your song months before you listened to his."

Also, a writer/agent may be so busy writing, editing, and submitting his/her own manuscripts or working on a deadline that your manuscript may not carry the importance it should. Select a professional agent whose sole business is to sell his clients' books.

How Do You Find An Agent?

Ask your writer friends. If they have an agent, are they satisfied with his or her representation? Does he or she keep in touch with them on a regular basis, letting them know to whom the manuscripts have been sent and the response?

Attend writers' conferences where agents are present and set up an appointment. You usually have only fifteen minutes so be prepared with a brief, well-prepared book proposal, bio, and business card. They won't have time to look at a complete manuscript (many will look only at the first one or two pages), nor will they want to haul dozens of manuscripts away with them. However, if they ask you to send them your proposal and sample chapters, follow up as soon as you get home.

Sally Stuart includes several pages of literary agents and agencies in the *Christian Writers' Market Guide*. Another source is the *Insiders Guide to Book Editors, Publishers, and Literary Agents*. You can also check the Association of Authors' Representatives which requires their members to follow a specific code of ethics.

If you are contacting an agent via snail mail, be sure to enclose a self-addressed, stamped envelope (SASE). Whether using that method or e-mail, write a one-page query letter, stating how you heard about him or her and why you think your book would be a good fit. Include a brief description of your manuscript and a bio sketch listing publishing credits. Also let him know if you are sending this proposal to other agents.

Study the markets, be willing to rewrite (Hemingway rewrote *A Farewell to Arms* thirty-nine times), don't give up, and you will discover that you, too, can be a published author—*with or without an agent!*

Finding a Publisher

I received three calls in one week from would-be authors. "I've written a book," they all said. "Can you tell me where to send it?"

I thought back to the hundreds of hours and days I spent poring through marketing guides searching for publishers and then sending query letters. Wouldn't it be great if we could finish typing the last page, then pick up the phone and call a writer friend who would give us the name and address of a publisher? Voila, instant sale!

Before you begin to write your book, have a possible publisher in mind. While attending writers' conferences, I watch conferees eagerly grab up sample magazines and put them in their already overcrowded bags—leaving behind the publishers' catalogs.

These catalogs contain a wealth of information: type of books the company publishes; books they have recently published (you won't want to send them one on the same subject unless yours has a different slant); length; price range; and if they print "series" books.

Another way to find a publisher is to scour the latest *Writer's Market* and the *Christian Writers' Market Guide*. Select those who buy the genre of book you are writing and send for their catalogs and guidelines, or obtain this information online. You also can check the library and bookstores to see who publishes books dealing with your subject.

Follow the guideline requirements to the letter. Don't think your manuscript will be the exception. Editors diligently send their specific needs to writers' marketing guides, writers' magazines, and prospective writers. If you send them a manuscript longer than what they publish, they'll assume—and rightly so—that if you don't follow directions on length, you probably won't follow them in the content of your manuscript.

After you've studied these guidelines, select two or three to whom you can submit your manuscript. Determine first: 1) if they want a proposal or the entire manuscript, 2) if they accept simultaneous submissions, and 3) if they accept submissions via e-mail.

After you've completed the first two or three chapters, consider sending a book proposal. There are several advantages to this:

It saves time. Some publishers take up to six months or more to consider a query letter or book proposal. During this time you can be writing the rest of your book.

You can receive an advance based on this proposal. It's possible, at this time, to get an advance that will help on typing and research expenses, and also to allow you to put aside other obligations and spend more time writing.

The publisher can make suggestions to help you write your book. When a publisher sent me a contract for three devotional books based on samples I had submitted, he also sent me the exact specifications for typing the manuscript (this was in pre-computer days): margins, number of characters per line, lines per page, total pages, and format.

That same year I sent another publisher a query letter and table of contents for a proposed book entitled *Ten Commandments for Sunday School Teachers*. The editor suggested six chapters instead to fit their study program and, upon completion of the manuscript, he bought it. The new title was *Winning Souls Through the Sunday School*.

While writing the typing and income tax books, several times the editor sent me material she felt I could use in the books.

Book Proposal

A book proposal is composed of a query letter, a chapter-by-chapter synopsis, and two or three chapters (check publishers' guidelines for proposal requirements). (See Chapter 2 for a sample book proposal for fiction.)

Query Letter

Your query letter should be no longer than one page (see sample on page 155). The letter should cover: 1) the need for the book, 2) a brief description of the book, and 3) why you're qualified to write it. Qualifications can include previous writing credits or, if you have none, list other experiences that qualify you to write this book. For example, if it's a children's book, mention that you're a parent and/or a grandparent; you're a schoolteacher; you've taught Sunday school for a number of years. Your qualifications may just include a deep interest in the subject.

Address your query to the *current* editor. A phone call to the publisher can supply this information. And *spell the editor's name correctly.* Nothing detracts more from a first impression of an author than spelling the editor's name wrong. Follow this name with the title, i.e., senior editor, acquisitions editor, and so on.

If the editor has a name that could be male or female, simply begin the letter with: Dear . . . and give the full name.

The first two paragraphs of this query letter give the reasons this book is needed. Use statistics if they pertain to your subject. Make sure, however, that they are current. My 1981 query letter included 1972 statistics. They should have been more up to date.

The third paragraph gives a brief description of the book. However, I left out two things that should have been included: the approximate word count (not pages) and when the book would be finished.

The fourth paragraph gives my qualifications. I don't think, though, that my background of previous books published sold this book to the editor as much as the fact that I had twenty-four years of experience operating a typing service in my home.

Sample Query Letter

Street address
City, state, zip
Date

Name of editor/title
Name of publisher
Street address
City, state, zip

Dear Mr./Mrs., Ms.:

In 1900 there were approximately 1.67 million business firms in the United States. In 1972 there were about eight million small businesses. Of all new businesses, about one-third went defunct within one year; about one-half within two years, and approximately two-thirds within five years.

Why? Lack of planning, failure to know the customer and what he/she wants, wrong personality to manage a business, not enough capital set aside for downturns, lack of time management. All these reasons and more contribute to business failure.

Prospective entrepreneurs should ask themselves two questions before opening a business: What do I need to get started? And, Where will I find customers? These points, along with others, are covered in my proposed book, *How to Set Up and Run a Typing Service*. The outline for this book is enclosed. I have a more complete fourteen-page summary I can send upon request.

My background includes twenty-four years of operating a typing service in my home. I am also an income tax preparer and a freelance writer with ten books and over six hundred stories and articles published.

Thank you for your consideration.

Sincerely,

Donna Clark Goodrich
Phone number

I signed the letter with my name and phone number. (This was before e-mail.)

Use your letterhead stationery for this query, and don't forget to include a business card.

If you've met this editor at a conference and he or she asked you to submit your manuscript, be sure and remind him of that in the query letter. Let him know, too, if you were referred to him by another writer or editor.

If you're sending this query via e-mail, use a professional e-mail name (bigflirt@yahoo.com may not impress an editor too much), and indicate on the subject line what you are sending, i.e., query on article submission, query on short story submission, query on novel/nonfiction submission, and so on.

Chapter-by-Chapter Synopsis

For a nonfiction book, include a brief description of what each chapter covers. However, often the chapter titles are enough as shown in the Table of Contents I sent with my typing book (see page 158).

Sample Chapters

The third thing to send with your book proposal is one to three sample chapters—the first three chapters, or whatever the publishers' guidelines require.

Make sure that these sample chapters are in tiptop condition. Don't feel you'll have time later to put them in better shape. You may not have a second chance. I almost lost the sale on the typing book because of outdated material and sloppy writing in the proposal. On the second how-to book for the same publisher, however, I edited my sample chapter so thoroughly before sending it in with the query letter that when I received a contract and sat down to write the book, I didn't have to do anything else with that chapter. It was in final form.

One other thing editors like to see in your proposal is a list of other books currently on the market on the same subject, and how yours differs.

This book proposal can be the key to opening the door to a published manuscript. Edit it, take it to your critique group, put in their suggestions, then read it over one more time before clicking "send" on your e-mail!

Cover Letter

If you've already sent a query letter and received a go-ahead, then you can send a *cover letter* with your manuscript. In this case, you won't have to repeat all the information you gave earlier in the query as the editor already has a copy of this. It's okay to send photocopies of your letter or e-mail and the response, however. The cover letter merely tells the editor you are enclosing the manuscript referred to in your letter of such-and-such a date, and thanks him for his consideration.

What Happens After My Book Arrives at the Publisher's?

A publisher's consideration of a book manuscript involves several steps. First, it may go through a "reader." This person weeds out any books that are totally unacceptable for that publishing house—either because of poor writing, lack of organization or research, or it just doesn't fit that particular publisher.

Manuscripts that pass this test will be passed on to an editor or—depending on the size of the staff—an assistant editor, and eventually a senior editor. A book that reaches this third stage usually has a fair chance of making it. The editorial staff then meets at regular intervals, reviews the manuscripts that have been submitted, and selects those that will fit their book program. At the same time they take a look at similar books already in print and see how this one differs.

A minister wrote and sold his first book. Going to a preachers' retreat, he eagerly awaited the comments from fellow ministers, but no one said anything. He wanted to bring up the subject of the book himself, but didn't want to appear proud.

As the weekend wore on, he tried in vain to work the book into the conversation, but to no avail.

Finally it was the last evening, and the clergy gathered together for a banquet. At the end, the emcee asked this particular minister to give the benediction.

Standing to his feet, the preacher began, "Dear God, Thou who has also written and published a book . . . ."

Sample Chapter-by-Chapter Synopsis
(machines in use in the year 1982)

How to Set Up and Run a Typing Service

Chapter

1. To own or not to own: That is the question
   Advantages and disadvantages of owning your own business; sole proprietorship or partnership; hiring good employees; labor laws.

2. "Backward, turn backward, O time in your flight."
   (I must have this thesis typed by tonight.)
   Time management

3. "Go tell it on the mountain" (and colleges and copy places)
   Advertising hints

4. "Double, double, toil and trouble."
   (Clips and bands and ribbons double)
   Supplies needed to start your business

5. QWERT—Which typewriter is for me?
   Models and prices of typewriters

6. Thanks for the memory
   Word processing machines

7. The cloning of a dissertation
   Copiers

8. "Friends, Romans, countrymen. Lend me your ears."
   Transcribing and dictation units

9. "Nothing is certain except death and taxes"
   Record keeping hints; tax laws, deductions

10. Old customers never die. They come back and bring others with them.
    General hints on typing, proofreading, making satisfied customers; how to charge—by page, hour, job, etc.

    Appendix A: Sample pages from style books (Turabian, APA, Campbell, etc.): Title page, contents, footnotes, bibliography.
    Appendix B: Filled-in tax forms with step-by-step instructions

The manuscript must then pass the most rigorous test—the marketing committee. This panel studies who will purchase the book and the projected estimated cost—cover design, typesetting, printing, artwork and so on. From these numbers they determine the book's price, and then the ultimate figure—the profit margin.

So while you are sitting at home waiting for a decision, and wondering why it is taking so long, things are going on behind the scene.

How can you help the publishing staff reach a positive decision?

- Send a well-written, neatly typed, and carefully proofread manuscript.
- List other books on the same subject and show how yours offers a new slant.
- Show how you can aid in the marketing of the book by speaking engagements, radio/TV interviews, your Web site/blog, and mailings.

Contract

C-Day! You may have received several rejection letters up to this point, but now you've received a contract! Before you sign on the dotted line and rush off to the post office, however, take time to study it. Show it to a professional writer friend or a lawyer who specializes in literary contracts. (Two people I personally recommend are Sally Stuart [stuartswmg@aol.com] and Susan Titus Osborn [susanosb@aol.com]). Don't be afraid to question anything in the contract and don't hesitate to turn it down if you have any doubts.

A writer friend received a contract for a children's book, but she was hesitant to sign it. Looking it over, I realized she had a valid reason to be skeptical. The publisher wanted to buy all rights, not that unusual as, at that time, the publisher held the copyright. But she wanted to buy the book outright for THIRTY DOLLARS!

We estimated how much my friend would lose if the book sold for $5 (low for a children's picture book) and if the publisher sold 5,000 copies (a normal first run) at a 10 percent royalty.

She returned the contract, stating her reasons for refusal. She realized that day that there are worse things than not selling a book. The pride of seeing her name on a book cover wasn't worth what she would lose in the long run.

Things to Look for in Your Contract

- What rights are the publishers buying—reprint, film, etc.?
- What percentage royalty are they offering?
- Will the royalty be based on net proceeds or gross?

- How many free copies do you get?
- Can you buy more copies at a discount?
- Does the publisher offer an advance (this is simply an advance *against* future royalties) or a grant for typing and research expenses?
- Will the copyright be in your name?
- Does the publisher ask for "rights of first refusal"—in other words, does the contract require that you submit your next manuscript to them *first?*
- When the book goes out of print, can you buy the remaining inventory at a reduced price?
- When the book goes out of print, do all rights revert to you?

Remember, any clauses in the contract are negotiable.

Angela Hoy, publisher of the *WritersWeekly* newsletter, suggests a clause stating, "If I die while this contract is still in effect, please assign editorial and contractual control and future royalty checks for this book to (family member or other beneficiary)."

If you receive a contract before you complete your book, it will include a date for the completed manuscript to be in the hands of the publisher. This deadline now will take precedence over anything else in your schedule as the publisher will plan its advertising based upon that date.

Make sure you get everything in writing. I once signed a contract for an eighth-grade textbook. The editor wanted it to cover church leaders from the early church to the twentieth century. I protested—in person, over the phone, and in writing—that this was too long a period to cover, but he didn't relent. I spent the entire summer in research before beginning the actual writing.

I turned in the finished manuscript on deadline—but to a new editor. He called me and said the book covered too many years; he wanted it cut off at the Reformation. Later he tried to reduce my royalties from 10 to 5 percent because of "necessary rewriting." Luckily I had kept all my correspondence and I ended up receiving the promised royalty.

What Happens Next?

The next correspondence with your publisher (doesn't that sound good?) may be a request for information on your personal and writing background—education, awards, club memberships, previous writing credits, and so on. The questionnaire also may ask for a brief description of the book, and names and addresses of magazines and newspapers to whom you'd like the publisher to send press releases and review copies.

Most publishers send page proofs to the authors. Ask also to see the cover and back cover copy and check details for accuracy. At this time you may want to ask an eagle-eyed friend to give it a final proof to catch any typos that may have occurred in editorial changes.

Also by this time you should have received the requested permissions. Make sure all the credit lines are included and delete material for which you could not obtain permission.

E-Books

An alternative to publishing your book is an e-book—short for electronic book—an e-text that forms the digital media equivalent of a conventional printed book, and is usually read on personal computers, smart phones, or devices known as e-book readers. They are generally written for a limited audience. (See http://en.wikipedia.org/wiki/e-book for more information on e-books, including advantages and disadvantages of this type of publishing.)

A Published Author

You're now on a first-name basis with the mail carrier as you stand waiting every day at the mailbox. Finally, the package arrives, with more tape than you thought could possibly cover a box. You rip it open as fast as you can and hold your treasured baby up for all to see. It will then be given a prominent place on your coffee table ready to show at a moment's notice to everyone who enters your house for any reason: friends, relatives, neighbors, plumber, exterminator, door-to-door salesmen.

You're convinced that as soon as you get your book, you'll sit down and read it from cover to cover. It may surprise you to know that many authors do not read their own books for many months—if ever. They leaf through it and all they can remember are the long hours of writing and rewriting. They're almost sick of it—for the time being. But you can still look at it and feel pride that it is your book.

Don't rest on your laurels too long though. There is still work ahead. You can play an important part in the marketing of the book. Donate a copy to your library, with a newspaper photographer present. Offer to appear on a local radio or television talk show, or hold a book signing at a local bookstore. Send news releases to those on your personal and business mailing lists.

Remember, the more you sell, the more you'll see on your first royalty check. Then you'll know you are a published author. By that time, however, you'll be so busy writing your second book you'll hardly have time to spend the royalties from the first.

Chapter 14

Where to Get Ideas

IDEAS ARE EVERYWHERE! You'll discover as you write, ideas will pop up in unexpected places. The secret is to train yourself to *think like a writer.*

During the eighteen years I operated a tax preparation service, I constantly reminded my customers, family, and friends to "think taxes" whenever they got into their car or pulled out their checkbook. (My son-in-law said going places with me was like traveling with H&R Block.)

It's the same with a writer. Whenever friends tell me a story, they see the gleam in my eye and ask, "Are you going to write about it?" I reply, "If you're not going to, with your permission I will."

While teaching at a conference one year, I sat at the lunch table jotting down notes. No one questioned what I was doing. (I'm sure they all thought that my creative juices were out of control, and I just *had* to get my thoughts down before they escaped.) In reality, however, I was eavesdropping on some very interesting conversations and making note of all the writing possibilities.

Imagine the surprise on the faces of some conferees attending my "Where to Get Ideas" class that afternoon when they heard me mention parts of their lunchtime chats. They hadn't realized that many of the stories they were sharing with friends contained the seeds for saleable manuscripts.

Almost everything I read or see or hear can end up as a short story, an article, or a devotional or filler. I write on scraps of paper wherever I find them—napkins at restaurants, corners of newspapers, church bulletins. Sometimes, the thought will flit around in my mind for years before I get it down, but eventually it will fit into something I'm writing.

> When you're a writer, nothing bad happens to you because it's all material.
> —Garrison Keillor

Where are ideas found? Let me mention a few places and share some devotionals and fillers gleaned from those sources.

Newspapers and Magazines

Reading a newspaper article can set your writer's mind awhirl. For example, I read a short item in our local paper about a town in Florida that had a problem with its water supply. Giving this filler a spiritual connotation, I came up with the following:

Tapping Our Unused Power

For ten years, residents of a Florida subdivision had very little water pressure. When they turned on the faucets, the water just trickled out.

Then one day while checking for pressure in the fire hydrants, someone noticed that two valves had not been turned back on after installation of a new water system a decade earlier. A work crew dug up a section of line. When the valves were opened, pressure rose.

Is our Christian life a struggle? Do we have enough power to meet our everyday needs? . . . The problem may be in two unopened valves—prayer and Bible reading. We may be so busy with legitimate tasks that our Bibles are dusty and the knees of our clothing shiny instead of worn through.

If these two valves are opened in our lives, instead of a trickle, we can start receiving the showers of blessings God has for us.

The above filler has been rewritten in various lengths, depending on periodical requirements, and resold over twenty times.

I mentioned earlier about the box we found in my mother's closet marked, "Save for Donna" and the dozens of poems, anecdotes, and advice columns she had saved for me. A gold mine, indeed. I've kept most of them and have referred back to them many times.

The secret to this is *organization!* On page 166 is a suggested list of topics for a clippings file. Depending on your genre of writing, you may have more or fewer topics. Whether you are writing or speaking, these quotations will prove to be invaluable.

You can use them for illustrations for devotionals and articles or as a springboard for short stories. But make sure you write the date, the name of the magazine or newspaper, and the page number on each clipping as you'll need to cite the source when you use it. If you don't have time to file the clippings right away, at least write the topic at the top.

If you don't have access to a file cabinet, use a cardboard box. And as a good steward, take every opportunity to save money. Why buy a box of new file folders when many businesses and schools toss out their old ones at the end of the year? Ask around!

Children's Activities

Halfway through a song at one of our children's grade-school concerts, a young boy lifted his cymbals in anticipation. Suddenly, a disappointed look crossed his face and he lowered the instruments. He had missed his cue, along with his chance to perform for family and friends. From this event (years later) I wrote the following filler:

One Chance—Missed

My husband and I sat watching the elementary school children struggle through their first band concert of the year. I especially was interested in a little lad standing with the other band members, a set of cymbals in his hand.

Halfway through the number he raised the cymbals, preparing for his big moment. He waited . . . and waited . . . and waited. Then a look of disappointment crossed his face, and he slowly lowered his instruments. The song had ended, and he had missed his chance to perform for his family and friends.

My heart went out to the small boy. I also felt a twinge of regret for myself for chances I had missed: to speak a word of encouragement to a friend, to be polite to an over-tired salesclerk, to show friendship to a newcomer at church.

I knew the boy would have another chance to clash his cymbals, and I prayed the Lord would also give me other chances to show His love.

An afternoon spent with my daughters cleaning canister cans and cupboard shelves led to a devotional on the importance of keeping both the inside and the outside of a person clean. I also wrote a devotional using the theme of taking my junior class on a hike, following the leader who had hiked that trail before and knew the path.

Clippings Topic File

Abortion	Empty Nest	Judgment	Rest
Aging	Estate/Wills	Justice	Resurrection
Alcohol	Excuses	Law (legal)	Retirement
Ambition	Failure	Letter writing	Revival
Anger	Faith	Life	Sanctification
Animals	Family	Love	Second Coming
Atheism	Father	Marriage	Service
Babies	Forgiveness	Ministers	Sex
Baseball	Fraud	Miracles	Sin
Biographies	Friendship	Miscellaneous	Singles
Burdens	Games	Missions	Small Business
Child Abuse	God	Money	Sports (general)
Children	Government	Mother	Stewardship
Christ	Grandparents	Movies	Stress
Christian Living	Greed	Moving	Success
Christmas	Grief	Music	Suffering
Church	Guilt	Names	Suicide
Coincidence/Fate	Habits	Nationalities	Sunday School
Communism	Healing	New Year	Taxes
Contentment	Health	Organization	Teachers
Contests	Heaven	Parenting	Teen-agers
Conversation	Hell	Patriotism	Television
Conversion	Heroes	Persistence	Temptation
Courage	Holidays	Personality	Ten Commandments
Crime	Holy Land	Poetry	Thanksgiving
Crucifixion	Home Business	Pornography	Time Management
Cults	Homosexuality	Positive Thinking	Tobacco
Death (children)	Household Hints	Prayer	Travel
Death (general)	Human Interest	Pregnancy	Welfare
Depression	Humor	Procrastination	Witnessing
Diet	Incarnation	Quotations	Women
Divorce	Inspiration	Religion	Work
Drugs	Insurance	Remodeling	Worry

Children's Quotations

You can get ideas not only from your own children, but from neighbor children, students in your Sunday school class, and children's programs on television. Be carefully, however, not to use copyrighted quotations verbatim, only as springboards to develop a larger thought.

One filler I sold came from our young son's statement that, "Yes, God can help me if I want to be a preacher because He knows more big words in the Bible than I do." Another quotation that could easily be used in an article on self-esteem came from our four-year-old daughter's lips. One evening we were watching the Miss Universe contest. I had had recent surgery and hadn't gotten out of my pajamas and robe for several weeks. When they crowned the winner, I told my daughter, "There's the most beautiful woman in the world." "Uh, uh," she disagreed. "She's not as pretty as you, Momma." Think of how many places you could use a quotation like that.

Everyday Events

This will more than likely be your most frequent source for ideas.

When I owned a secretarial service, a graduate student brought his doctoral dissertation to me to type. The next day his wife called me several times: "Did you remember to . . . ?" "Don't forget . . . " "Are you sure you'll have it done in time?" I finally said to my husband in disgust, "If they didn't trust me with it, why did they leave it with me?" Then God reminded me how many times I left something with Him, only to come back and ask Him, "Did you remember . . . ?" "Are You sure You'll have the answer in time?" That incident went into a filler simply called "The Typing Job."

> Want to succeed at anything without going nuts? Be passionately involved in the process; emotionally detached from the results.
>
> —Donna Partow

After my mother died, I went through a period of depression. It was difficult to read the Bible or spend time in prayer. It felt as though I was facing a brick wall. Standing at the sink one day doing dishes, my tears flowed almost as steadily as the water from the faucet. Finally I shook my fist toward heaven and yelled, "Are you there, Lord? Is anyone even listening?" Suddenly, I heard these words from the television set in the living room, "The audio portion of our program is temporarily disrupted. Please stand by!" I thanked God for the reminder and the thought was turned into a devotional to help someone else in a time of need.

The following is one of my favorite fillers taken from a true experience:

The Ugly Bedspread

The bedspread was ugly.

I bought it in desperation at a garage sale for $5.

"Yuk," I said, each time I made the bed. I grimaced as I spread the cover.

Then one day while leafing through a Penney's catalog, I saw the same bedspread with a well-known designer's name. Price $85.

Suddenly the bedspread took on a new beauty—once I discovered how much it cost.

At one time I didn't think much of myself. I felt ugly.

"Yuk," I said each time I looked in the mirror.

Then one day I heard the story of salvation—how Christ gave His life on Calvary just for me. And suddenly my life took on a new beauty—once I discovered how much it had cost.

Can you see how the above story could also be used as an illustration in a longer article on self-esteem?

Ideas are everywhere. A twenty-mile drive for a medical test gave me three saleable items. I ignored a detour on the way to the clinic, complaining that it would take me too far out of my way, only to find myself on a street under construction and filled with potholes. This reminded me that sometimes God may take me on paths that seem to be longer and out of the way, but He knows the potholes I would encounter if I took the path of my choosing. I called this filler "The Rocky Road."

The following devotional was taken from an incident that happened on the way home from the test. When submitting it, I used the verse, "Draw nigh to God, and he will draw nigh to you" (James 4:8 KJV).

No Reception

"Where is that ballgame?" I fiddled with the knobs on the car radio. I had turned the dial to the right station, but no announcer's voice came through.

Then I realized I was about twenty miles from where I usually received the station and it was too far away for the signal to come through. I left the radio on and in about fifteen minutes I heard the call of the balls and strikes.

Sometimes it's hard to hear God's voice. A story is told of a married couple out for a car ride. "We don't sit close to each other like we used to," the wife complained.

"I haven't moved," the husband replied from the driver's seat.

Just as I was too far away from the signal to get the program I wanted, so too have I sometimes moved too far away from my spiritual Source to get the help I needed.

Lord, help me remember that You haven't moved. Keep me always tuned in to You.

The third experience, while not a filler, helps illustrate how almost everyone you meet has a story. While talking to the lab technician that day, she mentioned that few patients know what to expect after a breast surgery, even a simple procedure as a lumpectomy. Sometimes a swelling or a black and blue mark after the surgery can send them into hysterics, she said, because the doctor didn't warn them it might happen. Then she added, "I'd like to write a booklet to hand to patients before surgery."

"Why don't you?" I asked.

She did and I edited it.

The ideas are there. As the motto says, "Stop, look, and listen!"

God's Mysterious Ways

We all have experienced incidents that the world calls "coincidences" but in which we can see the hand of God.

I remember sending my dad's second wife a "Thinking of You" card after my father died, telling her how much we appreciated her care for him during his final year-long illness. He was married to her for twenty-two years. This was the first time, however, I was able to tell her I loved her.

She wrote back, thanking me for the birthday card, saying it was the only one she received. I did not know it was her birthday. I just knew God brought her to my mind one particular day and impressed on me that I should write and thank her for all she had done. And it had arrived on the day she needed that encouragement the most—her first birthday alone without my father.

This is only one of many such events in my life and I'm sure you, too, have had your share. These brief incidents, which help remind us that God is still in charge, can be used as illustrations for a devotional, an inspirational filler, or in an article.

The Bible

One of the best sources for ideas is God's Word. However, as my nephew tells students in his workshops, "You don't read the Bible to get ideas for songs. You read it because you have a desire to communicate with God. The ideas are a fringe benefit."

In going through my mother's things after she died, I found some letters I had written her years before. In one letter I told her that my devotions earlier that evening had given me ideas for three short stories. I realized later while reading this letter that I had eventually sold all three of these stories to our denominational weekly take-home paper.

My intention in reading the Bible that night was not to get ideas for stories, however. I was 750 miles away from home, living in a strange city, attending a strange church, and working at a strange new job, and I needed the strength I knew I could find in the Scriptures.

Keep a pad and pencil handy when you read the Bible. You will come up with many ideas for fillers and devotionals.

An Event from the Past

You feel you would like to write a book to share with others how God brought you through a particular situation, especially in your childhood. These stories, however, though interesting, will probably never see print as the thought of "writing a book" terrifies you.

If this is the case, begin by using some of these highlights as the personal illustration portion of a devotional or article. In looking through various Christian magazines and take-home papers, you can see how authors many times use events from their lives to illustrate the text.

Get into the habit of jotting down events in your life—no matter how small. Sue Monk Kidd says, "We look at our experiences as plain, ordinary, and routine. We don't look deep enough to catch the *hidden holy*."

Zechariah 4:10 tells us not to "despise the day of small things." Ideas are everywhere. You just have to look for them!

Chapter 15

Editing Hints

THIS CHAPTER INCLUDES the most common errors I find in manuscripts I edit. Perhaps they will be helpful as you edit your own manuscript or to use as guidelines in a critique group.

Show, Don't Tell

- Which is better? "The giant looked around the room. When he saw the boy, he got angry and bellowed a threat to eat him." Or, "Fee, fi, fo, fum. I smell the blood of an Englishman. Be he alive, or be he dead, I'll grind his bones to make my bread."[1]
- Don't just say people are fat. Show it! Show them out of breath while climbing steps, their faces red, perspiring, buttons popped off their dresses or shirts, or rips under their sleeves.
- "He was a bushy-haired, massive man." What color hair? How massive? What did he weigh? How tall was he? Did he tower over someone? To someone who is only five feet tall, "tall" could be five feet six inches. Paint a picture readers can see in their minds.
- Telling: I felt sad.

Following is one of the best examples I've ever seen of showing, not telling. The author, Max Lucado, could have merely said, "Tears are necessary to show our emotion." But instead he wrote:

Tears.

Those tiny drops of humanity. Those round, wet balls of fluid that tumble from our eyes, creep down our cheeks, and splash on the floor of our hearts. They were there that day. They are always present at such times. They should be; that's their job. They are miniature messengers; on call twenty-four hours a day to substitute for crippled words. They drip, drop, and pour from the corner of our souls, carrying with them the deepest emotions we possess. They tumble down our faces with announcements that range from the most blissful joy to darkest despair.

The principle is simple; when words are most empty, tears are most apt.[2]

And how about this passage from the Bible:

For ye shall go out with joy, and be led forth with peace; the mountains and the hills shall break forth before you into singing, and all the trees of the field shall clap their hands.
—Isa. 55:12 KJV

Use Specific Adjectives

Okay: Small jar.
Better: A *two-ounce* jar.

Don't Overuse Adjectives

Pick out the strongest. Instead of "a pleasant and friendly voice," "pleasant" is enough.

Don't Overuse Adverbs

Replace an adverb with a strong verb.
Okay: She read the page quickly.
Better: She scanned the page.
"Get out of here!" he said angrily. Don't need "angrily" as your words show the anger.

Use Strong Verbs

Okay: She closed the kitchen window.
Better: She *slammed* the kitchen window.

Okay: She looked at her husband.
Better: She *stared* (or *glared*) at her husband.
　　　　She *gazed* at her husband.
Okay: Judy came into the room where her friend sat . . .
Better: Judy *burst* into the room . . .
Okay: Jesus was sad.
Better: Jesus *wept*.
Okay: He walked through the water.
Better: He *sloshed*.
Okay: He walked down the hall.
Better: He *darted* through the crowded corridor.

Instead of saying someone "picked" something up, say, she "grabbed it" or "lugged" it.

An adjective is an opinion, while a verb is a fact.

An angry dog attacked me.
The growling dog *leaped* at me and *tore* my pant leg to shreds.
Don't just say a character is beautiful. Describe her so thoroughly that the reader will say, "She must be beautiful."

Avoid passive voice whenever possible

Wrong: If your manuscript *is sent back*, try again.
Right: If your manuscript *comes back*, try again.
Wrong: The printer *was used* by several administrative assistants.
Right: Several administrative assistants *used* the printer.

Get to the Point

Bob went to his car, opened the door, and sat down behind the wheel. Closing the door, he fastened his seatbelt, then he adjusted his rearview mirror, and looked in his glove compartment for his sunglasses. Finally finding them, he took a tissue from the cupholder and cleaned the glasses. Then he put the car in gear and backed out of the driveway. Reaching the end of the driveway, he looked to the right and to the left, before heading east down the street. Reaching the corner, he stopped at the stop sign. Seeing no one coming, he continued on his way. After stopping at several traffic lights, he finally arrived at the restaurant where he was to meet his client for lunch.

Better: John pulled out of the driveway, and ten minutes later he arrived at the restaurant where he found his client waiting.

Good Transition Words

That morning, the following day, however, therefore. When the bus arrived . . .

Pet Words (words you tend to overuse)

Began to, sort of, kind of, just, a little, some, it, thing, I guess, I think, I began, I started, only, actually, also, both, certainly, indeed, in fact, of course, quite, really, surely, truly, very.

Time Sequence

When you have a lapse in time, leave extra space between paragraphs or center * * * on page.

Count Prepositions. Eliminate as many as possible.

Ever so gently she penned her name *with* the tip *of* her finger *in* the dust *on* the pew *in* front *of* her.

Rewritten: Ever so gently her finger penned her name *on* the dusty pew *in* front *of* her. Same meaning, three less prepositions.

Wordiness

I've chosen some samples of wordiness from manuscripts I edited. They are used with the permission of the authors.

Wordy: He did not take the time to file a flight plan, which he usually did just before take-off.

Better: He did not take the time to file his usual flight plan.

Wordy: She set the table and placed two mugs of water into her microwave oven, preparatory to brewing tea. When the water was sufficiently hot, she inserted a tea bag in each mug and closed the door while the tea steeped.

Better: . . . then she prepared two cups of tea. *How much does your reader need to know?*

Wordy: She raised her hand and stiffened her finger that was shaking and pointing to a crude sign nailed to the top of a cross.

Better: She pointed a shaky finger to a crude sign nailed to the top of a cross.

One of the best ways to improve on wordiness is to enter contests in which the entry has to be fifty words or less. You discover how many words are absolutely unnecessary.

Sometimes in typing term papers for students, I'd end up with one word to go onto the next page. In most cases, it was simple to omit a word without changing the meaning. However, while typing a book for a friend, this was not the case. She had written so tightly that not one word could be removed without changing the context. Strong writing, indeed.

Don't Use the Same Word too Close Together.

For example,
She and her brother had always been close. Before her brother married, they had done everything together, gone places together. Then her brother moved out of state and she had gone to college, and everything changed.

Better:
She and her brother had always been close. Before he married, they had done everything together, gone places together. Then he moved out of state and she had gone to college, and everything changed.

Use your thesaurus to find just the right word, and be specific. The one time it's proper to repeat a word over and over is in children's writing. They love it. Look at the success of Dr. Seuss's *The Cat in the Hat.*

Use Descriptive Words

As the sun goes down, a stillness falls over Egypt. Water channels that cross the fields turn to the colour of blood, then to bright yellow that fades into silver. The palm trees might be cut from black paper and pasted against the incandescence of the sky. Brown hawks that hang all day above the sugar-cane and the growing wheat are seen no more and, one by one, the stars burn over the sandhills and lie caught in the stiff fronds of the date palms.[3]

- She had made a soft landing into the real world of today.
- My mouth's so dry I could spit enough cotton to knit a sweater.

- It's a ten-hanky crying jag.
- One eye that, like his tie, always drifted to the left.
- We're all different. Did you think God made a paper-doll pattern from Adam and Eve?[4]

Pronouns

- Whenever you use a pronoun such as "they," "he," "it," etc., make sure the reader knows who or what the pronoun is referring to.
  Linda says that her sister always gives *her* children too many presents. Whose children is the sister spoiling?
- "It's" needs an apostrophe only if used as a contraction, not in possessive:
  The dog lost its bone.
  I'll be glad when it's (it is) payday.
- *I or me?*
  John, Eunice, and I were all sick.
  Father sent for John, Eunice, and me. (To determine which one should be used, delete "John, Eunice, and" and see how it reads as "Father sent for I.")
- *We or us?*
  We girls will be waiting for you. (Delete "girls" and it reads okay.)
  He waited for us girls. (Delete "girls" and it reads okay.)

Abbreviations

In nonfiction, the first time you use the name of an organization, spell it out, then show the abbreviation in parentheses. The next time you can simply use the initials. For example, Alcoholics Anonymous (AA) thereafter can be simply AA.

Numbers

- Use your publisher's style guide. Decide whether you're going to spell out numbers under ten or one hundred and under and be consistent.
- Always spell out numbers at the beginning of a sentence, unless it is a year.
- Use numbers for dates (August 13, 1960), monetary amounts ($140), percentages (10 percent), and ratios (3-to-1).
- When giving a phone number, use the prefix 555 as there is no such prefix and people won't mistake it for a real number.

Avoid Beginning Sentences or Paragraphs in a Row with Same Word

You can find examples of this every morning in the obituary section. Try your hand at rewriting the following paragraph:

She was born in Jackson, Michigan. She moved to Arizona in 1969. She was a proofreader for the Arizona State House of Representatives. She was a former associate editor for a trade magazine. She was on the advisory board of American Christian Writers.

Try Not to End Sentences in a Row with the Same Word

When I worked for a newspaper, the editor had a rule that we couldn't begin or end more than two sentences in a row with the same word. This is a good rule to follow.

Redundancy

Costlier in price. Costlier.
Exact same size. Same size.
Red in color. Red.
Taller in height. Taller.
Two twin girls. Twin girls.
Shouted loudly. Shouted.

Correct order

Wrong: A luncheon will be served in the executive dining room so that new employees can eat as well as meet their supervisors.
Right: . . . so that new employees can eat lunch and meet their supervisors.
Wrong: Skateboarding along the sidewalk, a dog ran in front of the boy.
Right: As the boy skateboarded along the sidewalk, a dog ran in front of him.

Avoid

Starting sentences with "There was," "It is," "It was."
It was shortly after that I tried to run away from home. (Delete "It was.")
There is a special path the Lord has for your life. (The Lord has a special path for your life.)

Avoid use of linking verbs

Michael Hemmes calls these "The Terrible 20":

is, am, was, were, be, been, are, has, have, had, may, can, must, might, would, could, should, shall, will, do. He says they add little to your writing, and they force you to use the passive voice.[5] Writing "actively" takes more thought, but results in a stronger presentation.

Viewpoint

Unless you use omniscient viewpoint (showing the thoughts of all the characters), you can only get into the mind of the main character. Thus, the only way the reader can know what other characters are thinking is either by dialogue or facial expressions.

* "He knocked, and then opened the door, surprising the woman inside who was shocked to see him since she had not heard any vehicle drive up." How do we know she was shocked? How do we know she couldn't hear the car drive up?
* Even though you use omniscient viewpoint, you still shouldn't put *your own viewpoint* into story, i.e., "The meal was scrumptious." How do we know it's scrumptious? That's your opinion as the author. Have someone at the table say, "This meal is scrumptious," or describe the food so thoroughly as to make the reader see how scrumptious it is.

Avoid Overuse of "ing" Words

First draft:
The hail was pelt*ing* against the windows. Betty was sing*ing* while iron*ing* John's jeans. Complain*ing* about gett*ing* to work on time, John kept open*ing* the closet door and look*ing* for another pair hang*ing* from the rod. Betty glanced up, try*ing* unsuccessfully to hide a frown. "Give me a break, John. You're irritat*ing* me."

Rewrite:
The hail pelted against the windows. Betty sang while she ironed John's jeans. He complained that he'd be late for work again if she didn't hurry. He opened the closet door for the third time, and pulled out another pair of pants off the rod. Betty tried to hide a frown. "Give me a break, John. I'll have these ready in time." (Cut down from ten to zero.)

Proofreading Hints

- Use ruler—one line at a time.
- Use ruler with opening thin enough to read only one line.
- Read sentence backward.

Avoid Changing Personal Tense

He is returning for *us* . . . so *you* can be with Him in glory.
Correct: He is returning for *us* . . . so *we* can be with Him in glory.

Commas

Always use a comma after dialogue and before identifying the speaker, i.e., "I don't want to go," Susan said to her mother.

If your dialogue ends with an exclamation point or question mark, then no comma is needed.

See what a difference a comma makes in the following Scripture verse:

"Truly I say to you, today you shall be with Me in paradise" (Luke 23:43 NASB).
"Truly I tell you today, you will be with me in Paradise" (New World Translation used by Jehovah's Witnesses).

Insert a comma where needed in the following sentences:

Man wanted to wash cars and two cashiers.
Briefcase lost by writer full of ideas.

Colon

A capital letter is used in the first word following a colon if that word begins a complete sentence. For example:

I bought the following items at the store: bread, milk, and jelly.
I heard some good news today: One of the writers in our critique group received a contract for her novel.

Exclamation Point

This has been described as "writing at the top of your voice." Rather than have your characters shouting, let their actions show the emotion. "Julie stomped across the room," or, "Julie slammed the door." William G. Tapply says, "An exclamation mark is the author jumping up and down waving his arms. It's a poor substitute for words . . . It shouts to your reader: 'This is really important [startling, surprising, scary, loud, dramatic, whatever], but I don't know how to convey it with words . . . or I'm too lazy to try.'"[6]

Quotes

Use single quotes inside double quotes and leave a one-half space between the two. (To do this, highlight the two sets of quotation marks, go to Format, Font, Character Spacing. Change the spacing from Normal to Expanded, and the amount to .5, and this will put a half space in between.)

In nonfiction, if the quote is more than four lines, indent on the left or both sides and delete the quotation marks. In this case, any quote within this quote would require double quotation marks.

Apostrophes

Do *not* use apostrophe for plurals: lots of love, the girls.
Do *not* use apostrophe for "its" except as a contraction for "it is."
In using an apostrophe for singular possessive, place *before* the "s": Mary's coat.
In using an apostrophe for plural possessive, place *after* the "s," i.e., (many birds), the birds' freedom.

Dash

A dash is two hyphens with no spaces before, between, or after. A Word program will automatically make this a dash, or you can click on Ctrl, Alt, and the minus key on your number pad.

Ellipses

Ellipses indicate an incomplete thought or something omitted in a quotation. It is composed of three periods with spaces before, between, and after. If it appears at the end of a sentence, use the required period, then three more with spaces before, between, and after.

Thoughts

Thoughts may be placed in italics without quotation marks, or without italics and using quotation marks. Or you can say, "He said to himself" or "He asked himself" and place the thoughts in quotation marks. If you write, "he thought," you do not need to add "to himself."

Capitalization

- Only proper nouns need initial capitalization. It's not used in "He is our pastor" but it's needed in "I went to see Pastor Smith" because it's being used as part of a name.
- Use a capital letter when you're using a pronoun as a proper name. For example, you don't need a capital "m" and "d" in "My mom and dad said no" but you do when writing, "Can I go to the store, Mom?" (Here "Mom" is used in place of her name.)
- The names of geographical regions are proper nouns and need to be capitalized, i.e., "He settled in the West." However, when used only as a direction, use lowercase, i.e., "I turned west to go to the store."

   What words need to be capitalized in the following sentence?

   She used to be a Teacher's Aide for a Biology class in Junior High School.

   Answer: none. However, if the names of a specific class and junior high school are listed, then they would be capitalized; i.e., She was a teacher's aide for Biology 101 at Fremont Junior High School.

Small Caps

The following all use small caps (or go by publisher's style sheet):

A.M., P.M. B.C., A.D., NIV, KJV (and other abbreviations for Bible translations), and LORD ("ord" in small caps). (In Microsoft Word, small caps are made by clicking on Ctrl, Shift, k, and typing in lowercase.)

Awhile or a while

"A while" is used after a preposition (in a while, for a while); "awhile" is an adverb that follows a verb: I read awhile, then I took a break.

If you study the suggestions in this chapter and incorporate them into your manuscripts, you can experience a successful writing career—and be a friend of editors forever.

Mnemonic Spelling

Affect, as v., *alter*, *sway*; as n., psychological state
Effect, as v., *establish*; as n., *end result*
All right, two words; remember its antonym, *all wrong*
Anoint, use *an oint*ment
Balloon, two *l*'s as in ba*ll*
Battalion, two *t*'s, one *l*, as in *battle*
Capit*o*l, building as in d*o*me
Capit*a*l, city as in an *a*rea
Connecticut, first I *connect*, then *I cut*.
Deductible, *i* as in *IRS*.
Dependent, take depen*dents* to the *dent*ist.
Descendant, descend*ants* come from *ancestors*.
February, "*Br*! It's cold."
Friend, a fri*end* to the *end*.
Grammar, bad gram*mar* will *mar* your progress.
Gray, *a* as in America; grey, the English spelling, *e* as in England.
Inoculate, one *n*, one *c*, as in in*ject*.
Memento, *mem* as in *mem*ory.
Minuscule, contains *minus*.
Piece, a *piece* of *pie*.
Privilege, a privil*ege* gives you a *leg* up.
Recommend/recommendation, contain the word *commend*.
Rhythm, divide six letters into two groups, each with an *h* in the middle.
Separate, break into *parts*.
Stationary, st*a*nd still.
Stationery, writ*e* on it (or remember *e* stands for *envelope*).[7]

And a great way to remember the names of the Great Lakes: Sailors refer to them as their HOMES—Huron, Ontario, Michigan, Erie, Superior.

Chapter 16

How to Sell What You Write

I DON'T CARE if I get paid. I just want to share the message," Christian writers sometimes say. You may have said this yourself.

Spreading the gospel should be our number one reason for writing. However, the goal for many of us is to become full-time writers and this won't happen if editors give us only a byline and a thank-you.

Writers have expenses, and we cannot continue to write unless we are paid. Luke 10:7 says, "The laborer is worthy of his hire" (KJV).

There are exceptions, of course. If the editor of a new magazine asks us to write an article and says he can't afford to pay, we'd probably say yes. Most writers I know are willing to help a Christian magazine get started. Later, when this editor can begin to pay, he will remember writers who supported the magazine when it was struggling.

Let me add: Checks are not the reward, nor are the bylines. The reward is when a reader tells you, "What you wrote changed my life!" That's worth more than any check. That's the stamp of approval I'm doing what God has called me to do.

Marketing Your Manuscripts

It is said that when P. G. Woodhouse wrote a letter, he sealed it, affixed a stamp, and threw it out of a third story window, convinced that a passerby would mail it. He insisted that not one letter got lost.

Crazy? Yes. But that's often the way we submit manuscripts. We may not toss them out a window, but if we don't send them to appropriate markets, we're like a driver going in the wrong direction who refused to turn back because he was making such good time. It doesn't do any good to make good time if you're going in the wrong direction.

Christine Tangvald, best-selling author of over ninety children's books, once told writers at a conference, "If you don't take time to learn something about a magazine, why should the editor take time to read your manuscript?"

In talking about submitting a manuscript to the wrong market, she said it's like entering a chocolate cake in a banana pie contest. "It may be the best chocolate cake you can make, but it's sent to the wrong place."

The secret to success is to study the magazines themselves, rather than just the guidelines. Once I realized this, I pored over the leads, transitions, endings, slant, and style, and filled out a "Periodical Analysis Sheet" for each one (see page 189).

Marketing Tools

Books

Two popular books—both updated annually—are available to help you in your marketing. The most widely-used resource for Christian writers is the *Christian Writers' Market Guide* edited by Sally E. Stuart. The first section of this guide gives the name of book publishers, along with considerable information about each one. A sample listing is shown below. (Note: This is a *sample listing* only. Updated information on this particular publisher can be obtained by writing to the publisher or by going to its Web site.)

ACTA PUBLICATIONS, 5559 W. Howard St., Skokie, IL 60077-2621. Toll-free (800) 397-2282. (847) 676-2282. Fax (800) 397-0079. E-mail: acta@ actapublications.com. Website: www.actapublications.com. Catholic. Gregory F. Augustine Perce, pres. & co-pub. Wants books that successfully integrate daily life and spirituality. Publishes 10 titles/yr; hardcover, trade paperbacks, coffee-table books. Receives 100 submissions annually. 50% of books from first-time authors. Prefers 150-200 pgs. Royalty 10-12% of net; no advance. Average first printing 3,000. Publication within 1 yr. Responds in 2 mos. Prefers NRSV. Guidelines; catalog for 9x12 SAE/2 stamps.
Nonfiction: Query or proposal/1 chapter; no phone/fax/e-query.
Tips: "Most open to books that are useful to a large number of average Christians. Read our catalog and one of our books first.

The second section of the book divides periodicals into topical categories, such as marriage, ministry, finance, church leadership, women, teens, and so on. This magazine section gives the same information as the book section, along with specific details on reading audience, frequency of publication, circulation, how much freelance material they use, and whether they accept entire manuscripts or queries only. Listed also are pay rates and editorial schedules, rights purchased, and specific needs, i.e., articles, short stories, poetry, book reviews, and so on, with the requested length for each. These listings state, as well, how long editors take to report, deadline for submitting seasonal material, if they accept reprints, and how to obtain guidelines and sample copies.

Additional information in this guide includes a glossary (see Appendix B), greeting card markets, Internet Web sites for writers, correspondence courses, agents, editorial services, and writers' clubs and conferences across the United States and other countries.

A second marketing book is the *Writer's Market* published by Writer's Digest Books (available also on CD). This book lists religious markets, but not as many as are found in Sally Stuart's book, and they are harder to find among the pages of other magazine and book publishers. You may want to purchase this book, however, if you also write for the general market.

Writer's Digest Books also publishes specific market guides for fiction, poetry, children's writers and illustrators, artists, photographers, songwriters, and science fiction writers.

The *Writer's Market* can be found at bookstores and public libraries. Editors suggest purchasing secular guides at least every two years but I recommend buying the *Christian Writers' Market Guide* annually as religious markets change at a more rapid pace. If your library doesn't have this book, you might consider donating a copy. It also includes a CD.

Neither of the above books gives *complete* requirements for book publishers and magazines. It is now up to you to go through the listings, select those that interest you, and obtain guidelines, sample copies, and catalogs—either by writing and requesting them or going online to their Web sites.

Magazines

Many writer's magazines are also available. The children's librarian in my hometown introduced me to *The Writer* when I was nine years old. Other magazines include *Writer's Digest, Writer's Journal,* and *Christian Communicator (CC)*. All of these, with the exception of *CC*, can be bought on the newsstands.

These magazines contain excellent instructive articles on various fields of writing, along with marketing information. However, *CC* also contains a section each month called "Write Markets" in which Sally Stuart gives up-to-date information on editor/ address changes, new magazines, magazines no longer published, and current needs. After each listing, she gives the page number this book or magazine is listed on in the current *Christian Writers' Market Guide,* so you can keep this guide up to date all year. She also gives information on contests, conferences, and writers' clubs.

Another Christian periodical—*Cross & Quill*—is available from the Christian Writers Fellowship International. (See page 199 for more information on these marketing tools.)

Most of us cannot afford to subscribe to all these writers' magazines. Select those you find most helpful and put them on your Christmas list, purchase individual issues at a bookstore or newsstand, or read them at the library. Or members of your critique group can subscribe to different ones and share them. I recommend a personal subscription to *CC,* however, for the excellent articles and marketing information.

Periodical Analysis Sheet

You've sent for sample magazines or picked up a selection at the last writers' conference you attended. Now what?

First, sit down and read them. Then file them in a cabinet or sturdy box—alphabetically, or by category such as children, marriage, general, and so on.

Second, fill out a periodical analysis sheet on each of these periodicals. If you do this with your samples, you will never again wonder where to send your manuscripts.

Start out by filling in the *name* and *address* of the publication and the *submissions editor.* (Check *CC* each month for editorial changes. An article or book previously rejected may find a home with a new editor.)

Also fill in the *e-mail address* and the *Web site* of the periodical. Most editors now accept manuscripts either as an e-mail attachment or enclosed within the e-mail itself. Many will also accept e-mail queries. The magazine Web sites may contain the latest issue and sometimes offer a trial subscription.

PERIODICAL ANALYSIS SHEET

Name of Publication _____

Address _____

E-mail Address _____ Web site _____

Submissions Editor_____

Frequency of Publication _____ Denomination _____

Audience_____

Taboos _____

Rights Purchased _____

Payment _____ When _____

Table of Contents: _____

Percent Staff Written?_____ Percent Freelance?_____

Check photos, illustrations, and ads

Read Letters to the Editor? Reactions? Like to see article on?

	Yes/No	Length
Articles		
Fillers		
Fiction		
Columns		
Puzzles		
Poetry		
Book Reviews		
Other (Personal Experience, etc.)		

How often does this publication come out—weekly, monthly, quarterly? It's only logical that a weekly magazine or Sunday school take-home paper needs more material than a monthly or quarterly. The Sunday school papers usually use at least three or four short stories, a couple of short fillers or devotionals, one or two poems, and a puzzle. One week I saw the names of eight authors in our denominational take-home paper. Multiply this by fifty-two weeks, then multiply that number by all the denominations that publish these papers. Because the majority of the manuscripts used by these editors are written by freelancers, the field is wide open.

Who is your audience? Some magazines provide a survey sheet describing their typical reader—thirty years old, two children, two years of college, and so on. Think of a friend who fits these qualifications and write your article for him or her. This helps avoid the feeling that you're writing to an unseen audience.

Age of your audience. Is the magazine aimed at singles, young married, middle-aged parents whose children have left the nest, retirees? The guidelines will give you most of this information; however, the sample magazine will tell you more.

This criteria is especially important when you are writing for children. In times past, children's periodicals were divided into kindergarten, primary, and junior. Now the divisions are preschool (separated by two- and three-year-olds, and four- and five-year-olds), kindergarten, primary, middlers, junior, pre-teens (or 'tweens), and so on.

Denomination. Many denominations have specific "taboos." Some won't accept a manuscript mentioning movies or dances. Others will reject anything dealing with women ministers, eating meat, or going to war. If you want to be published in their magazine, you must follow their guidelines. The second reason you need to know this is so when you begin selling reprints, you won't submit your manuscript to a magazine with an overlapping readership.

What rights do they purchase? (See page 192ff for more information on rights.)

How do they pay? Do they pay by the word, by the published page, or a flat rate? Payment can be from 1/2 cent a word up to as much as $1 a word. Those that pay more usually require a higher caliber of writing and may be harder to sell to.

A note on payment: I've had writers ask me why they received a certain amount for an article when a friend sold one to the same periodical and received a larger check. The amount could be based on two things. If you've written for this same magazine for a long time, you'll often receive more than the rate given in their guidelines. The amount may also be based on the amount of editing necessary. If the market guide says they pay four to seven cents per word, and you send them a clean, well-edited article in their format, you may receive the top figure. Remember, however, the check is based on the *printed* article. If you send them a 1,500-word article and they cut it down to 1,000 words, they will pay you for the 1,000 words.

Do they pay on publication or acceptance? Some magazines pay on publication; some when they schedule your piece for publication—which can be as much as six months ahead of time; others may pay a set time after publication. But be careful of those who buy all rights and pay on publication. You can't send it to anyone else because the first editor bought all rights, and you don't see any money until it's actually published, which can be a year or more.

It's in a writer's favor if a magazine pays on acceptance. But it's also nice to have several articles accepted by publishers who pay on publication because you receive checks even when you haven't been sending out manuscripts.

Table of contents. What type of articles do they use? How many fiction and nonfiction per issue?

Masthead. Look at the list of editors, then the bylines. How many articles are staff written? How many are written by freelance writers?

To whom are the *photographs, illustrations,* and *sidebars* aimed? This tells you your audience.

Also check the *advertisements,* if any. Before a company invests money to advertise in a periodical, a marketing representative has thoroughly studied the readership and the focus of the magazine. Writers should do the same.

Is it written in *first person* or *third person; informally* or in *theological language*?

Study the *leads* and *transitions.*

Read the *letters-to-the-editor* column. Note readers' reactions to past articles, what they liked and didn't like and why, and the type of articles they'd like to see in upcoming issues.

Complete this Periodical Analysis Sheet by listing the types and length of manuscripts the magazine publishes: fiction, nonfiction, book reviews, poetry, fillers, puzzles, and so on.

Put this completed form in your folder along with the corresponding sample magazine. Later, when you consider this periodical as a possible market, you can look at the analysis sheet and the magazine to see if your manuscript fits. Then you can write in your query letter, "I've read your magazine and I feel this article is one that would interest your readers." Mention the name of a particular article you read. This will show you have done your homework.

Each issue of *Christian Communicator* includes a profile of a publisher or editor. Clip these articles, and place them in the folder with the sample magazine and analysis sheet. If you go to a conference and talk to an editor from that magazine, or if you obtain guidelines, file this information in the same folder.

Studying the sample magazines instead of only the guidelines, filling out a Periodical Analysis Sheet for each one, and keeping this information up to date helped me sell 100 percent of what I submitted one fall. It can do the same for you.

Rights

Writers may become confused when they read about first rights, reprint rights, all rights, one-time rights, and simultaneous rights, but it really isn't as complicated as you might think. Understanding what rights to offer an editor can increase your writing income many times over.

The majority of the time, you will be concerned with only two of these rights: first rights and reprint or second rights.

First Rights. Type First Rights in the top, right-hand corner of your manuscript the first time you submit it. This means that the editor buys the *right* to be the *first* to publish your manuscript. Then *after* it is printed, you may resell it using reprint rights, but not to a competing market. For example, if you sell a manuscript the first time to a Southern Baptist periodical, you can sell a reprint to American Baptist or Conservative Baptist, but not to another Southern Baptist publication because it likely will have the same readership.

Many denominations publish a general magazine, as well as periodicals for teens, children, missions, and church leaders. So it is possible to sell an article to one magazine, then *change the slant* and sell it to another in the same denomination because the readership will be different. I sold an article on the dynamics of prayer to our general church magazine, then I rewrote it using a different slant and illustrations and sold it to the teen magazine.

Another time I sold an article about my mother to a preacher's magazine for the "Parsonage Queen" page. Eighteen years later, I sent it to the church's general magazine, after letting the editor know where and when it was published before. Because the first article had a limited readership—pastors—the editor of the denominational magazine bought it, knowing this time it would have a larger audience.

To resell an article using first rights, you have to change the *title, slant,* and *illustrations.* Only the idea remains the same.

Reprint Rights. An advantage of writing for Christian periodicals is that you can sell reprints. This is more difficult in the secular field as many have the same reading audience. For example, if you sold an article to *Woman's Day,* you couldn't sell a reprint to *Family Circle* because many women read both of these every month. The weekly periodical

Woman's World asks that you wait a year after it publishes your article before submitting it to a similar market.

After your material has been published the first time and you're getting ready to resubmit it, type Reprint Rights or Second Rights in the upper right-hand corner.

Hint: When you look for markets to send your manuscript the first time, jot down markets for reprints once your article has been published. When I sold an article about my mother to a take-home paper and the editor bought it for use the next Mother's Day, I wrote down names and addresses of other possible markets. The day I received my published article, I sent out reprints to these markets. With Mother's Day coming up, I knew editors were thinking about the holiday and buying for the next year.

An editor may pay less for reprints, but it depends on the magazine and how much time has elapsed since you first sold the manuscript.

Some people ask, "What if this article has just been published in my local newspaper, or my church bulletin, or online?" In that case, I would type Reprint Rights with an asterisk, then at the bottom of the page, type * published one time in our local newspaper (church bulletin, online, etc.). It helps to give the circulation figures if you know them.

I received two surprises when I began to sell reprints. Not only had the dollar amount of the checks increased, but in reading those I sold years earlier, I shook my head in disbelief that they ever sold. Your writing skills do improve (or should) between the time you first sell the article and when you resubmit it as a reprint.

You can sell an article or short story written from a mother's point of view, then rewrite it from a child's point of view and sell it to a teen or children's magazine, using first rights. Or you can take a short story, add some statistics, and turn it into nonfiction. An event that happened in your life or a friend's life can be written as fiction, nonfiction, an illustration for a devotional, a poem, or even a song. You're using the same idea with a different slant.

You'll reap your profits with reprints. One author I know has sold over 2,000 short stories to take-home papers and now supports herself with checks from reprints.

Remember, if you're using the same title, the same illustrations, and the same slant, it will be considered a reprint. Only if you change the title, illustrations, and slant, can you submit it again as first rights.

One-Time Rights. You may use one-time rights for sales to newspapers. The advantage is that you can sell your material to many newspapers all over the country at the same time; no one editor is buying the right to use it first.

For one year I wrote devotional fillers for the church page of a weekly newspaper. Later, when we moved to another state, I sold these same devotionals to another newspaper.

Although these devotionals were published in different years, I could have sold them to newspapers in different areas at the same time, giving each editor one-time rights.

I also use one-time rights when I submit book reviews to magazines of different readerships. If I sold first rights, then waited for the reviews to be published before sending out reprints, the books would be old. Publishers want their readers to know about *new* books.

All Rights. When you sell a manuscript to a periodical that buys all rights, you forfeit any further use of that manuscript. Publishers can do whatever they want, as often as they want, without further payment to you. Your article can be included in an anthology or sold to another periodical without your permission. If, at a later date, you want to use all or part of this piece in an article or book, you will have to write to that publisher for permission. Depending how you want to use it, they will most likely grant their permission.

Editors read publications from other denominational groups. If they see an article or story they want to publish, they write to that periodical's editor and ask to use it. If you have sold first rights, you will receive a check from the second editor. However, if you have sold all rights, the original publisher will receive the check.

Sally Stuart says that there are four occasions when you might want to sell all rights.

a) If the price is right.
b) If you need a credit line.
c) If it is a specialized article.
d) If it is a timely article.

Let's expand on these.

a) *If the price is right.* Editors usually pay more for all rights because they know you can't sell it again. If the price is agreeable and you're willing to sell all rights, go ahead.
b) *If you need a credit line.* Editors often want to know what you've sold and to whom. Because it is more difficult to sell to a magazine that buys all rights, it may be important to you to have this market on your list of credits.
c) *If it is a specialized article.* If you've written an article on nuclear warheads, not many editors will scramble for it. So, in this case, you wouldn't hesitate to sell all rights because you probably won't sell reprints.

d) *If it is a timely article.* If your manuscript is written to coincide with a current event, you could sell all rights as it would be difficult to sell a reprint without a rewrite. You would need to bring the facts of the story up to date, and perhaps also change the title and illustrations. This rewrite would then be an entirely new article and you could sell it to another market using first rights.

Simultaneous Rights. Another method of selling an article is as a simultaneous submission. In this case, you submit your manuscript to several editors of noncompeting markets *at the same time.*

If you do this, remember several things. First, as in all your writing, keep good records. Second, some editors will not accept simultaneous submissions (check your market books or publishers' guidelines). Third, if they do accept them, they often pay less.

Some authors use simultaneous submissions or one-time rights for holiday material. If you sell first rights on a Christmas story, then wait until it is published, it can be a year or more before you can send out a reprint. Offering simultaneous or one-time rights can result in multiple sales to periodicals with different reading audiences.

Record Keeping

You should always know the whereabouts of your manuscript. Some writers use index cards to keep track of their submissions, others use notebooks, and some computer programs. I use the form on page 197, adapted from one developed by Dennis Hensley.

If you submit something and it is returned, how long do you wait before sending it out again? If you're like some discouraged writers, you throw it in a drawer, not having—or wanting to take—the time to research other markets. This form has space to list six markets. When you select your first market, complete the rest of the page. If the manuscript comes back, you already have five other possible markets. And if it sells the first time out, you have five markets for reprints. Don't let your manuscript lie around collecting dust.

Fill in the top part with the name of your manuscript and the length. Include postage information (weight, rather than cost) if sending it through the postal service. This saves you from having to go to the post office every time you send out the manuscript.

On the "mail to" line, put the name of the editor, the magazine, the address, and the denomination. Fill in the date you send it. If it's accepted, record the date. If it's rejected, recording the date shows how long this particular editor keeps a manuscript before responding.

Place this record keeping sheet in the folder with your manuscript so you can see at a glance the status of your manuscript.

This form works when you have only one or two manuscripts circulating, but if you have several, you can use the form on page 198, which shows the dates and markets to whom you sent your submissions. You can look at this sheet any time and see what manuscripts are still out.

Computerized record keeping programs are also available. My publisher for this book, WinePress Group, offers a proprietary Web based software called *The Organized Writer: A Record Keeper for Busy Writers*. All the record keeping tools I've mentioned, plus a lot more, in one place, online! Visit www.theorganizedwriter.com for more information.

This may seem like a lot of work, but it pays off. Especially if you send things out in bunches, it's even more important to keep your records up to date.

With all the emphasis on marketing and selling in this chapter, let me leave you with the following advice:

- Be obedient to what God wants you to write.
- Go to your knees before you go to your keyboard.
- Write to the best of your ability, then take it to a writer friend or critique group for a final reading.
- Pray over which market to send it to.
- Once it's gone, leave it in God's hands and begin work on another manuscript.

MANUSCRIPT SUBMISSION SHEET

Title _____ Length _____

Type of Piece _____ Weight _____

Mailed to: Date:	Mailed to: Date:
Length _____ Pay _____	Length _____ Pay _____
Denomination: _____	Denomination _____
Age/Audience _____	Age/Audience _____
Accepted _____ Rejected _____	Accepted _____ Rejected _____
Mailed to: Date:	Mailed to: Date:
Length _____ Pay _____	Length _____ Pay _____
Denomination: _____	Denomination _____
Age/Audience _____	Age/Audience _____
Accepted _____ Rejected _____	Accepted _____ Rejected _____
Mailed to: Date:	Mailed to: Date:
Length _____ Pay _____	Length _____ Pay _____
Denomination: _____	Denomination _____
Age/Audience _____	Age/Audience _____
Accepted _____ Rejected _____	Accepted _____ Rejected _____

MANUSCRIPT SUBMISSION (by date)

Date	Title	Type	Sent to	Acc'd	Amt.	Rej'd

MARKETING BOOKS AND PERIODICALS

Books

Christian Writers' Market Guide (updated annually). Sally E. Stuart. Order from Sally Stuart, 1647 S.W. Pheasant Dr., Aloha, OR 97006. (503) 642-9844. (Monthly updates in *Christian Communicator*.) Web site: www.stuartmarket.com/BookPublishers.html

Writer's Market (updated annually). F+W Publications, 4700 East Galbraith, Cincinnati, OH 45236, or at bookstores. Also publishes market guides for: fiction, poetry, children's writers/illustrators, artists, photographers, and songwriters. Same address, or at bookstores. Web site: www.writersmarket.com

Periodicals

Christian Communicator (eleven issues/year). American Christian Writers, PO Box 110390, Nashville, TN 37222. Web site: www.wordprocommunications.com/CC.htm. (Updates the *Christian Writers' Market Guide*.)

Cross & Quill (bi-monthly). Christian Writers Fellowship International, 1624 Jefferson Davis Rd., Clinton, SC 29325-6401. (864) 697-6035. Web site: www.cwfi-online.org

The Writer (monthly). Kalmbach Publishing, 21027 Crossroads Circle, PO Box 1612, Waukesha, WI 53187. Web site: www.writermag.com

Writer's Digest (monthly). F+W Publications, 4700 East Galbraith, Cincinnati, OH 45236. Web site: www.writersdig.com

WRITERS' Journal (monthly). PO Box 394, Perham, MN 56573. Web site: www.writers'journal.com

Part IV

Other Sources

of Income

Chapter 17

Other Sources of Income

Proofreading

WHENEVER I TELL someone I'm a proofreader, I get one of two reactions: They think I look for mistakes in everything they send me, or they look for mistakes in everything I send them.

Perhaps proofreading as a full- or part-time job interests you, and you wonder what qualifications are required. Good spelling is important, of course, but it takes more than that. It takes . . .

The Ability to Read Slowly

If you are a fast reader, you'll have to unlearn this skill. In proofreading, you must read one letter at a time, and realize that each one is a potential mistake. Using a ruler works for many proofreaders.

Knowledge of Events, Past and Present

For eighteen years I typed papers for university students. From this, I absorbed a myriad of information that has proven useful in proofreading. Because you will be working with materials covering a variety of subjects, it helps to be widely read.

Also you should keep up with current events. Sometimes from the time a book is edited to when it is finally published, facts have changed. Or a book is reprinted from a previous edition and the author has failed to update information, such as people who have died or the names of leaders and countries that have changed. Editors will appreciate you bringing these facts to their attention.

A Good Library

A wise investment for a proofreader is a good selection of reference material. My library includes such books as atlases, travel guides, poetry and quotation collections, a world almanac, and a one-volume encyclopedia, *The Chicago Manual of Style*, and the latest dictionary, along with dictionaries from various professions. If you are working with religious materials, you also may want to purchase a hymnbook and different translations of the Bible. Of course, most of this information is also available on the Internet. Just be sure the Web site is up to date.

A Good Memory

The ability to remember details is important. For example, if you see a hyphenated word, do you recall that you saw that same word spelled earlier as one or two words? Or is the name of an author spelled one way in the book and another way in the endnotes or bibliography? What about capitalization? Was a word capitalized in one chapter, but lowercase ten chapters later? Because rules for such things as commas and capitalization may vary among publishers, it's your job to know each publisher's style and proofread accordingly, but consistency is critical.

Common Sense

As a proofreader, you will not do any editing (correct grammar or change sentences around); however, if you see an obvious error, let the editor know. For example, I read a novel that took place over the course of a month. Three different times during that month the author—in describing a romantic setting— wrote that there was "a full moon" (three full moons in a month?). In another book, a twelve-year-old had broken her arm in a fall. The author wrote, "The next day as Judy braided her hair . . . " Braiding her hair with a cast on her arm? The next day?

Does the color of a character's hair or eyes change during the book? Did she age two years in the space of a year? Catching these mistakes will get you a gold star from publishers.

Know the Proofreading Symbols

I've included a list of proofreading symbols at the end of this section, or publishers may send you specific symbols their house uses. Use these symbols to make your corrections in the margin of the manuscript.

Develop a System

If you develop a consistent system in your work, you will be less likely to overlook anything. I use the following method when proofreading book manuscripts.

First, I go through and make sure I have all the pages. If not, I notify the publisher immediately. It's much easier to do this at the beginning than to arrive at page 323 of a 330-page book you have to return that day and notice that page 324 is missing.

Next, after reading the title page, dedication, acknowledgement, and other preliminary pages, I check the table of contents to see if the chapter titles are the same on this page as they are throughout the book—including chapter headings at the top of the page and, later, in the endnotes section. Then I make sure the page numbers in the table of contents are correct.

Next I go to the end of the book and pull out the bibliography. As I go through the manuscript and see the name of a book or an author, I check to see if it's spelled exactly the same in the appendices. I also separate the endnote pages and as each endnote appears in the manuscript, I compare the numbers (and author and book title, if mentioned) with those on the endnote page. If an endnote has been deleted in the book, I make sure that endnote material has been deleted on the endnote page and the following notes renumbered accordingly.

When I begin the first page of the actual manuscript, I jot down the time. After an hour, I note how many pages I've read, and this gives me an idea of how long it will take to proofread the entire book. From this, I can decide if I have time to accept another job and meet both deadlines.

How to Start Your Business

First, invest in business cards. Your address isn't as important on this card as your name, business name, phone/fax number, and e-mail address, if applicable. Don't crowd the information, but do list your qualifications: proofreader, editor, typist, and so on.

Next, compose a resume. Include any previous jobs and volunteer work that relate to proofreading: brochures, annual reports, newsletters, and so on. For references, use previous employers or friends who are knowledgeable of your proofreading aptitude. Obtain permission from them so they will be prepared when a prospective employer calls.

How to Find Work

Start with people you know. If you're now in a similar line of work, make a list of those who already know your capabilities and reliability. Tell them you are available and ask them to pass your name on to others. In the long run, you'll find that word-of-mouth is the best advertising. Remember, however, that it works both ways: If your customers are happy, they'll tell others—maybe; but if they're unhappy with your work, they'll tell others—definitely.

Look in the Yellow Pages under such categories as book publishers, printers, copying services, clubs, charitable organizations—any business that publishes anything. Send a cover letter briefly stating your qualifications, and include your business card and resume. Follow up a week or so later with a telephone call or personal visit.

If you are interested in proofreading book manuscripts, go through the various writers' market books for a list of publishers. To reach writers who may want their manuscripts proofread before sending them to publishers, place an ad in writers' magazines or leave fliers at local writers' clubs.

I picked up several jobs by making a list of typos I found in books and sending this list to the production manager (not the editor) of the publishing house, along with my cover letter, business card, and resume. This also worked with a local magazine. One day, I circled in red all the typos I found in the magazine and took it to the publisher, who hired me on the spot.

Before a company places your name on its list of proofreaders, the production manager may send you a proofreading test to complete. The following suggestions will help in taking these tests:

- If a publisher requires you to use a red pen, for the sake of neatness, first make a photocopy of the test. Then, after you locate all the mistakes, copy the corrections onto the original test to return to the publisher.
- If you find a mistake on one line, look carefully for another mistake close by. It is a trick of test givers to have a second misspelled word closely following the first, as often your eye will skip over the next few words to the end of the line.
- Look for the same word or letter repeated in a row. Can you find the mistakes in the following sentences?
  "When proofreading, look for the same word or or letter repeated in a row."
  "David thought that he had been given too much responsibillity for his age."
- Another mistake easily overlooked is the spelling of the same word two differ-ent ways, especially if both ways are correct. Find the error(s) in the next two sentences.
  "I'm going to the store," said Frances. "Do you want anything, Terri?"
  "Oh, yes, Francis," Terry said. "I need a loaf of bread."

- Look carefully at words in a title or heading. It's easy to assume that because letters are in a large font, they are right. At one place I worked, my desk was next to the advertising department. The graphic artist was working on an oversized poster for a new hymnbook entitled "Rejoice and Sing." When she showed it to me, I read, in large letters, the words: REJOICE AND SIN.
- Read the instructions before beginning the test. One proofreading supervisor used an interesting test. She gave applicants a sheet of paper that included twenty questions asking for such information as name, address, phone, education, and work experience. The instructions at the top of the sheet said: "Read the *entire* sheet before you begin." At the bottom of the page, after the last question, were the words: "You do not have to fill in any of the above blanks. Just put your name on the first line and return the test." As soon as I saw a person hurriedly going down the sheet and answering every question, I knew she wouldn't be hired as she hadn't followed the instructions.

How to Charge

Don't quote prices in advance without seeing the job. If you are proofreading for individuals, decide how much you need to make an hour. Proofread one chapter or a small portion of the work, keep track of the time, then estimate how long the job will take and charge accordingly. You can charge by the hour, by the page, or by the job. If you're proofreading for publishers or companies, however, they will tell you what they pay. If this is acceptable to you, accept the job. After six months or a year, if they appear happy with your work, ask for a raise.

Is proofreading for you? To help you answer this question, take the following three tests. First, read this sentence:

FINISHED FILES ARE THE RESULT OF YEARS OF SCIENTIFIC STUDY COMBINED WITH THE EXPERIENCE OF YEARS.

Now count the F's in that sentence. Count only once. Don't go back a second time. How many F's did you count? (Answer at end.)

Second, read the following nine sentences taken from actual manuscripts sent to an editor and find the error in each sentence.

1. He bent over the sink, washing the dusk from his face.

2. The moon and stars were whining brightly.
3. Ask children to form a circle and sin.
4. The farmer in the deli.
5. We must be sensitive to a new generation of convicts in the church.
6. The battle is raging all around us, but many are perishing because Christians have failed to engage the enema at the point of attack.
7. My family and I are from a country in Africa. We have had no raid for seven years.
8. Why were their bodies scattered all over the dessert?
9. Backyard Bible clubs were held in pubic parks.

Third, in the following article, there are seventeen typos. (Note: this does not include editing, only misspelled words and inconsistencies.)

A Thankful Hart—or a Heart if Praise
bye
Donna Clark Goodrich

"Develop an attitude of praise,' our pastor told us in his Sunday message. "It will change your life"

I tried it. If it rained, I tried to be thankful it didn't flood. If it was to hot, I gave Thanks for our air conditioner. For the ornery boy in my Sunday school class, I thanked god that his parents cared enough to bring him. It seemed to work—for a while!

Then in the next few years, I found it harder to be thankful? My mother died of cancer. My husband had a serious car accident that put him out of work for three months. Then, a few years later he had a heart attack which—along with a number of other health problems—led to his retirement At the age of 48. Having three teenagers for seven years increased the stress.

"How can I be thankful?" I otfen asked. Then one Sunday morning while listening to the the words of a song a friend was singing at church, the answer came to me: Being thankful is for *things* God gives to us; but a heart of praise is giving thanks for *who He is.*

Have we lost our sense of awe when we are in God's presence? I remember when our family first moved to Arizona. All baseball fans, we were thrilled to learn that several major league teams held their spring training our in area.

My son grabbed his baseball autograph book and we took off for a batting practice where young players where more than happy to sign their names. Suddenly a tall, imposing figure walked toward us. I stopped, frozen in my tracks. *Joe DiMaggio!* I couldn't speak, but our son—who knew no fear—ran up to him. "Hey, Joe!" he yelled. "Can I have your autograph."

I thought later, if I felt that much awe for a man who merely played baseball, how much more awe should I feel when I come before God.

I can still have an "attitude of gratitude," but now I realize that God deserves my highest praise—not because of what He gives me, but because of who he is.

Answers:
Test 1: There are six F's in the sentence. A person of average intelligence finds three. If you spotted four, you're above average. If you found six, you're a genius!
Test 2: Misspelled words in the nine sentences are, in order: dusk/dust; whining/shining; sin/sing; deli/dell; convicts/converts; enema/enemy; raid/rain; dessert/desert; pubic/public.
Test 3:

A Thankful <u>Hart</u>—or a Heart <u>if</u> Praise
<u>bye</u>
Donna Clark Goodrich

"Develop an attitude of praise,'' our pastor told us in his Sunday message. "It will change your life<u>.</u>"

I tried it. If it rained, I tried to be thankful it didn't flood. If it was <u>to</u> hot, I gave <u>Thanks</u> for our air conditioner. For the ornery boy in my Sunday school class, I thanked <u>god</u> that his parents cared enough to bring him. It seemed to work—for a while!

Then in the next few years, I found it harder to be thankful<u>?</u> My mother died of cancer. My husband had a serious car accident that put him out of work for three months. Then, a few years later he had a heart attack which—along with a number of other health problems—led to his retirement <u>At</u> the age of 48. Having three teenagers for seven years increased the stress.

"How can I be thankful?" I <u>otfen</u> asked. Then one Sunday morning while listening to the <u>the</u> words of a song a friend was singing at church, the answer came to me: Being thankful is for *things* God gives to us; but a heart of praise is giving thanks for *who He is*.

Have we lost our sense of awe when we are in God's presence? I remember when our family first moved to Arizona. All baseball fans, we were thrilled to learn that several major league teams held their spring training <u>our in</u> area.

Proofreading Symbols

OPERATIONAL SIGNS

⟋	Delete
⌒	Close up; delete space
⟋	Delete and close up (use only when deleting letters *within* a word)
(stet)	Let it stand
#	Insert space
(eq #)	Make space between words equal; make space between lines equal
(hr #)	Insert hair space
(ls)	Letterspace
¶	Begin new paragraph
☐	Indent type one em from left or right
]	Move right
[	Move left
][	Center
⊓	Move up
⊔	Move down
(fl)	Flush left
(fr)	Flush right
⹀	Straighten type; align horizontally
‖	Align vertically
(tr)	Transpose
(sp)	Spell out

TYPOGRAPHICAL SIGNS

(ital)	Set in italic type
(rom)	Set in roman type
(bf)	Set in boldface type
(lc)	Set in lowercase
(caps)	Set in capital letters
(sc)	Set in small capitals
(wf)	Wrong font; set in correct type
X	Check type image; remove blemish
V	Insert here *or* make superscript
∧	Insert here *or* make subscript

PUNCTUATION MARKS

∧	Insert comma
⌄ ⌄	Insert apostrophe *or* single quotation mark
⌄ ⌄	Insert quotation marks
⊙	Insert period
(set) ?	Insert question mark
⦀	Insert semicolon
⌄ *or* ⦂	Insert colon
=	Insert hyphen
M	Insert em dash
N	Insert en dash
{⦀} *or* (⦀)	Insert parentheses [1]

My son grabbed his baseball autograph book and we took off for a batting practice where young players <u>where</u> more than happy to sign their names. Suddenly a tall, imposing figure walked toward us. I stopped, frozen in my tracks. *Joe DiMaggio!* I couldn't speak, but our son—who knew no fear—ran up to him. "Hey, Joe!" he yelled. "Can I have your autograph<u>.</u>"

I thought later, if I felt that much awe for a man who merely played baseball, how much more awe should I feel when I come before God<u>.</u>

I can still have an "attitude of gratitude," but now I realize that God deserves my highest praise—not because of what He gives me, but because of who <u>he</u> is.

Editing

There are two types of editing. One may be a reading of a manuscript and a one- or two-page letter spelling out what needs to be corrected without offering suggestions on how to do it. The second is a line-by-line edit in which you're correcting misspelled words, inconsistencies in hyphenation and other punctuation, incorrect grammar, overworked words, sentence structure, and paragraphs not in chronological order.

When I critique authors' manuscripts, I am careful to point out their strengths, along with their weaknesses. And I tell them that my suggestions are just that—suggestions. (As one writer said, "It's my baby and babies cry when you cut off their fingers and toes.") I never want it to sound like my work when it's done. I also send along a copy of the proofreading symbols, a copy of my "Editing Hints" booklet, and a letter summarizing the changes. It's always enjoyable to receive a second manuscript from the same author in which they've used suggestions from the first editing.

If this is something you would enjoy, make sure you have a strong English background. You should also have legible handwriting so authors can clearly comprehend your corrections.

To obtain work, it's good first to belong to a writers' group and learn from the critiques of your manuscripts. Then ask the other writers how they feel about your editing of *their* work and how you can improve.

Next, contact local printers. Many of these handle books for people who wish to self-publish, perhaps for ministries or fund-raisers. Prepare a resume giving your qualifications. After your first job, ask if you can use their name as a reference in applying for other positions.

Because of the economy, many publishers today are hiring freelance editors as this saves them money in withholding taxes and benefits such as insurance, vacation, and sick days. E-mail them your resume, or meet with them at writers' conferences to discuss your qualifications.

The following hints will help improve your skills as an editor:

Commandments for Copy Editors

1. Thou shalt not change the author's meaning.
2. Thou shalt not introduce new errors; especially shalt thou not change something correct to something incorrect.
3. Thou shalt change nothing except to improve it.
4. Thou shall hearken to thy instructions and do precisely what is expected of thee.
5. Thou shalt honor and obey those in charge over thee.
6. Thou shalt mark clearly and write legibly in a color that photocopies well.
7. Thou shalt protect the manuscript from rain, hail, wind, coffee, children, pets, and all things damaging.
8. Thou shalt meet thy deadlines.
9. Thou shalt assume nothing but shalt seek answers to all things doubtful or unspecified.
10. Thou shalt read and study the English language continually.[2]

Speaking

Many publishers request—or even require—that their authors be willing to travel and speak on behalf of their books. If this experience is new for you, and you tremble at the thought of getting up in front of a crowd, the following suggestions by author and speaker Dr. Mary Ann Diorio may be of help to you.

Seven Tips for Speaking with Confidence

Public speaking ranks at the top of the list of the most common fears. In fact, a popular joke among speakers says that most people would rather be the corpse at a funeral than the one giving the eulogy!

Perhaps you're one of those people. If so, take heart. You can overcome your fear of speaking in public. Here are seven proven techniques to help you:

1. Prepare thoroughly. One of the most important keys to effective and powerful public speaking is to know your material. Solid preparation establishes a solid foundation, and a solid foundation goes far toward eliminating fear. Much nervousness in public speaking is caused simply by lack of adequate preparation. When

you are sure of what you're talking about, you will inspire confidence not only in yourself, but in your audience as well.

2. Practice your speech ahead of time. Find a family member or friend willing to listen to your speech and to offer constructive criticism. If you can't round up a relative or friend, invite your dog or cat. The point is to rehearse with an audience. A good practice is to videotape yourself as you rehearse your speech. When I taught public speaking at Rowan University in Glassboro, New Jersey, I would videotape my students so that they could see what they looked like and hear what they sounded like as they spoke. This feedback proved invaluable to them in polishing their speaking techniques and greatly boosted their confidence level.

3. Arrive early. Doing so will allow you to check out the location of your speech ahead of time. If you live close enough, you may want to visit the location a few days before your speech. Becoming familiar with the room in which you will speak, the equipment you will use, and the layout of the audience area will give you time to make any necessary adjustments before your speech.

4. Meet your audience ahead of time. When possible, I greet members of my audience before my speech. I move around the room, introducing myself and shaking hands with people as they arrive. I ask for their names and try to make them feel welcome. This practice helps build rapport with my audience before my speech and helps me focus on my audience instead of on myself.

5. Establish eye contact with the most interested people in your audience. While it is wise to look at all sections of your audience during your speech, establish more regular eye contact with one or two of the most attentive people. This will give your speech a more personal touch while providing encouragement for you from the most interested listeners.

6. Consider your speech as a gift to your audience. You are giving the speech not to bring glory to yourself but to minister to the needs of your audience. When you focus on the needs of your audience, you will forget your nervousness. As in other areas of life, getting your eyes off yourself and on to others is a sure antidote to fear and worry.

7. Pray at all times. Prayer is an essential ingredient to effective speaking. Pray as you choose a topic for your speech. Pray as you prepare your speech. Pray before you deliver your speech. And pray afterwards as well. The words you speak are seeds that will be planted in the hearts of your listeners. Prayer ensures that your words will be filled with truth and life, that they will take root, and that they will leave your audience glad that they came. And bottom line, that's your ultimate goal.[3]

One other suggestion is to consider having a book available on the topic you speak or teach on. This is another pefect time to consider custom self-publishing with a reputable Christian publisher.

Responding to an Invitation

When someone calls or e-mails and asks you to speak, even though the invitation sounds like a dream come true, don't answer yes on the spot. First seek God's will on the matter, and then ask yourself the following questions:

- If you are a wife and mother, or husband and father, is this a good time to leave your family?
- Can you fit this into an already overloaded schedule?
- Is this a freebie and, if so, can your budget afford any necessary, unreimbursed expenses?
- Do you have enough time to prepare properly?
- Can you arrange another talk nearby, thus reducing expenses for both yourself and your host?

If you can answer yes to the above questions, then accept the invitation. At this time, it is important to obtain all the necessary information. Completing the form on the next page, adapted from one developed by writer/speaker Kathy Collard Miller,[4] will ensure that you have all the facts at hand when you board the plane for your speaking engagement.

What Will I Speak About?

The invitation for you to speak may come in a variety of ways. Perhaps people heard you speak at another meeting and liked what they heard. In this case, they may want you to repeat the same talk for a different audience. Or a leader may have heard about you by word-of-mouth and will invite you for a themed dinner, giving you an assigned topic. Another option may be in response to promotional brochures you have mailed, listing your qualifications along with titles and brief descriptions of talks you've given in the past.

Other Sources of Income

Information for Speaking Engagement

Date _____ Location (city, state, country) _____

Contact person/title _____

Telephone/cell of contact person _____ E-mail _____

Address of contact person _____

Name of church or place of meeting _____

Address _____ Phone _____

Directions _____

Ship books to _____

Leave home on _____ Airlines, flight # _____,

Time _____

Change at _____ to flight # _____

Arrive in _____ at _____

Stay at (or with) _____ Phone _____

Address _____

Leave for home on _____ Airlines, flight # _____,

Time _____

Change at _____ to flight # _____

Arrive in _____ at _____

Number of talks _____ Length of each _____

Days and times of talks _____

Subjects of talks _____

Remuneration (yes/no; amount): Talks _____ Motel/meals _____
Airfare _____

Date acceptance confirmed _____ Bought tickets _____

Date books shipped: _____ How shipped? _____

Shipping cost _____

Titles and number of books shipped:

As a writer, your topic may be writing-related—how you got started in the writing field, advice on how to sell what you write, writing fiction or nonfiction, or perhaps just words of encouragement the audience needs to hear to persevere in their calling.

Whatever topic you choose, let it be one that you care about. It may be an overworked word in writing circles, but in speaking, you also need to have *passion*. Share some anecdotes, and use humor, if appropriate. If you're giving facts, intersperse them with illustrations. Don't put your audience to sleep. Leave them wanting more.

And don't talk above your audience. If possible, learn ahead of time the ages and genders of those attending and prepare your talk accordingly. Let them feel you're one of them and speak in a language they can relate to. Using personal examples lets your audience know you've "sat where they sat" (Ezek. 3:15 KJV) and, through your speaking, you're putting yourself in their place and offering encouragement.

Above all, stay humble and realize that your speaking ability is a talent on loan from the Lord. Don't be like the young pastor preaching his first sermon. Proudly, he strutted up to the platform and, using theological terms he had learned in seminary, he began his message. It wasn't long before he realized he had lost his audience so he quickly ended the sermon and walked down the aisle, his head low. An old retired preacher sitting near the back of the church came up to him, put his hand on his shoulder, and said, "Son, if you had gone up like you came back down, you would have had a better sermon."

Preparation

Learn to outline your talk—either on unstapled sheets of paper or on index cards. Using brief notes allows you to make frequent eye contact with your audience. One author/speaker says she always feels offended when she takes the time to attend a program where the speaker is reading a speech. "I feel like they could have just mailed out the script and I could have done something else with my time."

Jot down the main points and key words of any illustrations you plan to use. You may have a quotation or poem you want to read word for word, but other than that, your notes should be complete enough that the audience won't be seeing only the top of your head as you bend over your paper the entire speech.

Closing

No matter what your topic, always leave the audience focusing on God, not you. Whatever personal illustrations you use, whatever victories you share, whatever published manuscripts you mention, be sure to give God the glory.

Dave Clark, an award-winning gospel songwriter with twenty-five number-one songs on the charts, traveled the country giving concerts for many years. During much of that time, he suffered a painful throat disease for which doctors at various hospitals, including Mayo Clinic, could find no cure. Because of this, many of the songs he wrote were for hurting people.[5] However, his theme always centered on God's faithfulness. A pastor commented after one of Dave's concerts, "Dave is one of the few persons that can make people come out of a concert and say, 'Isn't God good?' instead of 'Wasn't that singer good?'"

Wouldn't you like to hear an audience say that after one of your talks? They will if you:

- Pray before accepting an invitation;
- Choose a topic you're passionate about;
- Prepare your talk well;
- Put yourself in the audience's shoes; and
- Leave the results in the Lord's hands.

Teaching

There's an old saying that "those who can't write, teach." If you're looking for another source of income, however, it is possible to do both. It's exciting to take the information and knowledge you've gleaned over the years from your own experience, from books you've read, and from conferences, and pass this on to eager listeners.

Much of my writing background came from on-the-job experience (book editor's secretary, proofreader at a publishing house and magazine, associate magazine editor, and newspaper columnist/reporter), rather than a college education. I didn't realize how much I had learned until our first writers' group met in 1981 and they threw questions at me.

After the group had met for a few months, they asked if I would teach a writing class and we set up a six-week schedule. Between the fifth and sixth class, I spent eight weeks in another state, helping my mother after her cancer surgery. I took my class notes and, during this time, I held my first daylong workshop. This was the beginning of my "teaching" career.

To teach is to learn twice.

—Chinese proverb

If teaching is also your desire, you can attain this dream in several ways:

- First decide what your specialty will be: fiction, nonfiction, poetry, children's writing, newspaper, interviews, personal experience, marketing, getting ideas, and so on.
- Contact your local college board and offer to teach night classes on one of the above classes for a semester or term.
- Volunteer to come in once or twice a semester at your local high school or college journalism class simply to hold a question-and-answer period. Elementary school teachers are also open to writers as guest speakers. (These appearances probably will be unpaid, but the experience will help you later in applying for paid positions.)
- Send your resume and CD of a class you've taught to Christian writers' conference directors. It helps if you have attended that particular conference and have met the director personally, or at least know how the conference is run.
- You can send this same material to directors of secular conferences as most of your material will also be applicable to writers for the general market. One class I've taught at these conferences that has proven popular is "Writing for the Inspirational Market" in which I list the various genres editors of Christian material look for and give examples of each. I've also taught marketing classes at secular conferences.
- You can also schedule and hold your own one- or two-day workshops—in your hometown or in other states. (See next section. More information is available in my booklet *How to Form and Run a Successful Writers' Club . . . Critique Group . . . Conference.*)

Teaching is rewarding in two ways: It not only allows you to share information you have gleaned, but you will have a little sense of pride when you see your students' byline in a magazine or on a book cover.

You, therefore, who teach another, do you not teach yourself?

—Rom. 2:21 NKJV

Holding a Successful Writers' Conference

"I learned a lot today. It was well organized."

You, too, can receive comments such as this after your writers' workshop. At the beginning, you probably will be the sole speaker. With more experience, you can expand this workshop to two or three days and invite others, including editors, to teach classes and meet with students in fifteen-minute appointments. The secret to a successful conference lies in advance planning, effective advertising, appropriate facilities, responsible staff, and a tight budget. You will learn to delegate responsibility and, from the very outset, to keep an ongoing list of things to be done. Don't trust anything to memory or chance.

Setting the Date

The time of year and the days of the conference will depend on the length of the conference and the location. If your conference site is in a mild climate, select a winter date to entice people from cold locales. Resort areas attract summertime visitors. Saturday is good for a one-day conference; Friday and Saturday for a two-day conference; and Thursday through Saturday for three days. If you have a local Christian newspaper, check the calendar so your conference doesn't conflict with another event held on the same day.

Advertising

- Prepare a mailing list of anyone who shows an interest in writing. Ask friends for names and addresses of prospects, and order mailing labels by area zip code from Sally Stuart (Stuartcwmg@aol.com).
- Send notices to magazines beamed toward writers, i.e., *The Writer, Writer's Digest, Christian Communicator, WRITERS' Journal, Cross & Quill.*
- Take advantage of free spots on radio and television "Community Calendars," and offer to appear on local radio and TV talk shows. Place fliers in store windows—especially Christian bookstores, and on supermarket and library bulletin boards. Give a phone number, e-mail address, or Web site where writers can contact you for more information or a brochure.

Brochure

Your brochure should include schedule, description of workshops, background of leaders, costs, food (bring sack lunch; catered lunch; nearby restaurants), address of conference and directions, and name, address, phone number, and e-mail of coordinator. Also include Web site if you have one.

Facilities

- How many are you expecting? How many rooms will you need? One big room with one large table or a number of small tables? Several small rooms for workshops?

- Will you need a cafeteria or fellowship hall? A sound system? A room with video equipment installed, or one that can be darkened for films or slide presentations?
- Is there sufficient parking? Ramps for wheelchairs?

Possible Facilities

Schools and churches both provide classrooms, cafeterias, fellowship halls, and adequate parking. For smaller workshops, a restaurant may provide a free meeting space if conferees buy meals. Utility companies also rent out meeting rooms. Other suggestions are hotels or motels, bank rooms, and libraries.

Note: Get everything in writing: date, cost, custodial duties (open facility and clean up afterwards, set up rooms with tables and chairs, set up sound system, stock restrooms with ample supplies), time (when does registration begin? when will you set up? when will you finish?). The conference may be 9:00 to 5:00, but you may need to come the day before or early on the day of the conference to unpack books and freebies, put up signs, set out drinks and snacks, and register early arrivals. And it could be long after 5:00 before you get the last person out the door (writers like to mingle!) and everything packed up.

Registration Hints

Make a checklist for incoming registrations:

- Put name and address on list or computerized spreadsheet with amount paid and whether check, cash, or credit card.
- Make two alphabetical lists of registrants for registrars—one for "registered and paid" and one for "registered, not paid."
- Prepare different color name tags for staff.
- Decide if you will send registration confirmation or if cancelled check will be receipt.

Approximately one week before conference, provide workshop leaders with the number of persons in their classes so they can prepare handouts. Or, ask them to send a master sheet and you prepare the handouts for them.

Give lists of registrants to each registrar. Try to anticipate any questions. Instruct registrars that if there is any question concerning amount due, rather than argue, embarrass the registrant, and hold up the line, to accept offered amount and discuss it later with you.

Make three signs for registration tables: "Registered—Paid"; "Registered—Not Paid"; "Not Registered." Assign at least one registrar to each table.

Book and "Freebie" Room or Table

If you will be selling books pertaining to writing, you can either display copies and take orders, or purchase enough to sell outright. Some publishers offer quantity discounts that give you a profit between the purchase price and the selling price.

Let the publisher know the date you must *receive* the books (allow yourself time for pricing) and the shipping address. If you phone in your order, use publishers' toll-free numbers. If you order through the Internet, print out a copy of the order, the final cost, and a confirmation number.

Make computerized perforated sales slips—one copy goes to the buyer as a tax receipt and the second copy stays with you as a record of books sold.

For the book table, you will need calculators, money box with change, and sufficient personnel. These personnel should not have other conference responsibilities as buyers may be visiting the site on and off during the conference. An alternative is to invite a local bookstore to set up a stand and give you a percentage.

Encourage published registrants to bring their books for an author's table or an autograph session. Introduce these writers during the conference and give them a distinctive name tag. (It's *not* a good idea to let writers introduce themselves, however, as it's often hard to get the microphone back!)

Many magazine publishers will provide samples for your conference. And in exchange for displaying their ads, local Christian bookstores may provide shopping bags for your conferees' books and periodicals.

Workshop Leaders and Speakers

Selection of your speakers will depend on your budget. However, quality does not always mean expensive. Many times you can find resource people in your own backyard. Local talent will help your budget as you won't have to pay travel expenses.

Out-of-state speakers may be able to work your conference in with one nearby and you can divide the transportation costs. Publishers may also help foot expenses.

Another method of locating speakers is to study other conference brochures and make a note of names that appear over and over, or invite speakers you have enjoyed hearing at conferences you have attended.

Begin building a file of prospective personnel. Request information, bio sketches, and costs. Even if some speakers are out of your price range now, keep them in mind for later years when your budget increases.

Honoraria vary across the country, so compare notes with other conference leaders. Speakers charge by the hour or by the day, plus transportation, meals, and hotel costs.

Some conferences give workers room and board, free tuition, and a small honorarium. Others reimburse airfare and lodging, but do not pay for teaching. Each conference differs according to length, budget, number of workshops, and so on.

Again, get everything in writing. Ask your speakers to sign a simple contract stating length of speech or workshop, topic, brief summary of talk or class, agreed-upon rates, and permission to tape their workshops, if this is an option. Give them their checks at the close of the conference.

Always follow up with a thank-you note. If you collected evaluation sheets, pass along some of the positive comments attendees make regarding classes and instructors.

Personnel Needed

- Pre-conference: people to collate and staple news releases; address, stuff, seal, and stamp envelopes for brochures; send out e-mail announcements
- Helpers for day before conference to unpack and set up books and freebies
- Signmakers
- Volunteers to make transportation and housing arrangements
- Cafeteria help, if not provided by caterers, to replenish coffee, tea, punch, ice, donuts, etc.
- Registrars—at least one for each table
- Bookstore personnel
- Gofers to take messages, go for supplies, etc.
- Maintenance to move furniture, adjust heat or air conditioning, set up microphone, etc.

Finances

Determine the total expenses, fixed and estimated, such as rent for facilities, custodian, drinks, donuts, catering, workshop leaders, helpers, photocopying, envelopes, mileage, postage, gifts, thank-you notes, and other costs. Estimate the number of hours you will dedicate to this project and how much you need to make an hour. Then estimate the expected attendance. From these figures, you can set a registration fee that covers your needs.

As soon as you begin planning your conference, set up a separate bank account. If this is a one-time conference, you can close the account as soon as your last check clears. If you hold an annual conference, it might be worth the monthly fee to keep it open all year.

The Big Day

The day is here! Is everything in order? To make sure you haven't forgotten anything, it helps to keep two checklists:

1. *Things to check out at the facility*: microphone; platform chairs, dais, table for speakers' materials; whiteboards, pegboards, bulletin boards; projection screens, projector (slide and opaque); PowerPoint/computer; electrical outlets; registration tables and chairs; tables for drinks.

2. *Things to take with you*: brochures; cash boxes and change for registration and books; registration slips; introductory notes on speakers; checkbook; signs—parking, registration, and classrooms; extension cords; nametags and pens; markers; Scotch and clear packing tape; scissors; and poster board. If the facility doesn't provide drinks, you'll want to take coffee—regular and decaf; tea—teabags, instant, with and without lemon, variety of herbal and spiced tea; punch; sugar; creamer; spoons and/or stirrers; can opener; measuring cup and spoons; pitchers; paper cups and napkins. (One year, as an afterthought, I took a jar of bouillon cubes. It turned out that one of the speakers got food poisoning at the airport and she said to me, "I wish you had some bouillon cubes here.")

On page 224 is a great icebreaker for conferees to get acquainted. It can be adapted to the number of attendees you expect.

Preparing for Next Year

Pass out an evaluation sheet, asking for comments on workshops, staff, facilities, meals, cost, date, and so on. Encourage registrants—and instructors—to turn these sheets in before they leave while details are still fresh in their minds.

After the conference is over, take a week or so to clear up loose ends. Send refunds for no-shows (if that is your policy), return unsold books, write thank-you notes, send appreciation gifts to helpers, and update your mailing list.

Savor the letters of appreciation you'll receive. Consider constructive criticism. Then take a couple weeks off to relax before beginning work on your next conference.

Manuscript Reviewer

When you submit a manuscript for consideration, the editor may give it to a "first reader" or a manuscript reviewer for a preliminary reading. If this person feels the manuscript fits that publisher's criteria, he or she will return it to the editor who will study it more in-depth. If it meets with his approval, he will pass it on to the marketing committee for further evaluation.

Getting Acquainted

Make new friends today! *Whoever completes this sheet first will receive a gift.* NO ONE CAN SIGN MORE THAN ONE LINE!

1. Took day off work to be here ⸺

2. Is attending first writer's seminar ⸺

3. Walks at least ten miles a week ⸺

4. Collects stuffed animals ⸺

5. Has published one or more books ⸺

6. Has ridden in a Model T Ford ⸺

7. Is/was a missionary ⸺

8. Worked on high school yearbook ⸺

9. Has five or more children ⸺

10. Has been married more than twenty-five years ⸺

11. Has a birthday or anniversary this month ⸺

12. Plays the accordion ⸺

13. Has collected over twenty rejection slips ⸺

14. Drove over one hundred miles to be here ⸺

15. Has never used a computer ⸺

16. Is a great-grandmother/father ⸺

17. Is left-handed ⸺

18. Has visited a foreign country ⸺

19. Has gotten more than two traffic tickets ⸺

20. Has never changed a baby ⸺

21. Plays a guitar ⸺

22. Likes frog legs ⸺

23. Has a hole in his or her stocking today ⸺

24. Has an address book in his/her purse/pocket ⸺

When John Wiley & Sons published my two how-to books, the following questions were included on the list the editor sent with the manuscript to an outside reviewer:

1. Does this book have a clear objective and fill a definite need?
2. Does the title express the purpose of the book? If not, can you suggest another?
3. What is your opinion of the overall organization?
   Is the order of the chapters generally acceptable?
   Would you reorganize the material in any way? (please indicate on the manuscript by renumbering the table of contents).
4. Have any major topics been omitted? Should any be deleted?
5. Take a look at the writing style:
   Is it clear and understandable?
   Is it sufficiently interesting and practical for the market?
   Is it written at the appropriate level?
6. What is your opinion of the figures/illustrations?
   Are there too many? Too few?
   Should they be redrawn or changed in any way to be clearer?
7. In regard to marketing:
   What are two or three leading books on the subject with which this book will have to compete?
   In what way is this book superior to (or inferior to) the competition?
8. Would you recommend publication?
9. Without considering it in any way a commitment, is this book one which you might consider using and/or recommending in training courses or in the study of this subject?

My manuscript on setting up an income tax business was reviewed by three tax preparers in New York City; the typing service book was sent to owners of secretarial services. And, because of my background, I have reviewed manuscripts dealing with working at home or setting up a business.

If this is something you would enjoy doing, and if you are an expert in a field a particular publisher specializes in, send in your resume and a cover letter, asking to be considered as a manuscript reviewer.

(For more ways to increase your income as a writer, see *83 Ways to Make Money Writing* by Beth Fowler: http://www.authorsden.com/bethfowler.)

Part V

The Challenges of

Being a Writer

. . . .

Chapter 18

Writer's Block

ONE QUESTION ARISES in almost every writers' conference: What do I do when I get writer's block?

What is writer's block? Wikipedia describes it as "a phenomenon involving temporary loss of ability to begin or continue writing, usually due to lack of inspiration or creativity." The article goes on to report, "The most notable example of writer's block in modern literary history was Henry Roth's writer's block which persisted for sixty years and was caused by a combination of depression, political problems, and an unwillingness to confront past problems."

There can be many reasons for writer's block.

Depression

Sometimes when writer's block hits, your body and mind are saying you need a break. You may have recently lost a family member or close friend. You or someone in your family might be dealing with a serious illness. You may be in the middle of a relationship problem with a friend or relative. Or you've lost your job and are facing a tough financial crisis. Although it's hard to write at times like this, try to jot down notes while you're going through these testings. They can be the seed for an article or short story later to help others experiencing similar situations.

Lisa R. Cohen suggests that "if you can't write because of pain or sorrow, you may need to concentrate your energies on healing yourself before you can get back into writing."[1]

A Difficult Assignment

Perhaps you have an assignment that is not to your liking or you feel you don't have the ability to write it. You can't get the impetus or courage needed to complete it—or even start it. A publisher offered a psychologist friend a book contract. She kept putting off returning the contract, and finally I asked her one day, "Do you *really* want to do this book?" She thought a minute, then said, "No!" and turned down the offer.

After completing two books for John Wiley & Sons on operating a typing service and an income tax business, the editor asked me to write a book on opening a computer store. Computers were rather new at that time—and I didn't even have one. I interviewed one store owner, but found that what he shared was pretty much Greek to me. I did not accept the assignment, feeling that the subject would be better covered by someone with more knowledge.

Too Many Assignments

You've sent out a number of query letters and received a go-ahead on most of them. They all have deadlines, causing you to feel totally overwhelmed. If this is the case, sit down and make a list of each one with the due date. Concentrate on the article that must be done first, and put the others out of sight until you're finished. If you need to obtain more facts and quotations for the remaining articles, send out your requests before you start the first assignment.

This problem can be avoided, however, by allowing yourself more time up front to finish the article. When the editor accepts your query, he may or may not have the article slated for a particular issue. If not, the deadline can be negotiated. Editors would rather have a well-written manuscript that doesn't require a lot of editing on their part than one that has been dashed off in a hurry to meet a deadline.

If an assignment requires considerable time and research, divide the job into smaller parts and set a goal for each day. Outline one day, the next day contact sources for interviews and set up appointments, write the lead the third day, look up some anecdotes and facts on another day—and soon you'll be looking at a finished article that earlier looked impossible to write.

No Inspiration

Kathi Macias says on the Writers' View Web site:

I'm journalism-trained. As a result, I learned early on that if we want to make a living by arranging words on paper, then few of us have the luxury of waiting for the muse to whisper, wrestle with writer's block, or write only that for which we have a passion. If I were a nurse, would I be able to work only on the days I feel a passion to patch up broken bodies? If I were a teacher, could I teach only on the days my pint-sized pupils stirred up my passion? If I were president, could I govern only on the days my polls were favorable?

If we've been called to do a job, we do it—period. On the days we have a passion for it, whoopee! Rejoice and enjoy it! On the other days, do it anyway. It's amazing how much steadier our writing income will be when we approach it with that attitude.

An anonymous author writes, "If you wait for inspiration, you're not a writer, you're a waiter."

You're Stuck in Your Writing

One of the biggest reasons for this happening is that you haven't planned in advance what you're going to write. As I wrote earlier, in my first nonfiction book on setting up a typing service, I got bogged down in the chapters until I realized that I could outline each chapter as I would an article. Once I did this, I found it easier to finish the book. On the second book, dealing with setting up and running an income tax business, I outlined so thoroughly at the beginning—heading, subheadings, even sub-subheadings—that when I sat down to write, I completed the book in thirty days.

Another problem—if you're writing fiction—may be that your characters have taken over the story and you don't know where they're going next. Or—if nonfiction—the details in your article or book just don't seem to come together like they should. If this is happening, go back and re-read your synopsis or outline to remind yourself of the theme and the takeaway you want to leave with readers. If you haven't developed an outline, now is the time to do so. Former baseball player Yogi Berra says, "If you don't know where you're going, you'll probably end up somewhere else." How true! If you don't know where you're going, the readers won't either—if it gets past the editor to the reader, that is.

If you're still stuck, pick up a book on the genre in which you're writing and follow some of the author's suggestions. Or join a group of writers who meet on a regular basis for encouragement and critiquing. You'll come away not only with help for your manuscript, but also a renewed desire to continue.

Fatigue

Get away from writing for a while. Take a walk or a nap, have a snack, go for a drive, work out at a gym, enjoy a lunch with friends, take a weekend vacation. Even getting away from your keyboard for an hour or so to do something in the house or workshop will recharge your creativity.

Whether you are a beginning or advanced writer, if you have faced the problem of writer's block, the following suggestions may help.

Hitchhike

Whenever you are working on a project, keep a pad handy to jot down related ideas. Our pastor calls this "hitchhiking on a thought." Do you need a Scripture verse for a devotional? While reading that portion of the Bible, a nearby verse may suggest another article. Write this verse down on your pad, along with a tentative outline and any other related scripture or song that comes to mind. Later, as you're working on a different article, you may come across other verses that fit the tentative outline you jotted down earlier.

If you get more than two ideas on the same subject, give it a working title and put it in a file folder—manila or computer. Then when you complete your first article, turn to your file with the tentative outline and you're ready to write. While you're working on this new article, a verse of Scripture may lead to a third article, and so on.

Don't Throw Anything Away

If you are working on a large project and end up with more material than you can use, save the rest for another project. Many years ago while writing two Bible study textbooks for a home school publisher, I accumulated pages of research. I have returned to these notes several times in writing other articles and devotionals.

Recycle

This is the day of recycling—in your writing as well as in your community. Don't ever be satisfied with selling something once! Continue to send out reprints until you know you have exhausted all the markets for that particular manuscript. Then rewrite it with a different slant.

Recall a time in your life when you struggled with a decision or a trial, but God brought you through. Write this as a personal experience article. Then, using the same incident, change the characters and location, make up a "what if" ending, and turn it into a short story.

If you've written this story from a mother's point of view for a woman's magazine, rewrite it from the father's point of view for a male-oriented periodical. If the story involves a family, write it from a teenager's point of view for youth magazines or take-home papers. Or change the dialogue and situations to that of a younger child for children's publications.

After you have sent to all the fiction markets, keep the same theme, do some research, add a few statistics, and turn it into a nonfiction piece. Or develop the main theme into a devotional or poem.

Dennis Hensley sold an article to a local newspaper about a high school boy who began a mobile horseshoeing business. He then sold it to a teen periodical. Because the young man was deaf, Hensley offered it to a magazine looking for stories on the hearing impaired. And since he was a Christian, the story next appeared in his denominational magazine. The teen used a Ford truck in his business, so Hensley then sold the story to *Ford Times*. And because he had offered only one-time rights to the local newspaper, he sold the story to other newspapers in the state, and eventually nationwide to the *Grit* newspaper. What a great example of recycling!

Type Something on Your Page

Some articles on writer's block suggest leaving your hero or heroine in a precarious situation. Then the next day you'll be eager to sit down at your keyboard to get him or her out of danger. Other writers suggest leaving off in the middle of a thought and picking it up the next day. (If I left a manuscript like that, I wouldn't be able to sleep! I'd either be too wound up or afraid I'd forget what I was going to write.)

The idea is to get *something* on that blank page. Some writers retype the previous page. This not only gets your fingers going but it also gives you a sense of continuity and makes it easier to begin your new material. Or you can write a letter to an editor, a friend, a manufacturer—anything to get the creative juices flowing.

Work on Several Projects at a Time

Have more than one project in progress. If you're writing a personal experience book, select a particular event and write it as an article. Select a character from a novel you're writing and put her or him in a short story. Write a filler or a devotional, then set it aside for further editing. Outline a chapter of a book or an article. Edit a rejected manuscript before sending it out again. Send a query letter.

Change Writing Locations

Your home office may be too noisy at times, or you have too many interruptions. An afternoon at a coffee bar, a fast-food restaurant, or the library may recharge your creativity.

Market Research

Market research is an important part of writing. If your mind goes blank when you sit down at the keyboard, read a book on writing. Go through your latest *Christian Communicator* and note new markets, editors, and contests, or study the listings in the *Christian Writers' Market Guide* or *Writer's Market*. The excitement of realizing that you've written—or are working on something—that will fit a specific editor's need will get your keyboard buzzing again.

By using one or more of the above suggestions, you'll find that your problem will change from writer's block to finding enough time to write. (And for that, see Chapter 19 on Time Management.)

. . . .

Time Management
Twelve Ways to Add More Hours to Your Writing Day

SOMEONE ONCE SAID, "Some self-employed persons work only half a day. It's up to them to decide which twelve hours it will be."

As writers, we are self-employed. However, many writers also work full time at an outside job. They struggle to fit their writing around this job, along with home and family responsibilities.

If you find yourself complaining, "I don't have time to write," this chapter is for you. It may be that you don't need *more* time; rather, that you make better use of the time you already have. How can you do this?

1. Keep Track of Your Time

T. Suzanne Eller tells of a time when she just couldn't settle down and focus on a writing project. Watching a favorite television program, she sensed God saying to her, "You're restless because you aren't making good use of your time." She decided to take an honest look at her life and her schedule, which, at that time, was overflowing with three kids in college, speaking engagements, teaching a discipleship class for teens, and volunteering at her church. God showed her that these activities weren't the problems; rather, it was the time stealers that had crept into her days.

When Eller looked closer at the flow of a typical day, she realized she operated at a spastic level—writing for thirty minutes, playing computer games for thirty minutes, starting a load of laundry, watching a half hour of television, then writing for another half hour. Eller shared her dilemma with a friend who called the problem "hummingbird head" syndrome—flitting from one activity to the next but accomplishing little.

After this discussion, Eller decided to tackle the situation head-on, identifying the time stealers that caused her to squander precious moments.[1]

Can you relate to Eller? If so, take one day and keep a minute-by-minute account of your activities—from the time you arise till you drop into bed at night. Include even minor things such as showering, brushing your teeth, and getting dressed. Also write down time spent on such things as television, phone calls, computer games, answering e-mails, and visiting social networks such as MySpace or Facebook.

After doing this for one or two days, you'll get an idea of where you're spending your time. Then comes the hard part of deciding which of those activities you can spend less time on or eliminate completely.

> There is no such time as *my* time if I truly want a life that God uses. I don't own my day; it's his. And time is nothing to him. He transcends it, and he can bring huge productivity out of a meager five minutes. When we allow him room to "mess" with our schedules, his time will always be enough. (Erin Keeley Marshall, *Negotiating Route 20-Something*)

2. Use Fifteen-Minute Increments

In the past I found it hard to begin work on a project when I had other appointments that day. On the other hand, if I had an empty day with no obligations, I flew out of bed, eager to get started. One day, while basically wasting a morning waiting for a luncheon engagement, the other party called and canceled. I moaned, thinking how much I could have accomplished in that time.

Often while working at especially difficult and eye-straining proofreading jobs, I take a break every couple of hours and set my timer for fifteen minutes. I am always amazed how much I can accomplish in that short period: cleaning my desk, attacking a pile of filing, writing a note of encouragement or thanks, looking up a market, printing a manuscript.

Charlotte Hale Allen gives a list of things that can be completed in a year in just fifteen minutes a day:

1. Read the entire Bible.
2. Plant and keep up a small garden.
3. Become physically fit.

4. Learn to play a musical instrument.
5. Paint a house.
6. Learn a foreign language.
7. *Write a book.*[2]

Note: We likely won't *find* these increments of time calling out to us; we have to put them into our schedules, the same as we would an appointment. Dig out your timer today, set it for fifteen or twenty minutes, and see how much you can get done. (And don't be surprised if you don't want to stop when you hear the ding.)

Daydreaming about something in order to do it properly is right, but daydreaming about it when we should be doing it is wrong.

—Oswald Chambers

---

3. Use Your Time on Hold

More and more phone calls today are answered by a voice mail saying, "Your call is very important to us. Please hold." What do we do while the music plays? Sing along with it? Gripe and complain?

This can be a good time to clean our desks, proofread or edit one of our manuscripts, or look up a market. With today's cordless phones, we can catch up on jobs all over the house.

A CNN survey shows that the average person spends sixty hours per year on hold. We can put that time to good use.

4. Check E-mail at Scheduled Intervals

Are you one who hurries to your computer every time you hear "You've got mail"? Then, once you've read the latest message, do you feel obligated to answer, even if it's a "that's cute" to a joke you received?

If so, your Internet is controlling you instead of you controlling it. Unless you are expecting an important letter or you receive work assignments through the Internet, why not schedule specific times to go to your "Read" file? And don't feel you have to answer every e-mail unless a question requires an immediate reply.

5. Prioritize Your Tasks

Our pastor told us that if we followed one rule, we could change our lives in a week. "Every night before you go to bed," he said, "make a list of what you have to do the next day, and rearrange the list in order of priority."

I tried this. I wrote out my list and *put* the jobs in order of priority, but it didn't work. Why? Because I didn't *do* them in order of priority. I skipped through the list, picking out those *I wanted to do*.

Then I read about a writer who made a similar list, but she made it a practice to complete the top three jobs on that list every day. I tried that too. My problem, however, was that the first time I made out my list and rearranged the items in order, I had thirty-nine jobs jumping out at me. I did what I could the first day, then recopied the list the second day, adding a few new jobs. Eventually, I felt all I was doing every day was recopying the same list, with many additions and very few deletions.

I finally found a method that works for me; perhaps it will help you too. I now make my list at the beginning of the week, then—depending on my schedule for the week—I assign jobs to specific days. If I'm working on a big project, I break it into smaller pieces for that day's schedule. This makes completing my list each day more manageable.

Emilie Barnes, in her book, *15 Minutes Alone With God*, suggests, "List only those things that need to be done today, not tomorrow or next week, *but just today*" (emphasis added).[3]

6. Plan Your Schedule

Writers who do not work outside of the home often say it is as difficult for them to find time to write as someone with a forty-hour-a-week job because of the interruptions. The secret is to plan our writing schedules around those interruptions, or use these interruptions to our advantage.

For example, I schedule my jobs depending on whether I'm going to be home, what's happening at home that week, or if I have to run errands. Jobs that require use of the computer I schedule for days I'm home. Editing jobs I do in early mornings and late evenings when it's quiet, or when I'm at my "away" office—a back table in a hospital cafeteria where my daughter works. (Fast-food restaurants and coffee shops work great for this too, as well as the library.)

Jobs that don't require as much concentration, such as research, scanning sample magazines, addressing and stuffing envelopes, or writing rough drafts in pencil, I can do while I watch a favorite program on TV. And I take advantage of time spent in doctors' waiting rooms to write, read magazines or books, or edit manuscripts.

If you work full time away from home, you can write during breaks or lunch. If you ride the bus, use the time to write or edit manuscripts. If you pick up your children at school or your mate at work, go fifteen minutes early and work while you wait.

Use the time you spend waiting in line at the supermarket to study the magazines on the racks. Read the titles on the covers to see what type of articles various magazines use on a regular basis. Watch and listen to the people around you. (This is a good idea in a doctor's office or on the bus too.) Fifteen minutes a day, five days a week, adds up to sixty-five hours a year—and that's a lot of extra time to write.

7. Set Goals

One author, who finds it difficult to carve out a block of time in a day, prefers to set a goal of writing two articles a week or a certain number of pages. This gives her the freedom to choose which hours or days she will write. Other writers set aside one day a week or a specific period, perhaps a week at a time.

What works for you? Regardless of what you hear at every writers' conference, there is nothing magic about "two hours a day." You shouldn't put yourself on a guilt trip if you have younger children or a spouse with health problems or aging parents and you can't spare that much time every day. Can you find one afternoon or evening a week? Can you exchange child care with another writer? Can a neighbor or friend sit with your spouse or parent for a few hours while you go to the library?

Members of a writers' club set individual goals to be met before the next meeting. This goal may be to read a book on writing or in their favorite genre, update marketing files, outline an article, send a query letter, or complete a chapter of a book—anything connected with writing.

Do you want to write a book? Make a list of what needs to be done *before* you can start the actual writing. What research do you need to do? Who will you need to interview? Now set a goal for each month; for example, by the end of January you'll complete research for Chapter 1. Even with limited time, you can finish this book. One page a day, five days a week, will give you a 261-page book at the end of the year. Long-range goals can include sending out a specific number of fiction or nonfiction pieces a month, taking a correspondence course in writing, or setting up a marketing file.

If you have a number of projects in mind and don't know where to begin, make a list and study it. Which project is the most important to you? To God? Which book or article, story or poem, does a hurting world need today? Decide, and start writing.

8. Organize

One author writes that we spend six weeks a year looking for things![4] Think of what you could do with those six weeks—organize your marketing files, write a book proposal, perhaps write a chapter or two of a book, a short story or article, read some writing books. The list goes on.

A file cabinet is the simplest method of organization. Buy one at a "crash and dent" sale; it doesn't matter what it looks like. Set up files for clippings, for ideas, for manuscripts, for sample magazines, for workshop notes, and an "A to Z" file for correspondence. (As Emilie Barnes says, "File, don't pile!")

9. Learn to Say No

There is nothing wrong with church, school, and community involvements, but what takes precedence in your life? Do these jobs crowd out what God wants you to do? My mother used to say that God sometimes takes away the good so He can give us His best. We can keep saying yes to so many things we enjoy doing that we end up not having any energy left over for what God has called us to do.

Jan Johnson said that she kept committing herself to projects that left her feeling empty. "I grew afraid," she said, "that I would wake up at the end of my life and wonder why I hadn't accomplished my dreams—or even attempted them."

In his book, *When I Relax I Feel Guilty*, Tim Hansel says:

I was dominated by "shoulds," "ought to's," and "musts." I would awaken unrefreshed in the morning, with a tired kind of resentment, and hurry through the day trying to uncover and meet the demands of others. Days were not lived but endured. I was exhausted trying to be a hope constantly rekindled for others, straining to live up to the images of me. I had worked hard to develop a reputation as one who was concerned, available, and involved—now I was being tyrannized by it. Often I was more at peace in the eyes of others than in my own.[5]

Kim Thomas agrees. "There is way too much shame associated with rest in our culture," she says. "The busier we are, the more pious we feel about how busy we are. We wear our to-do lists like proud medals telling the world that 'Hey, I'm important because I have a lot of things to do!'"[6]

Don't be afraid to say no.

Don't feel guilty when you say no.

And don't feel you have to defend yourself. For years, whenever someone asked me to do something, I responded with a long list of my "to do's." It was almost as though

I felt I had to justify my reason for saying no, and was too embarrassed to tell them I wanted to write. One evening I turned down a typing customer, telling the caller I had another job. "I didn't know you had a job to do for someone," my husband commented when I hung up. "I don't—for someone else," I replied. "I plan to write tonight—and that's a job!" And I felt no guilt in turning down the customer.

10. Occasionally Forget Writing

Sometimes you need to get away from writing entirely and recharge your batteries. In one "Winnie the Pooh" comic strip, Rabbit carries a ladder past Pooh and says, "No time for talk, Pooh! I'm busy, busy, busy fixing my roof."

Pooh says, "My goodness, Rabbit! Don't you ever take time out just to smell the flowers?"

"By George! You're right, Pooh!" Rabbit agrees.

Later, when Piglet stops to talk, Rabbit breathlessly says, "No time for talk, Rabbit. I'm busy, busy, busy smelling the flowers."

Get away from the computer for awhile. Read a good book. Attend a concert. Watch a favorite TV program. Go for a walk. Take your children or grandchildren to the park or the zoo. Browse the mall. Take time for yourself, and your writing will be better for it. You'll pick up a lot of new ideas as well!

11. Treat Your Writing As a Calling from God

Earlier in this book I tell about the talk Harold Ivan Smith gave at a conference that literally changed my writing career. Up to that time I had treated writing only as a hobby, to be done when and if I had the time. Then I heard these words: "We are called to write, and I feel we will be held responsible at the Judgment for the people who are hurting that we could have helped but didn't, because we didn't write what God laid on our hearts to write." That took writing out of the hobby category for me and made it a calling.

I have never heard a preacher say, "I don't have time to prepare my sermon." He takes the time, because God has called him to preach.

Cecil Murphey—who calls himself a "curmudgeon"—admits on the Writers' View Web site that

> . . . occasionally we get slammed against a deadline wall; however, I'm bothered that professional-types use that as an excuse for submitting less than the best. It's as if they excuse themselves by saying, "It should have been better but God only gave me 19 hours today."

Something is wrong if time excuses become the constant wail. Instead of blaming deadlines, maybe they need to say, "Maybe I should have started earlier." "Maybe I yakked too long on the phone." "Maybe I should have turned off the TV an hour earlier."

He continues,

Lack-of-time excuses trouble me because it's an easy way to avoid responsibility for lesser-quality work. If God calls us to write, surely God provides the time to get it done. We don't please God by turning in less-than-polished work. Jeff Adams [named the Sherwood Eliot Wirt Writer of the Year by the San Diego Christian Writers Guild in 2008] has a saying, "Strive for perfection; settle for excellence." Instead of that standard, some writers imply, "I dream of excellence, but I settle for mediocrity."

> It is a wretched taste to be gratified with mediocrity when the Excellent lies before us.
>
> —Isaac D'Israeli

12. Prioritize Your Life

Isn't this the same as prioritizing our tasks discussed in point #1? you ask. No, there we talked about prioritizing *tasks*. Now we must determine where writing fits into our lives and realize that, at times, we may have to place some things *ahead* of our writing. These things include:

Friends

A writer friend has a sign above her computer that says, "Writing can wait; relationships can't." This lady is an excellent writer and has sold many articles. She is also a compassionate person, and people often knock at her door for counseling and prayer.

I'm not saying that you should allow others to constantly interrupt your writing time for trivial reasons. You need to be firm and tell them you are working. However, when a friend or loved one has a need that can't wait, your writing can. This is well expressed in the following poem by Milo Arnold:

His Interruptions

Today I toiled from morn till setting sun,
And in the gathered night saw nothing done.
My tools and hands were worn without success;
Unfinished tasks but mocked my busyness.

I'd met old age, been greeted by a child,
So oft lost time, by friendship's call beguiled.
I'd dried an urchin's tear and tried to understand
The burdens of a man—and lend a hand.

Tonight, aweary, when I knelt to pray,
I begged God's mercy for the fruitless day.
He whispered that the hours were in His hands;
His interruptions were the day's real plans.

Family

I've heard many speakers at conferences say to write two hours a day . . . or an hour a day . . . or even fifteen minutes. And you go home feeling guilty because you can't find that time.

One summer I was in a situation where I wanted desperately to write, but our family was experiencing numerous family illnesses. My husband—who already had nine diseases—added two more that year. Our youngest daughter was diagnosed with diabetes, and our oldest daughter and her husband—who had multiple sclerosis—were in a car accident, resulting in my daughter's second miscarriage of the year. I literally could not find time to write.

That summer I taught at a Midwest writers' conference. The first evening a friend asked about my family, knowing some of their medical problems. I gave her an update, then she asked, "How is your writing?"

"I'm really frustrated," I told her. "I just haven't had time to write. I've been busy taking care of my family."

This friend said just four words that entirely changed my attitude and gave me a new perspective on my situation. She said, "God will honor that."

The next morning I shared this experience with another friend. She began to cry. "Thanks for telling me that," she said. "My dad's been real sick. He lives forty-five miles away. Every time I sit down to write, he calls and says he needs me. I was beginning to resent it. He was interrupting my writing and I feel I'm called to write."

Then in the plenary session that morning, the speaker reminded us that "families are more important than writing."

Yes, we may be called to write, but we're also called to be a wife, a husband, a mother, a father, a son, a daughter. One of our family's favorite songs is "We Have This Moment Today." In the chorus, Bill Gaither reminds us that yesterday is gone and tomorrow may never come. Your children are only young once; your parents are aging; your spouse needs you. Allow room for them.

If your situation permits, it is good discipline to set aside a specific time each day or week. But when your mate needs to talk or your son or daughter comes to you with a problem, take a break. You can always come back to writing; the family won't always be there. This was vividly brought home to me one day when I was again complaining that I didn't have time to write (I don't always learn lessons right away!). The sobering thought came to me: *Someday you'll have all the time you want, and you won't want it!*

If you're going through a situation right now and you cannot write, at least try to keep notes. The day will come when you will have the time and that journal will give you the material you need.

I truly believe that if God gives you something to write, He will help you find the time to write it.

God

In a conference talk entitled, "Keeping the Sparkle in Your Writing," Sally Stuart warns, "You can't write from an empty cup." What sets us apart from secular writers is that we have first touched God. It's easy to rely solely on our own talent when beginning a project without asking for God's guidance in what we should write, how we should write it, and where we should send it. Someone once wrote, "Go to your knees before you go to your typewriter [or keyboard]." Don't leave God out of your writing.

Prioritize your life and put writing in its proper place.

How do you find time to write? The minutes are there, waiting. Make the best use of them. Christian novelist and physician Brandt Dodson said that when he first began medical school, his instructor told them that they would have to sacrifice in the present if they wanted a secure future. "You may have to give up time with friends," the instructor said. "Turn off the TV. Eat out less often. Put your hobbies on hold. Or you will need to find a process for renewing your mental energy."[7]

If this is true for medical students, shouldn't it be as true for those of us God has called to spread the gospel message through the printed page? We are called to write and He will help us make time for this important calling.

If our work does not come through Jesus, it counts for nothing—zero. Our fruit-producing has to go beyond our natural talent. Each of us has been called for a unique ministry. We need not copy another's ministry, because that isn't our calling. Remember, our calling is just for us, and it will not produce fruit if Christ isn't in agreement. (Emilie Barnes, *Tea Lovers Devotional*)

A Prayer for Living Out God's Plan

1. *Pray over your priorities*—"Lord, what is Your will for me at this time in my life?"
2. *Plan through your priorities*—"Lord, what must I do today to accomplish Your will?"
3. *Prepare a schedule based on your priorities*—"Lord, when should I do the things that live out these priorities today?"
4. *Proceed to implement your priorities*—"Lord, thank You for giving me Your direction for my day."
5. *Purpose to check your progress*—"Lord, I only have a limited time left in my day. What important tasks do I need to focus on for the remainder of the day?"
6. *Prepare for tomorrow*—"Lord, how can I better live out Your plan for my life tomorrow?"
7. *Praise God at the end of the day*—"Lord, thank You for a meaningful day, for 'a day well spent,' for I have offered my life and this day to You as a 'living sacrifice.'"[8]

Chapter 20

How to Handle Rejection

I READ ABOUT several authors attending a romance writers convention. A group was in a crowded elevator that stopped on one floor to allow people to get in. One of the writers said, "You'll have to wait for the next one." After the door closed, another writer said, "*Those were editors!*" to which the first writer replied, "I know, *and we rejected them!*"

A writer named Linda Bosson came up with the following response to a rejection letter:

Dear Editor:
Thank you for sending me the enclosed rejection slip.
Although I enjoyed reading it, it is not quite the type of material I am looking for.
In any case, my desk drawer is currently overstocked with rejection slips, so I am returning this one to you, hoping you may be able to place it elsewhere.

We've all received rejections. (In my critique group, we call them "pre-acceptances.") If it makes you feel any better, many great manuscripts were rejected numerous times before they found a home.

- Richard Bach's book *Jonathan Livingston Seagull* was rejected by twenty-six publishers before it was finally accepted. It sold thirty million copies worldwide.
- J. K. Rowling received fourteen rejections for her first *Harry Potter* book.
- Stephen King received more than thirty rejections for his first novel, *Carrie*.
- Madeleine L'Engle's *A Wrinkle in Time* received over thirty rejections.

- Margaret Mitchell's *Gone with the Wind* was turned down by more than twenty-five publishers. One claimed that "the public is not interested in Civil War stories."

The book titles and authors below all received rejection slips, also with uncomplimentary words about their writing.

- *Carrie* by Stephen King ("We are not interested in science fiction which deals with negative utopias. They do not sell.")
- *The Diary of Anne Frank* ("The girl doesn't, it seems to me, have a special perception or feeling which would lift that book above the 'curiosity' level.")
- *Animal Farm* by George Orwell ("It is impossible to sell animal stories in the USA.")
- *Lust for Life* by Irving Stone ("A long, dull novel about an artist.") Rejected 16 times but found a publisher and went on to sell about a million copies.[1]

One editor told Rudyard Kipling, "I'm sorry, but you just don't know how to use the English language." Editors also turned down Theodore H. White's *The Making of the President,* Thor Heyerdahl's *Kon-Tiki,* and J. R. R. Tolkien's *Lord of the Rings.*[2]

Why Manuscripts Are Rejected

Following is a list of reasons editors give for rejecting manuscripts:

Too wordy. If this is your weakness, check some of the exercises in Chapter 16 on Editing Hints. I also recommend *Make Every Word Count* by Gary Provost, published by Writer's Digest Books. One of the best ways to improve on this weakness is to enter contests in which your submission must be in fifty words or less. You'll be surprised how many words are unnecessary.

Connection between paragraphs is poor. Learn to use proper transitional words, such as "In the meantime," "Therefore," "However," "When Janet arrived home," and so on. Don't just change thoughts or locations on your reader without warning.

Sloppy thinking. What do you mean? Our family used to watch a program in which one of the most frequent sentences uttered was, "What are you trying to say?" Let others read your manuscript before submitting it and ask them if the meaning is clear.

Sentences too long. I attended a class in which the instructor mentioned Charlie Shedd's statement that a sentence should not be over fifteen words. He asked us to count the words in our sentences and see who had the longest. I won with a sentence of forty-seven words.

After returning home, I was reading a Bible study book, and I thought, "I wonder what the longest sentence is in this book." After finding one with sixty-four words, I turned to the front page of the book, and discovered it was written by the same instructor who had taught our class. (He said, in defense, that he wrote the book before he heard of Charlie Shedd.)

A good rule to follow is this: Your sentence shouldn't be so long or so short that your reader is conscious of how long or short it is. You can have a very short sentence that is choppy, or one that fits the context. On the other hand, you can have a long sentence, but with the proper punctuation, the reader is not conscious of the length of the sentence. If it's so long that the reader has to go back and read it again and again, and stop at the commas and dashes and parentheses, it needs to be divided into two or three shorter ones.

Important thought not in emphatic position. One author of writers' books said that whatever thought you want your reader to retain should be placed at the end of the sentence. If it is at the beginning, the reader may have forgotten it when he reads through the rest of the exposition.

Thoughts in paragraph not related to each other. When you change thoughts, begin a new paragraph.

Used passive voice instead of active voice. (See more on this in Chapter 16 on Editing Hints.)

Author "oversaid" his or her words. One of our ministers years ago often said, "I only said that to say this," and I wondered, *So why didn't you say what you meant the first time?* Write your words succinctly the first time, and you won't have to repeat them in a different wording in the next paragraph. As my mother used to say, "I've told you once and that's enough!"

Author used clichés. Self-explanatory.

Wrong market. Manuscript is geared to a different readership.

Doesn't fit our needs. Won't appeal to our audience.

Inept writing. Poor opening, transitions, grammar, sentence structure. Poorly conceived and written.

Badly organized. Needs major reworking.

Incomplete. Not a real story; no plot; just an incident.

Unexciting. Lacks sufficient drama to sustain interest. Story is not dramatic enough.

Duplication. Too similar to material already published or on hand.

Overstocked. I'm sure we've all received rejection slips with this reason checked, and it can be true. An editor will reject a manuscript if he has too many already on hand. I've heard editors say that they will not accept a manuscript unless they feel they can use it within a year.

You might ask if it is all right to submit the same manuscript to this editor later if he says he's "presently overstocked"? I feel it's okay if enough time elapses. Or you can resubmit it to the same publisher if a new editor joins the staff. If it is written well enough and the timing is right, the second time may result in a sale.

Too preachy. In my twenties, I sold regularly to a teen take-home paper. In later years, the editor began rejecting all my submissions. I asked him what I was doing wrong and he replied that my stories were "too preachy." It occurred to me that in my previous stories, I could still remember what it was like to be a teenager. Now I was writing in a "turn down that stereo" tone of voice.

I encouraged a friend of mine to submit devotionals to a children's magazine. When I looked over the finished pages, I saw she had ended each one with the words, "Now boys and girls, the moral of this story is . . . " I told her that she had to work the lesson throughout the devotional so she wasn't hitting the children over the head with it.

Too many typographical errors. The writer mentioned earlier, whose book had five typos on page one, wanted to send a cover letter that read, in part, "I know this needs retyping but I don't have the money right now. If you buy it and I get an advance, I will pay someone to retype it." Neatness is especially important on the first page of your manuscript as that may be all the editor reads.

Misuse of punctuation. I heard a story (which was confirmed) about an old-time preacher and writer named Uncle Buddy Robinson, who was somewhat illiterate. At the bottom of each manuscript page, he placed a row of periods and commas and told the editor, "Put them where they belong. That's your job." We couldn't get away with that today (and he couldn't have either except his writing contained so much sparkle).

Didn't study the publisher's guidelines. My son and I were at the library and, as usual, he headed for the sports section. Eagerly, he pulled down a book entitled *The Big Red Machine* (he was a Cincinnati Reds baseball fan). Unfortunately, the book was about communist Russia. It's not enough just to look at the market listing in the various writers' guides and magazines as you can't always get a complete picture of what the editors are looking for. Send for, or check the Internet for a catalog, sample copy, and guidelines, and study them.

When I put out a call for devotionals for a book I was compiling on a specific Scripture verse, I gave the requirements: 250 words or less, double-spaced, and so on. I received handwritten devotionals, some as long as 1,000 words, some single-spaced, a few on other verses, and one even asked for a sample of what a devotional looked like so she could write one. Also, I received two I could have used, but the manuscripts contained no name or address.

One lady in a former writers' group I attended told us she sent an article to *Guideposts*. Along with it, she sent a letter saying, "I know this is longer than what you usually accept but if you buy it, I'll cut it down."

An editor of a new magazine said that when a writers' magazine put out his guidelines, he was immediately flooded with manuscripts. Writers thought, "Oh, here's a new market," and cleaned out all of their files. "I could only use 1-2 percent," he said. Don't risk an automatic rejection because you didn't follow the publisher's guidelines.

Poor packaging. I've received manuscripts with so much tape around the envelopes I thought the senders owned stock in 3M. Some editors tell of receiving manuscripts sprayed with perfume or envelopes containing chocolate.

Other reasons editors give for rejecting manuscripts are: postage due, editors' names spelled wrong (they wonder what other inaccuracies the manuscript contains), and weak opening paragraphs.

You may never know why your manuscript is rejected. Perhaps it is because of one of the above reasons, or maybe the editor was just under a lot of stress that morning. I mistakenly sent out a manuscript to an editor who had rejected it a month before, and *he bought it the second time!*

If an editor writes an encouraging note on a rejection letter, take it seriously, or if he suggests rewriting, do it! One take-home paper formerly bought 1,000-word stories. When I sent her one that length, she wrote back and said, "I like it, but it's too short. We're now buying 1,500 words." I upped it to 1,500 words and she bought it.

I sent another short story about a runaway wife to a monthly magazine. The editor wrote, saying, "I like your story but it is so short you haven't really given us an opportunity to get to know this woman . . . I like the idea, but can you expand it?" I doubled it in length, sent it back, and received an acceptance.

In this section we've included reasons editors reject your manuscript. Following are suggestions if you hire a *freelance* editor to go over your manuscript *before* you submit it to a publisher:

- Don't call her a few days after mailing your manuscript and ask what she thinks about it, or how much she's done, especially if she told you she can't begin it for a couple of weeks because of previous commitments.
- Double-space your manuscript.

- Number your pages consecutively throughout the book, not chapter by chapter.
- If you're sending it as an e-mail attachment, put the entire manuscript in one file instead of storing every chapter in a separate file. This makes it much easier for the editor to search and replace if he or she is also inserting the corrections.
- Checking Scripture verses isn't a normal part of a freelance editor's job. That's your responsibility. If he or she has agreed to do it, however, be sure to give the translation(s) you used.
- If you're sending your manuscript to a freelance editor you've worked with in the past, check first to see if he or she is still in the business, has time for your manuscript, and is at the same address. (One author whom I hadn't worked with in two years sent me a manuscript with a $400 check. We had already gotten our mail Saturday morning, but the carrier came back later and left this package in the mailbox without letting us know. Because I wasn't expecting it, I didn't find the envelope and check until Monday.)
- Determine the price ahead of time—whether by the page or by the hour. And be ready to pay a deposit if asked.
- Finally, do not quote your editor's price to other writers. All manuscripts are *not* created equal.

At writers' conferences, you often hear editors from various publishing houses and magazines share what type of article or book they're looking for. But one editor admitted he doesn't always know.

"It's like a young man who went into the army," he said. "From day one he acted really strange. He'd walk along, pick up a piece of paper, look at it, and say, 'That's not it,' and put it back down. He'd go into different barracks and pick up other pieces of paper, throw them down, and say, 'No, that's not it.' He'd even go into some of the offices, pick up something, and say, 'No, that's not it,' and throw it down.

"Finally the top brass decided, 'This guy really isn't suited for the armed forces.'

"So they called him in one day and said, 'Nothing against you personally, but we don't think you're adjusting. We think we should probably let you go. Here's your honorable discharge.'

"The private gave one look at it and said, 'That's it!'"

This editor told the conferees, "I can't always tell you or give you a sheet saying this is what I'm looking for, but when I see it, I'm going to know, 'That's it!'"

James C. Magruder says, "If you believe God called you to a writing ministry, regardless of your success or failure, you should never stop trying. This is, in essence, the secret to successful writing . . . . Relentlessly sharpen your writing skills. Diligently revise and polish your manuscripts. Meticulously research your markets. Pray for divine enablement. But, most of all, never stop trying."[3]

Chapter 21

Social Networking and Online Promotion[1]

T HERE IS NO denying it: Social networking is changing the way writers interact with agents, publishers, and fans, and build their brand on a global basis. Social-networking capabilities have fundamentally altered the way publishers search for talent and these capabilities can quickly build (or destroy) a writer's credibility.

Yet many writers hesitate to adopt networking and social-media strategies. Why? Often it's because as writers, we are focused on the writing. Sometimes we just don't know about the latest and greatest and we don't want to waste our time learning something that might be out of fashion next week. Or it can be fear based. Learning a new program and how to use it can be scary. But in today's world, *not* using social networking not only hurts your opportunities; it can cripple your chances of landing a contract.

One key point to remember about social networking and all it has to offer: You must carefully guard your reputation and credibility. One of the benefits of using social networking is creating your brand and creating new relationships. Sharing information about yourself that makes you a real person can really pay off. For example, if you love riding horses and you share personal tidbits about horses, you can more easily connect with an agent who shares your passion. On the other hand, sharing gossip about another horse lover can seriously damage your reputation. If you choose to use social networking, keep it professional. Before you post, ask yourself, "Is this something I would want published in the newspaper or read aloud at church on Sunday?"

Another point that needs to be mentioned is that social networking is constantly changing and adding new types of networks and groups. You need to be open to new ideas. Pick one idea to start with; learn it and use it; and then add new ones as you can. What features get your attention online? How can you use some of these same things in your own promotion plan? If the thought of entering this field overwhelms you, find a mentor or a high school student to help.

The following is a brief look at some important tools available to writers today and a few tips on how to put them to use.

LinkedIn

LinkedIn is a popular social network for business users. With more than forty million registered users, it was ranked one of the top five social-media sites for traffic growth in the past year. This is more than sixteen million unique visits per month.

The concept behind LinkedIn is a pyramid of visibility. If you are familiar with "six degrees of separation" (some people know this as the game "six degrees of Kevin Bacon"), this is the idea behind LinkedIn. LinkedIn allows you to see your contacts and your contacts' network of connections. This visibility creates a number of opportunities for writers via an extended network focused on writing.

Tip 1: Use the Introductions Feature

In theory, you should be able to connect to anyone who is on LinkedIn by using the "Introductions" feature. Let's say you wanted to meet my contact "Peter," who is an agent, and you are one of my connections. When you search for Peter, you will find that he is a second degree contact for you, and that I am a first degree contact for Peter. You can then ask me to introduce you to Peter. If I agree, I will forward your information to Peter and he can choose to connect with you (or not). Now you have the opportunity to talk directly to Peter, or for Peter to see what you are working on via your updates.

Sometimes you will need to repeat this step two or three times to get to the person you want to connect to. It is an easy process: Go to your "Inbox," hover on "Compose message," choose "Inmail or Introduction," click on "Search Now." From there you can search for a person, a company, a title within a company, and so on.

Tip 2: Use the "Status Update" box

One of the biggest and most common mistakes LinkedIn users make is posting a basic profile then collecting contacts. One of the quickest and most effective tools for networking with your direct connections is the Network Updates box, a.k.a. "What are you working on now?" These messages are distributed to your direct connections as updates on their home pages. This allows you to stay at the top of your contacts' consciousness.

Tip 3: Use your profile to highlight your projects, your talent, and your availability for assignments

The profile section is a great way for agents or publishers to see what you have published and what you are working on. Be brief but include enough information to paint a picture of you as an author. Ask someone you trust to review it and give you feedback. Sometimes this is not your family but may be your writers' group, a writing instructor, or your agent.

Tip 4: Join groups

LinkedIn offers a variety of professional groups. The most effective groups generally have three or four sections—for example, Writing Tips, Interesting Articles, Opportunities, and Critiques. Under this format writers can connect virtually to post ideas, find opportunities for publication, post their own work to get advice, or ask for help with a particular problem. If you don't find a group that matches what you are looking for, start one.

In summary, LinkedIn is a great way to network without ever leaving home and can help a writer overcome geographic limitations.

Blogs

Blogging is a multifaceted tool for your writing arsenal. The term "blog" is a contraction of the words "Web" and "log." Blogs are easy-to-use Web sites that display articles in reverse-chronological order. Because they are such an accessible, powerful way to get your message out, blogs provide writers with an easy way to showcase their work and create a fan base.

Unlike social networks, which are owned by others and require you to follow their rules of engagement, bloggers have the opportunity to create their own "publications," write their own rulebooks, and establish their own formats with their target markets and goals as parameters.

Tip 1: Just start

The first and simplest tip is to adopt blogging as an important tool and step into the technology. Many sites offer free blogs—Google, Yahoo, WordPress, and Blogger.com, to name a few. There are pros and cons to every site. Pick one that is easy to use, offers a template you like, and is free. Then start writing.

Tip 2: Pick a theme

If your writing genre is poetry, then ideally your blog would be about poetry. You could publish your original poetry one day, writing tips another, the challenges of writing on another day, and so forth. Theme sites tend to get the most followers, so pick a theme.

Tip 3: Publish your blog

Let your friends and family and professional connections know how to follow your blog. You can do this through an e-mail, by connecting your blog to your social media sites, by posting links to your blog, or by twittering the address (coming up next). The important thing is to build a base of followers for your blog.

Tip 4: Write often and write well

Your blog is there to showcase your writing. If you only publish once a month when the mood strikes, it will not be effective. If you write too often (multiple times a day), it will not be effective. Decide how often you will publish and then stick with it. If you decide to publish weekly, but you have ideas in between, write and save them, then post on your weekly schedule. This way you will always have material ready to go. Also, your writing must be of the highest quality. You do not want a potential publisher to be subjected to poor grammar, spelling, or just bad writing. Make sure your blog is professional, interesting, and highlights your talents.

Twitter

Twitter is a social network that lets users post messages with a limit of 140 characters. Although Twitter's registered user count, estimated at ten million, is far below that of Facebook's estimated 200 million+, as of this writing Twitter is the fastest-growing social network according to Compete.com. From March 2008 to March 2009, Twitter grew 2,565%.

There are two reasons for this incredible growth and popularity. First, it is easy to use. Twitter requires very little technical savvy, and it requires you to do far less writing than for a blog.

Second, Twitter provides valuable features, such as instantaneous broadcasting and connectivity. This makes Twitter a major component of any social-media campaign.

Tip 1: Just tweet

Your first step is to join Twitter and create a user ID. Some writers use their real name; others use their pen name or a name that will attract followers—for example, "mysterywriter." You will build your base using this ID so be sure to pick something you will want to use for a long time and that matches your brand. Now try it out. Tweet a message. You are now a twittering pro!

Tip 2: Read the handbook found at: http://www. twitterhandbook.com/

The Twitter handbook explains it all—from applications to make tweeting easier to how to link Twitter, Facebook, and your blog together.

Tip 3: Tune into conversations

To hear what's going on in any conversation hosted on the site, just make a list of keywords that would identify topics you are interested in following. Twitter is behind the new search term: "semantic conversational search." Semantic search lets people search for conversations, in real time, relevant to their keywords. Unlike a Google search, which can return links to outdated information, Twitter has a third party, open-source search tool called Twazzup.com, which identifies relevant conversations.

As of this writing, it appears Twitter is here to stay. It's a great way to get your message out and link to others in the publishing world.

Facebook

Facebook is currently the largest social network with more than 200 million active users. Facebook reports that 100 million users spend more than four billion minutes on the site every day. Today's fastest-growing population segment is age thirty-five and older and it is leading to our use of Facebook as a marketing tool.

Tip 1: Set up a Facebook page and start connecting

If you already have a page, review it to make sure it is aligned with your brand. For example, let's say you write books aimed at 'tweens. Your Facebook page would be a great place to present a 'tween friendly image, while your LinkedIn page would present your professional image to potential publishers.

Tip 2: Pick your Facebook URL

Like a web URL, you can now pick your Facebook URL. When you join, Facebook will walk you through this process. It is important to put some thought into this. For someone named John Doe, a URL that is majordoe would only make sense if all his friends and fans know him as majordoe.

Tip 3: Control your privacy settings

Many writers are concerned about how to draw a line between personal and professional networking. Networks like Facebook may encompass both types of contacts. However, you have control over who sees what. Facebook provides settings that let you select who can see the various sections of your profile and your update activity.

Tip 4: Keep it current

Like LinkedIn, blogs, and Twitter, it's important to keep your presence fresh and current. Let people know you are writing Chapter 10 in your new novel. Or that your article is being published this week in *Christianity Today*. Or that you are speaking at a bookstore or church this weekend.

I recommend you post daily updates. Two or three updates in a day on Facebook is not overkill as long as they have meaning and are aimed at either updating your audience or creating a relationship with your audience. At the same time, balance your workload so that you are actually writing and not spending your entire day on Facebook.

Video

We have covered various forms of Internet marketing, including blogs and social networking. Now it is time for what could be the most important in today's book marketing world—video.

Video marketing takes on many forms, including video podcasts, Web site videos, videos for your press packet to help getting TV interviews, and book trailers. While all are similar, they also share some differences.

Tip: Posting a video can dramatically increase book title and author name recognition on search engines

Online video is so popular, search engines are continuously searching the Web for new content. Because of this, your video content can show up in search results within a few hours after you post it. In addition, video content generally shows up before other types of content.

As an author, it is important to ask yourself why you want to post video content. What do you want to accomplish? What is your key message? Who is your target audience? How do you want to use the video content? How much time and money are you willing to devote to creating video content?

Once you have answers to these questions, it is time to research the various types of video content that may be right for you.

Book Trailers

In an article that appeared in the Christian Fiction Online Magazine, Kathi Macias confesses how she finally made the transition ("under pressure") to market her wares via written/radio/TV interviews, public speaking, influencer lists, blog tours—and the latest craze, video trailers.

"The first time I heard the term, I had no clue what a book trailer might be," Kathi admits, "and then I saw one and it didn't take long to get hooked. I realize we live in a visually-oriented, sound-bite generation, and if we want to sell our books, we need to appeal to our readers in a medium they like and understand."

Kathi has worked on four projects with designer Misty Taggart and *Trailer to the Stars*, with several more in the planning stages. (Go to Google.com to check out other video trailer designers.)

(To see Kathi's trailers on *Mothers of the Bible Speak to Mothers of Today, How Can I Run a Tight Ship when I'm Surrounded by Loose Cannons?, Beyond Me,* and *My Son, John,* visit her Web site at www.kathimacias.com.)

The term "book trailer" was coined and trademarked by Circle of Seven Productions in 2002. It refers to a short video clip aimed at selling your book. Think of it as a low budget and shorter version of the movie trailer.

Although statistics are hard to come by, the general thought process is that a good book trailer will increase sales and name recognition. Conversely, a poorly done trailer can seriously impact an author's credibility

Tip: Your video must first and foremost sell books

When making a trailer, the first thing to remember is that the video *must* refer to the book and its author. An amazing number of trailers seem to forget this basic premise of sales. Beyond that, the prevailing advice is to offer something more than a picture of the book cover, more than the marketing material on the cover, something that will capture the attention of the viewer and compel him to purchase your book.

When planning your trailer, watch other trailers for ideas. Find the most popular so you understand *why* they are popular. There are currently two types of trailers. One is the commercial video, designed to let viewers know a new book is coming soon. The second is a viral video, designed to entertain the viewer, who will then e-mail it to friends and family, thus creating even more interest in the book.

Tip: Remember, the trailer is about the audience, not the author

Whether you decide to do a commercial or a viral trailer, entertainment is key and boredom is your enemy. Look ahead—in the early 1980s, music videos were born. At the time, they were innovative. MTV saw the potential and a new industry was born. There are many who believe book trailers are the wave of the future—a short film that can be shown on a future version of the Kindle[2], hooking the reader into purchasing the book immediately. Use your creativity as an author to create an entertaining, innovative trailer.

Three remaining points: Stay on budget, have a test audience review a rough cut, and distribute widely. A trailer can cost as little as a few hundred dollars, or quickly become several thousand. Using a talented film or design student to do your video (and potentially give him or her a class project) can save a lot and make the piece appeal to a younger audience. On the other hand, using a seasoned marketing firm can ensure a professional product.

Just as you ask for input on your book, you must ask for input on your video. Friends and family can be good or not so good in this regard. If you feel you will take their feedback too personally and it may hurt relationships, then it is best to have an independent audience. Again, a film program will often have students who will watch and give feedback in return for snacks.

Once your trailer is finished, distribute, distribute, distribute. Posting it on your Web site is like holding a worm over water and expecting the fish to jump out to get it. The point is for people to see your trailer and immediately go to your site where they will fall in love with you and your work, and ultimately purchase your book.

Therefore, the first step is to post it on sites such as YouTube, other social networking sites, including your Facebook page, and send it as a Tweet. You should also look for communities on social networking sites that share a common interest in your product. E-mail to your mailing list, friends, and family and ask them to forward. Post it on blogs and message boards. Remember that a post ages quickly. Sending a couple of tweets a week with the link will reach different audiences than a single tweet. And of course, you will want to have it on your Web site.

Video Interviews

Another option for videos is the video interview. These range in length from three minutes to thirty minutes, depending on the purpose. A three-minute interview can be shown on your Web site, be included in your press packet to television stations, and of course be posted on social networking sites. A thirty-minute interview would typically be for publication on social networking sites as a way to connect with your readers.

Tip: If you are stiff or uncomfortable on camera, consider a media training class

There are a few things to remember when creating an interview video. First, it's important that it be relaxed and real. There is nothing worse than watching an interview that is stilted, over-rehearsed, or boring.

Next, use good equipment. While you can do a video from the camera on your computer, it's worth spending the money to rent a camera and studio if you can afford it. The video quality will be much higher and the setting will look more professional. Many local or public television stations have a studio with a desk set (think morning news show). Also, many art schools or community colleges have students in film programs who know how to use a camera. Even if you rent the studio and use your video camera to do the filming, the quality will be much higher. On the other hand, if you are trying to create a homey feel, a corner of your office or study may work just fine.

Tip: Consider professional editing, especially if you do the video yourself

An editor can add credits, fade in/out, add music and other touches to your interview. Again, it's a matter of what you can afford and what you are trying to accomplish.

Finally, the rules from the previous section apply. Set a budget and stick to it. You may have to make some compromises. Consider getting critiques from a test audience. You wouldn't send your book to press without a critique and editing, so treat your video the same way. Finally, distribute as widely as possible. The point is to get as many people watching as possible so that you can attract readers to your site.

Readings

The reading is a video where an excerpt from your book is read. There are two primary formats—a reading by the author filmed live, or a combination of book trailer and reading, where images are played while the audio is the reading of the book. The live reading is the easiest to film and will be the least expensive. However, a reading with video image can be extremely powerful and attract readers to your site. Once you have decided on the format, follow the rules: Stay on budget, have an audience critique the work, then publish widely.

Video podcasts

Any of your videos can easily be turned into video podcasts. If you are hiring someone to do your video, be sure to let her know you want a video podcast version. Then post your video podcast on the various podcast sites. This gives your readers one more option to watch and fall in love with you and your book.

Summary

How does social networking help? Macias shares how it has helped promote her books:

> I'm on probably every social network that I know, but I have to watch myself that I don't spend so much time on them, I don't actually write books I have under contract. It's easy to get sidetracked with this marketing stuff, especially when it has the word "social" in it. As do most writers, I love people, I love to talk, I love words—and that can be a deadly combination! As a result, I discipline myself to check my social "fave" (Facebook) only two or three times a day; the others I visit once in the morning. When I know one post feeds into other networks, I'll go to those networks once a week.

> One thing I've done that's really helpful is to watch for any and all names on these networks that might key into my particular books. For instance, *Mothers of the Bible Speak to Mothers of Today* is obviously going to appeal more to mothers' groups than to young singles. So if I stumble across a blog site with the word "moms" in it, I check it out. If it looks promising I leave a comment and offer a free copy of my book for review and/or a giveaway. Most take me up on it, and I've had a good response as a result.

> Another example is my novel, *My Son John*, about a young man accused of murdering his grandmother. I watch for prisoners' advocate groups and/or families of the incarcerated (not as numerous as moms' groups but prevalent nonetheless) and make the same sort of offer with that book.

The most successful online tactic for Kathi was a "God thing." As a member of CAN (Christian Authors Network), she was asked to consider serving as their spiritual adviser. When she accepted, she took on the task of gathering/dispersing prayer requests and praise reports from members once a week. She also added a brief devotional each week, and soon the members asked if they could pass these devotionals on to others outside the group.

> Soon I had people I'd never met e-mailing via my Web site (listed under each devotional) to ask if they could post the devotional on their blog. Of course I agreed, as long as they didn't change the wording without my permission, and they included my name and Web site so readers could contact me. Eventually I had an offer from a professional translator to help me get the devotionals out in Spanish as well as English, at which time Crosswalk.

com picked them up and started printing them in both languages every week. Christianity. com also prints them, as do countless other blogs and Web sites, bringing my readership to astronomical figures.

Does Kathi get paid for any of this? "No," she says, "but I couldn't buy better advertising. And it's all done online."

As the world changes, media will also change. The one thing we know is that social networking is here to stay. Take advantage of it and you'll see your writing profits increase.

(My publisher for this book has a full-fledged multimedia department, offering book trailers, author profiles, and more. Visit www.winepressproductions.com for more information.)

Conclusion

The one who calls you is faithful and he will do it.

—1 Thess. 5:24

ONE OF THE biggest obstacles to writing is discouragement. This can come from repeated rejections (see Chapter 20 on dealing with rejection), lack of time (see Chapter 19 on time management), lack of support from family and friends (see Appendix G on how to form a Christian writers' group), or you just feel like giving up.

There is no evidence that this really happened, but a story is told that at one of Paderewski's concerts, a restless five-year-old sat near the front of the huge hall. Waiting for the concert to begin, the boy slipped away from his mother and crawled onto the platform. Sitting at the grand piano, he began to play "Chopsticks" with one finger.

As the audience sat in shocked silence, the famed pianist walked out and stood behind the boy. Bending over the child, Paderewski improvised a beautiful arrangement of "Chopsticks" as he whispered, "Keep playing, son. You're doing a great job."

Do you ever feel like you're just playing "Chopsticks" in your writing? You take an article to a writers' group and the members tear it apart. You send manuscripts to editors and they come back with form rejection letters. You meet an editor at a conference, who sounds excited about your book and takes it back with him, but you never hear from him again.

"I'm giving up," you say, and stuff all your writing materials on the top shelf of the closet.

You may just be playing "Chopsticks" today, but maybe that is what someone needs to hear. God will fill in the missing notes as He whispers in your ear, "Keep playing, child. You're doing a great job."

A story is told about a violinist giving a concert and, partway through, one of the strings broke. He transposed to another key and continued the song.

None of us fully understands why we face trials in our lives. In fact, Christian writers often seem to endure more tragedies than any other group of people. Perhaps it's because God knows that when the trials are over, He can trust us to use them to help other people. We may just have to change keys and keep on writing.

Sometimes we wonder if our writing helps anyone. We pour out our hearts in a book, an article, or a poem, but unless readers respond, we don't know what effect—if any—our words have had.

Consider the story of a young woman who loved flowers. She planted a rare vine beside her back fence. Day after day she cultivated it, but it did not bloom. One morning an invalid neighbor, whose back lot adjoined the young woman's, called her. "You can't imagine how much I enjoy the blossoms of the vine you planted."

Walking around to the neighbor's backyard, the mass of luxurious flowers on the other side of the fence amazed the young woman. They were blooming—but she could not see them from her own yard!

In 1954, the Milwaukee Braves and the Cincinnati Reds played each other on the opening day of major league baseball. A rookie, playing in his first game for the Braves, went zero for five against Cincinnati pitcher Joe Nuxhall. The rookie's name—Hank Aaron![1]

What if Aaron had become so discouraged after his first game that he said, "That's it! I'll never be a big league player. I might as well turn in my uniform and go home today." He didn't, however, and the rest is history as he went on to break Babe Ruth's home run record!

Speaking of Babe Ruth—you may know that he hit 714 home runs, but did you know that *he also struck out 1,330 times?*

Here's another sports story that may encourage you:

I went to my room and I closed the door and I cried. For a while, I couldn't stop. Even though there was no one else home at the time, I kept the door shut. It was important to me that no one hear me or see me.

For about two weeks, every boy who had tried out for the basketball team knew what day the cut list was going to go up. We knew that it was going to be posted in the gym, in the morning.

So that morning we all went in there, and the list was up. I had a friend—his name was Leroy Smith—and we went in to look at the list together. We stood there and looked for our names.

Leroy's name was on the list. He made it. Mine wasn't on the list.

Who wrote the above? You may recognize the name of Michael Jordan, former player for the Chicago Bulls and one of the great basketball players of the century.[2] During a nine-year professional career, Jordan scored 21,541 points in 667 regular season games for a 32.3-point average, the highest in NBA history.[3]

Whatever your cause of discouragement today, take it to the Lord in prayer and remind Him that He has called you to write. Then ask Him for the strength to write the words that will help a hurting world.

God, grant me the desire always to desire to be more than I can ever accomplish.

—Michelangelo

When our granddaughter was young, she enjoyed watching "her" music video with "Jesus Loves Me" and other songs on it. One day she wanted to watch it at our house, but we were watching the baseball game.

"Pease," she begged.

"We're watching TV now," I told her.

Looking up at me, she said again, "Pease, Gamma, I wanna see Jesus."

That's what the world is asking of us as Christian writers. We shouldn't worry about being clever. We shouldn't get caught up in comparing with other writers how many manuscripts we have sold and the checks we've received. Before we go to our computers, we should go to our knees. The world is begging of us, "Please, we want to see Jesus!"

Appendix A
Using Scripture in Your Writing

Fourteen Hints on Using Scripture

1. *Give the version of the Bible you are using.* If you quote Scripture in an article or book, the version is shown in parentheses after the reference, i.e., "In the beginning God created the heaven and the earth" (Gen. 1:1 KJV). Note that no punctuation is used between the reference and the version, which is abbreviated and typed in small caps.

   If you're writing a book and using only one version of the Bible, the following statement may be shown on the copyright page: "Unless otherwise indicated, all Scripture quotations in this book are taken from the . . . ," then give version and credit line, i.e., "New King James Version, Copyright © 1997 by Thomas Nelson, Inc. Used by permission. All rights reserved." If you are using more than one version, double space and continue to list the others, i.e., "Verses marked NIV are taken from the New International Version," then include the credit line, and on down the list. Each publisher allows a certain number of verses to be quoted before permission is required (see pages 273ff); however, a credit line still is needed.

2. *Place the reference* after *the Scripture verse.* Sometimes you see the reference *before* the quotation, as in, "We see in Genesis 1:1 that 'in the beginning God created the heaven and the earth,'" but this may break the train of thought for your reader. It's more common to say, "We read that 'in the beginning God created the heaven and the earth'" (Gen. 1:1). Some authors put the reference in a footnote or endnote, directing the reader to the bottom of the page or the end of the chapter or book.

However, this creates a lot of switching back and forth for the readers and some may not do it.

3. *Spell out the name of the book of the Bible in your reference to avoid confusion.* Phil. could stand for Philippians or Philemon. The publisher will abbreviate these books according to its style guide (as has been done in this writing book).

4. *Spell out numbers at the beginning of a sentence.* If you're saying, "1 Thessalonians 1:1 says . . . ," spell the number 1, i.e., "First Thessalonians 1:1 says . . . "

5. *If your citation includes two consecutive verses, be consistent in the use of punctuation.* Don't use a comma one time and a hyphen the next; i.e., John 3:16-17 or John 3:16,17. Either is correct, but be consistent. Use a hyphen when citing three or more consecutive verses, i.e., John 3:16-18. If you're quoting from the same book but different chapters, use a semicolon, i.e., John 3:16; 4:15. If you're referring the reader to a passage consisting of two consecutive chapters, use an en dash, i.e., John 3–4. (Note: In Word, an en dash is made by clicking on Ctrl, and then the minus key on the number pad.)

6. *Type Scripture quotations in the same typeface as the rest of your manuscript.* Typing passages in bold is like shouting at your reader, and placing them in italics takes away from the smoothness of your writing and breaks the reader's train of thought. Some publishers place Scripture quotations in a smaller font, but let that be *their* decision.

7. *To stress certain words in the Scripture passage, place them in italics, then show this fact after the reference;* i.e., "In the beginning God *created the heaven and the earth*" (Gen. 1:1 KJV, emphasis added). If you do this consistently throughout the manuscript, place a note to this effect on the copyright page as follows: Italics in Scriptures have been added by the author.

8. *If you insert commentary within the Scripture, enclose it in brackets,* i.e., "For God so loved the world [and this means you], that he gave his only begotten Son . . . " (John 3:16 KJV).

9. *Place closing punctuation after the ending parenthesis,* i.e., rather than "In the beginning God created the heaven and the earth." (Gen. 1:1), type "In the beginning God created the heaven and the earth" (Gen. 1:1). (Note: Some publishers place the closing punctuation before the reference in a lengthy, indented quotation. Use their style guide and be consistent.)

10. *Place passages four lines or less in quotation marks within the paragraph, but if the quotation is over four lines, begin a new paragraph and indent on one or both sides.* In this format, you will not need opening or closing quotation marks. Double

space these quotations to allow the editor room for necessary corrections—for example, if she wants to use a different version.

11. *Citing long quotations.* Citing a long passage of Scripture may be done in several ways. 1) As one long indented paragraph, leaving out individual verse numbers; 2) as a long indented paragraph, including verse number in parentheses before the verse; or, 3) instead of using paragraph format, type each verse separately, with or without the verse number before it. Again, be consistent.

12. *Copy Scripture* exactly, *word for word, comma for comma, period for period.* Be especially careful in the use of capitalization as some versions do not capitalize pronouns for God or Christ as "he," "him," "his," "himself," "me," "my," etc., while other versions do. Go according to the version you are using, even if it isn't your personal preference. Especially be careful of the word "Lord" as the Old Testament often spells it with an initial cap and small caps, i.e., "LORD," which means "Jehovah," while "Lord" is "Adonai," which can refer to either God or a human leader. Always use it as it is found in the Scriptures.

13. *Do not overuse Scripture.* In writing for the religious market, you may think that the more Scripture you use, the better; however, this can turn off and distract your reader; it also lets the Bible do your writing for you and doesn't show the editor much of your own writing style.

14. *Most importantly, follow the style guide of the publisher to whom you are submitting your manuscript.* Do your homework. Send for authors' guidelines and/or check books that this particular company has published.

Permission to Use Scripture

Publishers of modern Bible translations allow you to use a specific number of verses without charge as long as you attribute the quote to them and give a credit line on the copyright page. Following are the number of verses permitted by publishers of the more widely-used translations, followed by credit lines for those and other translations.

The Holy Bible, 21ˢᵗ Century King James Version. May quote up to and inclusive of two hundred (200) verses without prior written permission of the publisher, provided that the verses quoted do not account for more than 40 percent of the work in which they are quoted, and provided that a complete book of the Bible is not quoted.

The text of the Amplified® Bible may be quoted in any form (written, visual, electronic, or audio) up to and inclusive of five hundred (500) verses *without express written permission of the publisher,* providing the verses do not amount to a complete book of the Bible nor do the verses quoted account for more than 25 percent of the total work in which they are quoted.

Contemporary English Version (CEV). The CEV text may be quoted in any form (written, visual, electronic, or audio) up to and inclusive of five hundred (500) verses without written permission, provided the verses quoted do not amount to 50 percent of a complete book of the Bible nor do the verses account for 25 percent or more of the total text of the work in which they are quoted.

New American Standard Bible® may be quoted and/or reprinted up to and inclusive of five hundred (500) verses without express written permission of The Lockman Foundation, providing the verses do not amount to a complete book of the Bible nor do the verses quoted account for more than 25 percent of the total work in which they are quoted.

New Century Version® (NCV®) may be quoted or reprinted without prior written permission with the following qualifications: Up to and including 1,000 verses may be quoted in printed form as long as the verses quoted amount to less than 50 percent of a complete book of the Bible and make up less than 50 percent of the total work in which they are quoted.

The *New International Version* (NIV) text may be quoted in any form (written, visual, electronic, or audio), up to and inclusive of five hundred (500) verses without express written permission of the publisher, providing the verses do not amount to a complete book of the Bible nor do the verses quoted account for 25 percent or more of the total text of the work in which they are quoted.

New King James Version® (NKJV®) may be quoted or reprinted without prior written permission with the following qualifications: Up to and including 1,000 verses may be quoted in printed form as long as the verses quoted amount to less than 50 percent of a complete book of the Bible and make up less than 50 percent of the total work in which they are quoted.

Holy Bible, New Living Translation, may be quoted in any form (written, visual, electronic, or audio) up to and inclusive of two hundred and fifty (250) verses without express written permission of the publisher, provided that the verses quoted do not account for more than 20 percent of the work in which they are quoted, and provided that a complete book of the Bible is not quoted.

Appendix A: Using Scripture in Your Writing

The Message text may be quoted in any form (written, visual, electronic, or audio), up to and inclusive of five hundred (500) verses, without express written permission of the publisher, NavPress Publishing Group, providing the verses quoted do not amount to a complete book of the Bible and do not account for 25 percent or more of the total text of the work in which they are quoted.

English Standard Version (ESV) may be quoted (in written, visual, or electronic form) up to and inclusive of one thousand (1,000) verses without express written permission of the publisher, providing that the verses quoted do not amount to a complete book of the Bible nor do the verses quoted account for 50 percent or more of the total text of the work in which they are quoted.

Credit Lines for Bible Translations

Verses marked KJV are taken from the King James Version of the Bible.

Verses marked NKJV are taken from the New King James Version. Copyright © 1982 by Thomas Nelson, Inc. Used by permission. All rights reserved.

Verses marked NIV are taken from the Holy Bible, New International Version®, NIV®. Copyright © 1973, 1978, 1984 by Biblica, Inc.™ Used by permission of Zondervan. All rights reserved worldwide.

Verses marked AMP are taken from The Amplified Bible, Copyright © 1954, 1958, 1962, 1964, 1965, 1987 by The Lockman Foundation. All rights reserved. Used by permission. (www.Lockman.org)

Verses marked RSV are taken from the Revised Standard Version of the Bible, copyright © 1946, 1952, 1971 by the Division of Christian Education of the National Council of the Churches of Christ in the USA. Used by permission. All rights reserved.

Scripture verses marked NRSV are from the New Revised Standard Version of the Bible, copyright © 1989 by the Division of Christian Education of the National Council of the Churches of Christ in the USA. Used by permission. All rights reserved.

Appendix B
Glossary of Terms[*]

Advance. Amount of money a publisher pays to an author up front, against future royalties. The amount varies greatly from publisher to publisher, and is often paid in two or three installments (on signing contract, on delivery of manuscript, and on publication).

All rights. An outright sale of your material. Author has no further control over it.

Anecdote. A short, poignant, real-life story, usually used to illustrate a single thought.

Assignment. When an editor asks a writer to write a specific piece for an agreed-upon price.

As-told-to story. A true story you write as a first-person account, but about someone else.

Audio books. Books available on CDs.

Avant-garde. Experimental; ahead of the times.

Backlist. A publisher's previously published books that are still in print a year after publication.

B & W. Abbreviation for a black-and-white photograph.

Bar code. Identification code and price on the back of a book read by a scanner at checkout counters.

Bible versions. AMP—Amplified Bible; ASV—American Standard Version; CEV—Contemporary English Version; ESV—English Standard Version; GNB—Good News Bible; HCSB—Holman Christian Standard Bible; ICB—International Children's Bible; KJV—King James Version; MSG—The Message; NAB—New American Bible; NAS—New American Standard; NEB—New English Bible; NIRV—New International Reader's Version; NIV—New International Version; NJB—New Jerusalem Bible; NKJV—New King James Version; NLT—New Living Translation; NRSV—New Revised Standard Version; RSV—Revised Standard Version; TLB—The Living Bible; TNIV—Today's New International Version.

Bimonthly. Every two months.

Bio sketch. Information on the author.

Biweekly. Every two weeks.

Bluelines. Printer's proofs used to catch errors before a book is printed.

Book proposal. Submission of a book idea to an editor; usually includes a cover letter, thesis statement, chapter-by-chapter synopsis, market survey, and one to three sample chapters.

Byline. Author's name printed just below the title of a story, article, etc.

Camera-ready copy. The text and artwork for a book that are ready for the press.

Chapbook. A small book or pamphlet containing poetry, religious readings, etc.

Circulation. The number of copies sold or distributed of each issue of a publication.

Clips. See "Published clips."

Column. A regularly appearing feature, section, or department in a periodical using the same heading; written by the same person or a different freelancer each time.

Concept statement. A fifty- to 150-word summary of your proposed book.

Contributor's copy. Copy of an issue of a periodical sent to the author whose work appears in it.

Copyright. Legal protection of an author's work.

Cover letter. A letter that accompanies some manuscript submissions. Usually needed only if you have to tell the editor something specific or to give your credentials for writing a piece of a technical nature. Also used to remind the editor that a manuscript was requested or expected.

Credits, list of. A listing of your previously published works.

Critique. An evaluation of a piece of writing.

Defamation. A written or spoken injury to the reputation of a living person or organization. If what is said is true, it cannot be defamatory.

Derivative work. A work derived from another work, such as a condensation or abridgement. Contact copyright owner for permission before doing the abridgement and be prepared to pay that owner a fee or royalty.

Devotional. A short piece that shares a personal spiritual discovery, inspires to worship, challenges to commitment or action, or encourages.

Editorial guidelines. See "Writer's guidelines."

Electronic submission. The submission of a proposal or article to an editor by electronic means, such as by e-mail or on disk.

Endorsements. Flattering comments about a book; usually carried on the back cover or in promotional material.

EPA/Evangelical Press Assn. A professional trade organization for periodical publishers and associate members.

E-proposals. Proposals sent via e-mail.

E-queries. Queries sent via e-mail.

Eschatology. The branch of theology that is concerned with the last things, such as death, judgment, heaven, and hell.

Essay. A short composition usually expressing the author's opinion on a specific subject.

Evangelical. A person who believes that one receives God's forgiveness for sins through Jesus Christ, and believes the Bible is an authoritative guide for daily living.

Exegesis. Interpretation of the Scripture.

Feature article. In-depth coverage of a subject, usually focusing on a person, an event, a process, an organization, a movement, a trend or issue; written to explain, encourage, help, analyze, challenge, motivate, warn, or entertain as well as to inform.

Filler. A short item used to "fill" out the page of a periodical. It could be a timeless news item, joke, anecdote, light verse or short humor, puzzle, game, etc.

First rights. Editor buys the right to publish your piece for the first time.

Foreign rights. Selling or giving permission to translate or reprint published material in a foreign country.

Foreword. Opening remarks in a book introducing the book and its author.

Freelance. As in 50 percent freelance: means that 50 percent of the material printed in the publication is supplied by freelance writers.

Freelancer or freelance writer. A writer who is not on salary but sells his material to a number of different publishers.

Free verse. Poetry that flows without any set pattern.

Galley proof. A typeset copy of a book manuscript used to detect and correct errors before the final print run.

Genre. Refers to type or classification, as in fiction or poetry. Such types as westerns, romances, mysteries, etc., are referred to as genre fiction.

Glossy. A black-and-white photo with a shiny, rather than matte, finish.

Go-ahead. When a publisher tells you to go ahead and write up or send your article idea.

Haiku. A Japanese lyric poem of a fixed seventeen-syllable form.

Hard copy. A typed manuscript, as opposed to one on disk or in an e-mail.

Holiday/seasonal. A story, article, filler, etc., that has to do with a specific holiday or season. This material must reach the publisher the stated number of months prior to the holiday/season.

Homiletics. The art of preaching.

Honorarium. If a publisher indicates it pays an honorarium, it means it pays a small flat fee, as opposed to a set amount per word.

Humor. The amusing or comical aspects of life that add warmth and color to an article or story.

Interdenominational. Distributed to a number of different denominations.

International Postal Reply Coupon. See "IRC."

Interview article. An article based on an interview with a person of interest to a specific readership.

IRC or IPRC. International Postal Reply Coupon: can be purchased at your local post office and should be enclosed with a manuscript sent to a foreign publisher.

ISBN number. International Standard Book Number; an identification code needed for every book.

Journal. A periodical presenting news in a particular area.

Kill fee. A fee paid for a completed article done on assignment that is subsequently not published. Amount is usually 25-50 percent of original payment.

Libel. To defame someone by an opinion or a misquote and put his or her reputation in jeopardy.

Light verse. Simple, lighthearted poetry.

Little/literary. Small circulation publications whose focus is providing a forum for the literary writer, rather than on making money. Often do not pay, or pay in copies.

Mainstream fiction. Other than genre fiction, such as romance, mystery, or science fiction. Stories of people and their conflicts handled on a deeper level.

Mass market. Books intended for a wide, general market, rather than a specialized market. These books are produced in a smaller format, usually with smaller type, and are sold at a lower price. The expectation is that their sales will be higher.

Ms. Abbreviation for manuscript.

Mss. Abbreviation for more than one manuscript.

Multiple submissions. Submitting more than one piece at a time to the same publisher, usually reserved for poetry, greeting cards, or fillers, not articles. Also see "Simultaneous submissions."

NASR. Abbreviation for North American serial rights.

Newsbreak. A newsworthy event or item sent to a publisher who might be interested in publishing it because it would be of interest to his particular readership.

Nondenominational. Not associated with a particular denomination.

Not copyrighted. Publication of your piece in such a publication will put it into public domain and it is not then protected. Ask that the publisher carry your copyright notice on your piece when it is printed.

Novella. A short novel starting at 20,000 words—35,000 words maximum. Length varies from publisher to publisher.

On acceptance. Periodical or publisher pays a writer at the time manuscript is accepted for publication.

On assignment. Writing something at the specific request of an editor.

One-time rights. Selling the right to publish a story one time to any number of publications (usually refers to publishing for a nonoverlapping readership).

On publication. Publisher pays a writer when his/her manuscript is published.

On speculation/on spec. Writing something for an editor with the agreement that he will buy it only if he likes it.

Overrun. The extra copies of a book printed during the initial print run.

Over the transom. Unsolicited articles that arrive at a publisher's office.

Payment on acceptance. See "On acceptance."

Payment on publication. See "On publication."

Pen name/pseudonym. Using a name other than your legal name on an article or book in order to protect your identity or the identity of people included, or when the author wishes to remain anonymous. Put the pen name in the byline under the title, and your real name in the upper, left-hand corner.

Permissions. Asking permission to use the text or art from a copyrighted source.

Personal experience story. A story based on a real-life experience.

Personality profile. A feature article that highlights a specific person's life or accomplishments.

Photocopied submission. Sending an editor a photocopy of your manuscript, rather than an original. Some editors prefer an original.

Piracy. To take the writings of others just as they were written and put your name on them as the author.

Plagiarism. To steal and use the ideas or writings of another as your own, rewriting them to make them sound like your own.

Press kit. A compilation of promotional materials on a particular book or author, usually organized in a folder, used to publicize a book.

Print on demand (POD). A printing process where books are printed one at a time instead of in quantity. The production cost per book is higher, but no warehousing is necessary.

Public domain. Work that has never been copyrighted, or on which the copyright has expired. Subtract seventy-five from the current year, and anything copyrighted prior to that is in public domain.

Published clips. Copies of actual articles you have had published, from newspapers or magazines.

Quarterly. Every three months.

Query letter. A letter sent to an editor telling about an article you propose to write and asking if he or she is interested in seeing it.

Reporting time. The number of weeks or months it takes an editor to get back to you about a query or manuscript you have sent in.

Reprint rights. Selling the right to reprint an article that has already been published elsewhere. You must have sold only first or one-time rights originally and wait until it has been published the first time.

Review copies. Books given to book reviewers or buyers for chains.

Royalty. The percentage an author is paid by a publisher on the sale of each copy of a book.

SAE. Self-addressed envelope (without stamps).

SAN. Standard Account Number, used to identify libraries, book dealers, or schools.

SASE. Self-addressed, stamped envelope. Should always be sent with a manuscript or query letter.

SASP. Self-addressed, stamped postcard. May be sent with a manuscript submission to be returned by publisher indicating it arrived safely.

Satire. Ridicule that aims at reform.

Second serial rights. See "Reprint rights."

Semiannual. Issued twice a year.

Serial. Refers to publication in a periodical (such as first serial rights).

Sidebar. A short feature that accompanies an article and either elaborates on the human interest side of the story or gives additional information on the topic. It is often set apart by appearing within a box or border.

Simultaneous rights. Selling the rights to the same piece to several publishers simultaneously. Be sure everyone is aware that you are doing so.

Simultaneous submissions. Sending the same manuscript to more than one publisher at the same time. Usually done with nonoverlapping markets (such as denominational or newspapers) or when you are writing on a timely subject. Be sure to state in a cover letter that it is a simultaneous submission and why.

Slander. The verbal act of defamation.

Slanting. Writing an article so that it meets the needs of a particular market.

Slush pile. The stack of unsolicited manuscripts that have arrived at a publisher's office.

Speculation. See "On speculation."

Staff-written material. Material written by the members of a magazine staff.

Subsidiary rights. All those rights, other than book rights, included in a book contract, such as paperback, book club, movie, etc.

Subsidy publisher. A book publisher who charges the author to publish his book, as opposed to a royalty publisher who pays the author.

Synopsis. A brief summary of work from one paragraph to several pages long.

Tabloid. A newspaper-format publication about half the size of a regular newspaper.

Take-home paper. A periodical sent home from Sunday school each week (usually) with Sunday school students, children through adults.

Think piece. A magazine article that has an intellectual, philosophical, or provocative approach to a subject.

Third world. Reference to underdeveloped countries of Asia and Africa.

Trade magazine. A magazine whose audience is in a particular trade or business.

Traditional verse. One or more verses with an established pattern that is repeated throughout the poem.

Transparencies. Positive color slides, not color prints.

Unsolicited manuscript. A manuscript an editor didn't specifically ask to see.

Vignette. A short, descriptive literary sketch or a brief scene or incident.

Appendix B: Glossary of Terms

Vitae/Vita. An outline of one's personal history and experience.

Work-for-hire. Signing a contract with a publisher stating that a particular piece of writing you are doing for him is work-for-hire. In the agreement you give the publisher full ownership and control of the material.

Writers' guidelines. An information sheet provided by a publisher that gives specific guidelines for writing for the publication. Always send a SASE with your request for guidelines.

* I would like to thank Sally Stuart for giving permission to use this Glossary of Terms. It is only one of the many resources offered in her *Christian Writers' Market Guide*.

Appendix C
Trademarks

Following are some common words that are trademarks and should be capitalized. A complete list may be found at http://www.inta.org/tmcklst1.htm. Print out this list or bookmark it for handy reference, and check it whenever you have a question about a product. (Imagine how impressed your editor will be when he or she looks it up and discovers you are right!)

A

Ace elastic bandages
AstroTurf synthetic turf
Atari video games and computers

B

Baggies plastic bags
Band-Aid adhesive bandages
Beanie Babies plush toys
Big Gulp soft drinks
Big Wheel toy vehicles
Books In Print bibliographic reference work series
Books on Tape pre-recorded audio cassette tapes
BOTOX injections
Breathalyzer alcoholic content measuring apparatus
Bundt baking pans

C

Cabbage Patch Kids dolls
Candy Land board game
Caterpillar farm machinery
Chap Stick lip balm
Claymation animated motion picture services
Clearasil acne medication
Cliff Notes study guides
Coca-Cola soft drinks
Coke soft drinks
Cracker Jack candied popcorn (note: singular Jack)
Crock-Pot electric cooking appliance
C-SPAN entertainment services

D

Dacron polyester fiber
Day-Glo inks, paints, pencils
Day-Timer time planner
DeskJet printers
Dictaphone voice processing product
DieHard batteries
Dr Pepper soft drinks (no period after Dr)
Dumpster trash containers
Dunkin' Donuts donuts, restaurants
Du Pont chemicals, fibers
Duracell batteries
Dustbuster portable vacuums

E

Easy-Bake toy oven
Etch A Sketch toy drawing screen
Eveready batteries

F

Federal Express (also **FedEx**) delivery services

Fiberglas yarns, fibers, insulation
Formica laminated plastic
Frigidaire appliances
Frisbee flying discs
Frito-Lay snacks (also **Frito-Lay's, Frito Lay**)

G

Game Boy computer video game
Game of Life board game
GLAD plastic wrap
Good Housekeeping Seal of Approval certification
Grand Ole Opry country music program

H

Häagen-Dazs ice cream
Handi Wipes towelettes
Handiwrap plastic film
Happy Meal dinners
Harley-Davidson motorcycles (also **Harley**)
Heimlich Maneuver anti-choking technique
Hewlett-Packard computer programs
Hide-A-Bed sofa beds
Hula-Hoop plastic hoops
Humvee trucks

I

Igloo insulated water coolers
IKEA furniture
IMAX motion picture theaters
Instamatic cameras (must be used with **Kodak**; otherwise, it's an instant-load camera)
Isotoner gloves

J

Jack in the Box fast food restaurant
Jacuzzi therapeutic whirlpool baths

Jaws of Life rescue tools
Jazzercise dance exercise services
Jeep all-terrain vehicle
Jell-O gelatin, pudding
Jet Ski personal watercraft

K

Kay-Bee toy stores
Kids "R" Us children's clothing stores
Kitty Litter cat box filler
Kmart retail stores
Kool-Aid powdered drink mixes
Krazy Glue adhesives
Krispy Kreme doughnuts

L

LaserJet printers
Laundromat self-service laundries
La-Z-Boy recliners
LEGO plastic construction toys
Levi's sportswear, jeans
LifeSavers (also **Life Savers**), candy
Liquid Paper correction fluid

M

Mac computer
Mack trucks
Magic Kingdom amusement park
Magic Marker felt-tipped pens
MapQuest online access to geographic information
MasterCard credit card services
Matchbox miniature die-cast toy vehicles
Meals-On-Wheels food services

N

Naugahyde artificial leather
No-Doz (also **NoDoz**) drowsiness relief tablets

O

One A Day vitamins
Opryland amusement park

P

Ping-Pong table tennis equipment
Play-Doh modeling compound
Playskool educational toys, children's clothing
PlayStation computer video game
Plexiglas transparent resinous material
Popsicle flavored ices
Pop-Tarts toaster pastry
Porta-John, **Porta Potti**, portable toilets
Post-it self-stick note pads
PowerBar energy bar
PowerPoint presentation graphics program
Pyrex glassware

Q

Q-tips cotton swabs and balls
Quarter Pounder hamburger sandwich

R

RadioShack retail store services
Range Rover all-terrain vehicles
Reader's Digest magazines, books
Realtor real estate broker, member of the National Association of Realtors
Rollerblade in-line skates
Rolls-Royce automobiles

S

Scotch adhesive tape
7-Eleven convenience stores
7UP soft drinks (also **7 UP, Seven-Up**)
Slurpee semi-frozen soft drinks
SpaghettiOs pasta
Styrofoam plastic foam (Note: Cups and other serving items are not made of **Styrofoam** brand plastic foam.)

T

The Home Depot home improvement store chain
Thermos temperature-retaining vessels
Toys "R" Us toy stores

U

U-Haul truck rental services
USA Today newspaper

V

Velcro hook and loop fasteners

W

Waldenbooks bookstore
Wal-Mart retail department store services
Whopper hamburgers
Windbreaker clothing, jackets
Wite-Out correction fluid
WordPerfect word processing software

X

X-Acto knives
Xerox photocopiers (Note: **Xerox** is a noun, not a verb. You do not **Xerox** material, you photocopy it.)

Appendix C: Trademarks

Y

Yahoo! on-line computer services

Z

Ziploc resealable plastic bags

Appendix D
Creative Collaborations

Two Heads are Better than One
by Jennifer Brown Banks

Creative collaborations can be a great way to expand your portfolio, increase your bottom line, and partner with someone whose artistic strengths complement your weaknesses. Whether the union involves a graphic designer teaming up with a writer for the creation of a Web site, several authors coming together to pen an anthology, or a lyricist providing just the right words to complement a musician's score, the team can become a win-win situation for everyone involved.

But much like a marriage, approach these alliances sensibly and with great caution. The wrong partnership can harm the creative process like Kryptonite to Superman.

This epiphany came to me after working with folks who had the best of intentions initially, but little compatibility in key areas. I learned the hard way what makes for a good personal union does not necessarily make for a good business relationship. The price for the mismatch? Strained relations, frustration, and lost productivity.

If you're considering joining forces with someone for future business growth and better opportunities, take heed. Here are ten ways to make your vision a reality and create a winning combination.

1. Get your project off to a good start by providing for the "right fit." Don't be fooled. Not everyone we like, or with whom we enjoy a friendship, makes a good business

partner. Is he or she like-minded? Do you have a similar work ethic? Are your temperaments compatible? Choose wisely.

2. Not sure where to start? Get recommendations for partners from people whose opinion you value—people in your creative circle or writers' group.

3. Put in writing who will be responsible for what and when. The more parameters you have regarding roles, the better.

4. Make sure your strengths and weaknesses complement and do not conflict.

5. Learn the art of compromise. Even in the best scenarios people disagree. Be willing to see your partner's perspective, and to find a happy medium.

6. Carry your weight. Nobody likes a slacker. Not only does laziness create internal strife, but it can also be a detriment to future referrals.

7. Brainstorm individually and collectively. (Some of my best creative ideas come to me when I'm in the solitude of a bubble bath, when my muse is not being pressured.) Your "genius" may come to you while working in your garden. On the other hand, the energy of another mind might set your muse free. Whatever works, work it.

8. Make sure that you and your partner not only have the same agenda, but also the same sense of urgency. If you are very deadline oriented and the other person has to wait for the "right mood," expect tremendous stress, and potential sabotage to the collective success.

9. Remember to treat your partner with respect and as a valued professional. In too many scenarios, one person wants to act like a parent or supervisor. Let go of your ego. "You are not the boss of me."

10. Cheer each other on. The support keeps you both motivated and bonded, and gives you a sense of fun until you reach that finish line.[1]

Appendix E
Copyright Information

The following information can be found in the booklet *Copyright Basics,* published by the U.S. Copyright Office, Library of Congress, 101 Independence Avenue SE, Washington, DC 20559-6000. Web site: www.copyright.gov

How Long Copyright Protection Endures

Works originally created on or after January 1, 1978

A work that was created (fixed in tangible form for the first time) on or after January 1, 1978, is automatically protected from the moment of its creation and is ordinarily given a term enduring for the author's life plus an additional seventy years after the author's death. In the case of "a joint work prepared by two or more authors who did not work for hire," the term lasts for seventy years after the last surviving author's death.

Works originally created before January 1, 1978, but not published or registered by that date

These works have been automatically brought under the statute and are now given federal copyright protection. The copyright duration is generally computed in the same way as for works created on or after January 1, 1978.

Copyright Registration

In general, copyright registration is a legal formality intended to make a public record of the basic facts of a particular copyright. However, registration is not a condition of copyright protection. Even though registration is not a requirement for protection, the copyright law provides several inducements or advantages to encourage registration. Among these advantages are the following:

- Registration establishes a public record of the copyright claim.
- Before an infringement suit may be filed in court, registration is necessary for works of U.S. origin.
- If made before or within five years of publication, registration will establish *prima facie* evidence in court of the validity of the copyright and of the facts stated in the certificate.
- If registration is made within three months after publication of the work or prior to an infringement of the work, statutory damages and attorney's fees will be available to the copyright owner in court actions. Otherwise, only an award of actual damages and profits is available to the copyright owner.
- Registration allows the owner of the copyright to record the registration with the U.S. Customs Service for protection against the importation of infringing copies. For additional information, go to the U.S. Customs and Border Protection Web site at www.cbp.gov/xp/cgov/import and click on "Intellectual Property Rights."

Registration may be made at any time within the life of the copyright. Unlike the law before 1978, when a work has been registered in unpublished form, it is not necessary to make another registration when the work becomes published, although the copyright owner may register the published edition, if desired.

Registration Procedures

Original Registration

To register a work, send the following three elements in the same envelope or package to:

Library of Congress
Copyright Office
101 Independence Avenue SE
Washington, DC 20559-6000

1. A properly completed application form.
2. A nonrefundable filing fee* for each application.
3. A nonreturnable deposit of the work being registered. The deposit requirements vary in particular situations. The general requirements follow.

- If the work is unpublished, one complete copy or phonorecord.
- If the work was first published in the United States on or after January 1, 1978, two complete copies or phonorecords of the best edition.
- If the work was first published in the United States before January 1, 1978, two complete copies or phonorecords of the work as first published.
- If the work was first published outside the United States, one complete copy or phonorecord of the work as first published.
- If at all possible, when sending multiple works, place all applications, deposits, and fees in the same package. If it is not possible to fit everything in one package, number each package (e.g., 1 of 3; 2 of 4) to facilitate processing and, where possible, attach applications to the appropriate deposits.

*For current information on fees, please write the Copyright Office, check their Web site at www.copyright.gov, or call (202) 707-3000.

Forms

Most Copyright Office forms are available on the Copyright Office Web site in fill-in version. Go to www.copyright.gov and follow the instructions. The fill-in forms allow you to enter information while the form is displayed on the screen by an Adobe Acrobat Reader product. You may then print the completed form and mail it to the Copyright Office.

Effective Date of Registration

A copyright registration is effective on the date the Copyright Office receives all the required elements in acceptable form, regardless of how long it then takes to process the application and mail the certificate of registration. The time the Copyright Office requires to process an application varies, depending on the amount of material the office is receiving.

If you apply for copyright registration, you will not receive an acknowledgment that your application has been received (the office receives more than 600,000 applications annually), but you can expect:

- A letter or a telephone call from a Copyright Office staff member if further information is needed or
- A certificate of registration indicating that the work has been registered, or if the application cannot be accepted, a letter explaining why it has been rejected.

Requests to have certificates available for pickup in the Public Information Office or to have certificates sent by Federal Express or another mail service cannot be honored.

If you want to know the date that the Copyright Office receives your material, send it by registered or certified mail and request a return receipt.

Appendix F
Microsoft Word Shortcuts

Following are some of the more widely-used shortcuts for Microsoft Word users:

Ctrl + B	Bold highlighted selection
Ctrl + C	Copy selected text
Ctrl + S	Save file
Ctrl + X	Cut selected text
Ctrl + P	Print
Ctrl + F	Open find box
Ctrl + I	Italicize highlighted section
Ctrl + U	Underline highlighted selection
Ctrl + V	Paste
Ctrl + Y	Redo the last action performed
Ctrl+ Z	Undo the last action performed. (This shortcut is great when you don't know *what* you did to cause that strange screen to pop up. It can also retrieve documents you've accidentally deleted.)
Ctrl + L	Align selected text to the left of the screen
Ctrl + E	Center selected text
Ctrl + R	Align selected text to the right of the screen
Ctrl + M	Indent the paragraph
Ctrl + Home	Move cursor to beginning of document
Ctrl + End	Move cursor to end of document
Ctrl + 1	Single-space lines

Ctrl + 2	Double-space lines
Ctrl + 5	Space-and-a-half lines
F1	Open Help
F7	Spell and grammar check
Shift + F7	Thesaurus check on highlighted word
F12	Save as
Shift + F12	Save
Alt + Shift + D	Insert the current date
Alt + Shift + T	Insert the current time
F2	Rename a file

More shortcuts can be found at http://www.computerhope.com/shortcut/word.htm

Appendix G
Forming a Christian Writers' Group

Two are better than one, because they have a good return for their labor. For if either of them falls, the one will lift up his companion. But woe to the one who falls when there is not another to lift him up.

—Eccl. 4:9-10 NASB

Yelling with excitement, a writer tore open the package of her newly published book. Running into the room and discovering the reason for the shouting, her daughter said, "Mom, it's *only* a book," then ran outdoors. When the second child came in, she said calmly, "I know. You got your book today." After the third child walked by without a comment, the writer kept silent when her husband came home from work.

Later, she called a writer friend, who sent her an e-mail the next day. "My husband and I went out last night and celebrated your book!"

No one understands you like another writer. At every Christian writers' conference I've attended, the director will ask the staff to share words of advice on "where to go from here." I usually tell them to find at least one other writer to meet with on a regular basis.

If you've ever attended a writers' conference, you know that you usually leave on a high and come home eager to share everything that has happened and what you have learned, only to be met with, "The garbage disposal broke." Poof! Like a pin in a balloon, your high is quickly brought low. You need to find someone with whom you can share your dreams, and who will rejoice with you on an acceptance or commiserate with you over a rejection slip. Unfortunately, all too often this *won't* be a family member.

> At times our own light goes out and is rekindled by a spark from another person. Each of us has cause to think with deep gratitude of those who have lighted the flame within us.
>
> —Albert Schweitzer

If you don't have a writing group in your town, perhaps, like Esther, you were brought into the kingdom for such a time as this. The value of a writers' club is fourfold:

1. Meeting regularly with persons who have common concerns and problems provides opportunities to share ideas, enthusiasm, motivation, and experiences. Fellowship afforded by face-to-face writers' clubs stimulates better writing and encourages personal Christian growth and ministry.
2. Spending time together reading and evaluating the work of others benefits beginning and advanced writers alike. They learn from their mistakes and from jointly correcting them. A strong bond is formed and a type of group therapy develops.
3. Listening to speakers and taking part in discussion groups offers information and training. Participation is one of the best ways to learn the latest market trends, and to profit from the experiences (good and bad) of others.
4. Sharing market news by passing around sample copies of Christian magazines or writers' guidelines from book publishers encourages other writers to complete stories, articles, and books to submit to these publishers.

If you would like to begin a Christian writers' group in your area, perhaps the following suggestions will help.

How to Find Members

Word of Mouth

Tell friends at church or work of your interest in forming a writing group. Many people have had a lifelong dream of writing but don't know how to get started. Telephone these friends, share your plan, then set a convenient day and time to meet for organization.

Phone or write a brief letter to Christian writers in your area who may be interested in forming a group. (For a small fee, Sally Stuart provides mailing labels, divided by zip codes. E-mail her at: stuartcwmg@aol.com.) One leader-to-be sent out the following self-addressed printed postcard:

Please fill out and mail back.

_____Yes, I am interested in being part of a Christian Writers' Group.

_____No, I am not interested in a Christian Writers' Group, but please keep me on the mailing list for future updates, mailings, and newsletters.

_____No, I am not interested; please take off mailing list.

Address change/update (or use to add a friend)

Name _____

Street _____

City _____ State _____ Zip _____

Phone _____E-mail _____

Newspaper

Send a news release to your local newspapers and/or weekly shoppers, describing the purpose of the group and inviting visitors. These announcements should be typewritten and double-spaced. Include the following information: Christian writers' organizational meeting, location, date, time, and the name and number of contact person.

At the top of the release, type your name, address, phone number, and e-mail address. Also state date you wish release to be published: i.e., on next church page, one or two weeks before meeting, first Saturday of month, etc. After your group has met for awhile, invite a reporter to do a story on the organization and members.

Churches

Place a notice on your church bulletin board or in your church newsletter. Ask friends to do the same at their churches.

God, help me realize how important it is to have a support system of fellow believers who have kindred spirits. I cannot walk the journey alone—I need friends who will encourage me and lift me up. I am not an island unto myself. Amen. (Emilie Barnes, *Tea Lovers Devotional*)

Schools/Organizations

Send a notice to the directors of your local community education program, senior citizen center, Parks and Recreation Department—or any organization that sponsors writing programs. Request that they tell their classes about your group. Also ask journalism and English professors at local colleges to share the information with prospective writers.

Radio/TV

Many Christian radio and television stations have a calendar of events and will announce your meetings. Notify them well in advance.

Offer to appear on local radio or TV talk shows. Share your writing background and your desires for the club. Allow time for listeners to call in, if program format permits.

Bookstores

Post a flier on bulletin boards or in store windows, especially Christian bookstores. It doesn't have to be fancy, but it does need to be readable and include all the information people need to know.

Book Clubs

Send an announcement to area book clubs.

Christian Communicator

Send an announcement to Sally Stuart at *Christian Communicator* and she will include it in her section on new Christian writers' groups.

Other

Place notices on bulletin boards in supermarkets, photocopy places, libraries, Laundromats. You'll find more writers than you ever knew existed in your area.

Meeting Place

Meeting places include the library, a local church or school, a bank conference room, a mobile home park clubroom, or a senior citizens center. Restaurants will often let you use a room free if participants buy a meal.

For now, eliminate facilities that charge a fee as your treasury will be small or nonexistent. Some clubs who use a church take a collection once a year to help with utilities and extra janitorial duties.

Meet regularly at the same place, if possible. At some facilities, you can book an entire year in advance, which helps in your planning and fliers. Other places, if they are in frequent demand, require you to rebook each month.

Your First Meeting

This basically will be a get-acquainted meeting. If enough people attend, you can divide into pairs. Let the two talk for five or ten minutes and then introduce each other. It's not as important in this introduction to know family details or occupations as it is to know writing accomplishments and dreams. You might wish to have attendees fill out the interest indicator on the next page.

There are four functions of a writers' club:

1. Fellowship
   a. Exchanging experiences
   b. Finding fellow writers

2. Reinforcement
   a. Meeting together with other professional writers
   b. Discovering and studying new markets

3. Improved writing
   a. Studying writers' books
   b. Listening to speakers
   c. Critiquing

4. Submit and Sell
   a. Keeping club records
   b. Giving awards
   c. Contacting editors

Interest Indicator

Name _____ Phone _____ E-mail _____

Address _____

City _____ State _____ Zip _____

Writing Status

___ Beginner (interested; have not submitted or published)

___ Advanced (published, paying markets, not as regularly as I want)

___ Professional (consider writing my calling, publishing regularly)

I am especially interested in writing for:
___children ___ teens ___ singles ___ senior adults ___Christian markets ___ other
Type of writing I'm interested in (1,2,3, etc.)
___poetry ___ fiction ___ personal experience ___ devotionals ___ novels
___ inspirational articles ___ songwriting ___ humor ___ nonfiction ___ other
Marital status _____ # and ages of children:

Education (writing classes, workshops/seminars, correspondence courses, college):

Occupation:
How I heard of club:
What I hope to gain from coming to club:

Ways I am willing to help: ___ publicity ___ hospitality
___ teaching ___ posters
___ secretarial ___ mailings ___ planning committee
___ newsletter ___ clean-up

Membership Questions

To begin with, you probably won't limit the number of members in your group, but as you grow, you might consider:

- dividing the group into beginning and advanced writers
- dividing the group into writing genres, i.e., poetry, fiction, nonfiction, and so on
- beginning a separate group at a different time for professional writers who want serious critiquing

> It takes so little to make us glad,
> Just a cheering clasp of a friendly hand,
> Just a word from one who can understand;
> And we finish the task we long had planned,
> And we lose the doubt and the fear we had—
> So little it takes to make us glad.
>
> —Ida Goldsmith Morris

When to Meet

Do not *ask* the members at your first get-together when they can meet. The ensuing discussion will take the remainder of the meeting as those present give various reasons why they can or cannot come on a particular day. Instead, ask members to write down a day and time they can meet, ascertain the most frequently given answer, and set that as your next meeting date.

Officers

Many clubs do not have any officers except a leader. However, these leaders may be extremely overworked because they haven't learned how to delegate. When they cannot be present, nothing is accomplished during that meeting. The leader may end up feeling like the one who wrote the following:

My group (with one or two exceptions) seems to lean on me. They love coming to the meetings, hang on to every word I say, participate in discussions, but month after month never come with anything to be critiqued, because they have written nothing.

I'm beginning to feel a little resentful of the amount of time I spend in preparation for each meeting, which could otherwise be more profitably spent writing. Do I sound greedy?

One way to avoid this is by selecting a new leader every year. This not only gives your present leader a rest, but also brings in new blood and new ideas to keep your group alive.

The leader, especially in a critique group, should be strong enough to keep things under control. It's easy for a group to stray from the work at hand.

One club set up a committee composed of the past president, present president, and a president already chosen for the next year. These three divided up duties, such as newsletter, secretary (keeping mailing list updated, and so on), and critique leader.

Critiquing Suggestions

A group I belonged to used the motto, "We critique with love." A newcomer said, "I have been 'critiqued with love' long enough and my writings haven't sold. I want you to be honest."

Most writers *do* want honest critiquing. "If I want a pat on the head and a smile, I can let my children read my manuscripts," said one Ohio writer. "But that *isn't* what I want. I want someone to evaluate my writing critically, the same way an editor would. That helps improve my writing and increases my chances for a sale."

Be extra careful of first time attendees and beginning writers. A visitor read a poem at a club one evening. The leader, sensing that the others were ready to offer much-needed suggestions, quickly jumped in with, "That poem sounds like it came out of a very difficult time in your life." The writer admitted it did, and added, "I know it needs a lot of work, but I just wanted to share it with someone." Be positive. At least congratulate the efforts and ideas.

Also, be tactful when a regular member tries a new form of writing. One member, who had sold a number of books and other writings, shared the first act of a play with her group. The leader asked if she had read a particular book on playwriting and when she said she hadn't, he remarked, "It didn't sound like it." Another writer read a chapter of her first novel. "It's a good thing you can write devotionals," one member remarked. "You'll sure never make it as a novelist." Be careful! Even advanced writers need kindness.

Encourage members to be specific. Instead of, "It wasn't clear," state *what* wasn't clear. If it was too long, suggest what could be deleted in the manuscript without changing the meaning. Perhaps it needed more dialogue or a stronger lead. One club leader will not allow anyone to give criticism of a manuscript unless he or she can also offer a way to improve it. While listening, encourage the group to suggest markets for that particular piece.

Discourage members from repeating a criticism. They can say they agree with a comment, but the author doesn't need to hear a weakness stated over and over. If two or more people agree on the same point, however, it's worth the author's serious consideration to rewrite that passage.

A critique group's job is to help the author improve his piece, not cut him down to size or discourage him so he never wants to write again. As someone wrote, "Writers need praising as well as pruning."

Don't argue with the writer's theology. Unless your group is made up solely of your own church members, you will have a number of denominations represented and a variety of beliefs. It isn't important that you agree with the *content* of the writing. Suggestions should be directed only towards the work itself.

In August 1995, a group of Arizona Christian writers, who call themselves "Tuesday's Children," formed a weekly critique group. They still meet at a local restaurant from 9:00 A.M. to noon. Their schedule involves socializing until 9:30, silently critiquing manuscripts until 11:30, then sharing prayer requests and a closing prayer. It has literally become a second family to these writers, or as one describes it, her "therapy group."

How to *Receive* a Critique

Bring your best work. Don't waste others' time with a rough draft you know needs more work, unless you only want to explore the idea further and desire their input. Depending on your group's format, you can either read your manuscript aloud or ask someone else to read it. If someone else reads it, you'll be surprised what *you* catch while listening. Also, while your work is being read, watch other members of the group for their reactions of interest, excitement, agreement, disagreement, laughter, boredom. If audible suggestions are made, let the critics finish. Don't interrupt in self-defense. Listen quietly, make sure you understand the suggestions, and say thank you. Later you can decide what changes you will make.

If your group prefers silent critiquing, bring enough copies of your manuscript for everyone so others can *see* any problems. And if you're bringing the first chapter of a novel, also include a synopsis of the book so members will know where you're heading.

Rewards

When I surveyed others for ideas on starting a writers' group, Marlene Bagnull wrote, "My prayer is that heaven will be different because of what happens through your group—because of the writers who will be helped and encouraged to get the bit of truth God has entrusted to them down on paper so that someone, somewhere, reading it will come to know the Lord. God has given us a tremendous privilege and opportunity to share Him with others. Let us faithfully use the gifts He has given us."

In World War II, Ed Sullivan produced shows for wounded troops at Staten Island Hospital. During one of these shows, as Jimmy Durante was performing, Sullivan poked his head through the curtain. He saw two young lieutenants in the center of the first row. They had each lost an arm and were applauding by clapping their two remaining hands together.

Find another writer. You'll both have a better return for your labor!

> He bids us build each other up;
> And, gathered into one,
> To our high calling's glorious hope
> We hand in hand go on.
>
> "All Praise to Our Redeeming Lord"
> Charles Wesley

Appendix H
10 Ways to Mentor Your Mentor

Mentoring writers is a two-way relationship. Lest you think that you—the person being mentored—receive all the reward, let me assure you that most mentors greatly enjoy this experience. Personally, it is exciting for me to meet new writers at a conference or via the telephone or Internet, encourage them in their writing, and then later open a magazine and see an article or short story written by them, or receive a copy of a published book with their name on the cover.

How do you find a mentor? There are three ways: 1) If you're fortunate, another writer may recognize your potential and offer to mentor you; 2) a friend may recommend someone to you; or 3) you may "click" with a fellow author at a writers' club or conference. It may even be an editor or agent who sees potential in your work and is willing to take the time to help you in your climb up the writing ladder. Be courageous, take the plunge, and ask if he or she is available from time to time to answer questions and offer encouragement. If the answer is yes, then the following ten hints will make this a rewarding experience for you both.

1. Before contacting your mentor with a question, look for the answer on the Internet or at the library. You'll remember it more if you dig for it. Do as much on your own as you can.
2. Make a list of your questions before you call or e-mail. This will ensure you get all the information you need, and you can jot down the answers on your sheet next to each question.

3. Be considerate in the timing if you're phoning. Try not to call on Sundays, holidays, or the day after a conference. Also, remember the different time zones if you're calling another state.

4. If you call, ask if this is a good time or if you should call later. She may have company, be preparing for a conference, or be facing a writing deadline.

5. If you write your mentor with a question, enclose a self-addressed stamped envelope, along with reimbursement for any expenses he may incur, such as photocopies.

6. If you send a manuscript to look over, give him a little time. Don't call three days later and ask what he thought of it. If you're using regular mail, enclose a self-addressed stamped envelope to return your manuscript. You might also include a self-addressed postcard he can stick in the mailbox letting you know he received the material and the approximate time it will take to go over it.

7. Whether sending your manuscript by e-mail or regular mail, to receive more complete feedback, call or write first. Let him know how many pages it will be and if you have a deadline to meet. Allow enough time before this deadline to insert any changes your mentor suggests. Rush jobs should be avoided.

8. If your mentor's services include editing, type the manuscript double-spaced, with at least a one-inch margin on all sides. Number the pages consecutively, not chapter by chapter.

9. When you get your manuscript back, go through it and make a note of any weaknesses your mentor points out. Correct these weaknesses in future manuscripts you send.

10. Sometimes mentors need encouragement too. A "Thinking of You" card or an occasional token of appreciation may arrive on a day when *their* spirits need a lift.

Why would a person be willing to give up valuable time to help a new writer? For me, the answer is that early in my life, many people gave of their time and knowledge to help me. One way of thanking them is to pass on to others what I have learned through the years.

Recently, a friend gave me a copy of her first published book. Inside she had written, "Here's the product of your encouragement. Thanks for your help and love during this project." This letter, and others like it in my file, are why I mentor.

Perhaps after you've been writing for a while, someone will come up to *you* and ask, "Will you be my mentor?" And, of course, you'll say, "Yes."

Appendix I
Guidelines for Devotional Periodicals

(More devotional booklets are listed
in the Christian Writers' Market Guide.
These are only the ones who responded
to my request.)

These Days **Writing Assignment Guidelines**

The Main Purpose of *These Days*: to help readers center their minds and hearts upon worshiping God and to help them have honest and prayerful communion with God so that they might thereby grow spiritually and follow God's will in their daily living. We strive to inspire, enlighten, encourage, and instruct. We are a nonprofit publication with a distribution of approximately 170,000 through church and private subscriptions, mainly within The Cumberland Presbyterian Church, The Presbyterian Church in Canada, the Presbyterian Church (U.S.A.), The United Church of Canada, and The United Church of Christ, but also including readers from many other denominations.

Length, Style, and Format of Devotions: Approx. word count: Devotions, including the prayer, 190; "These Moments," 475; "These Times," 850; bios 50. See the attached sheet and a recent copy of *These Days* for details.

Poetry: Poems should be short. In the devotions, add thirty characters per each line of poetry to the total character count. For the back cover, limit to twenty lines with a maximum of thirty-three characters per line.

Submission of Manuscripts: *We do not accept unsolicited manuscripts. We assign writers the scripture for each week based upon the Sunday Revised Common Lectionary readings. To be considered for an assignment, please request and fill out a Writer Information Form. Submit it with two sample devotions.*

Assigned Writers: Please submit your manuscript by ONE of these methods: (1) by mail on a disk with a printed-out copy enclosed or (2) a PC file attached to e-mail (MS Word file or WordPerfect 5.1 or lower, or PC text file) or (3) Devotions copied and pasted into an e-mail message or an attached file or a Word file on disk is best for us because it preserves the formatting. Devotions pasted into the e-mail messages come through with a return after every line, which has to be deleted. Be sure to keep a copy of the devotions for yourself. Send to: Vince Patton, Editor/*These Days*/100 Witherspoon Street, Louisville, KY 40202-1396, e-mail address: vpatton@presbypub.com.

Bio: Please include in your submitted computer file a short bio of yourself of approx. fifty words that includes your name and address as you want it to appear and denominational affiliation. You may mention some of your publications, organizations, or activities in the bio. We will edit as needed.

Inclusive Language/Biased References: Please avoid masculine pronouns to refer to God or to people in general. Also take care not to disparage, label, or make sweeping generalizations about any particular group of people.

Fact Checking, References: Please verify the accuracy of every fact cited in each devotion. This includes double-checking all names, spellings, dates, quotations, statistics, Scripture references, etc. *For quotations, statistics, controversial assertions, or little-known facts, please identify your outside sources by author, title of publication, publisher, and copyright date in a note* (and the page number if a quotation).

Permissions Needed for Quoting Poetry, Hymns, Prayers, or Other Prose: If you quote more than 250 words of prose or one line of poetry/hymns/prayers, *you must secure permission in writing from the holder of copyright of that source and submit it to us with your devotion;* otherwise, we cannot print it. An exception is a hymn from the Presbyterian Hymnal that does not list a copyright holder. We will not print anonymous quotations or poems.

Time Estimate: Experience has shown that it takes *two or more hours to complete each devotion.*

Researching/Citing the Scripture: Make sure that you understand the context of the passage—what is happening before and after your particular passage. Recommended commentaries include *The Interpreter's One-Volume Commentary on the Bible, The Westminster Bible Companion, The Interpreter's Dictionary of the Bible, The New Interpreter's Bible,* and the notes in the *New Oxford Annotated Bible.* We generally quote from the New Revised Standard Version of the Bible. If you quote from another translation, *please cite the translation beside the quotation. Try to avoid listing the same Scripture passage more than one day for the reader.* Some passages can be broken down to cover two or more days. Please *limit each day's Scripture reading to ten or fewer verses.*

Forward Movement Author Guidelines

For *Forward Day by Day:*
Selection of authors: We welcome new authors to our daily devotional guide. To be considered as a *Forward Day by Day* author, send three sample meditations to us, in care of the editor. The editor issues invitations to write for *Forward Day by Day,* usually between two and three years in advance.

Length: Space is limited. Each meditation, including the Scripture passage, contains approximately 215 words. This does *not* include the date at the top of the page or the lectionary citations and Anglican Communion prayer request at the bottom of the page. Please follow the *Forward Day by Day* format in what you submit (caps for day of week, italics for Bible quotation but not quotation marks, etc.).

Biblical text: Weekday meditations should be based on a verse or sentence of Scripture drawn from the Daily Office Lectionary of the Episcopal Church USA, found on pages 933 to 1001 of the *1979 Book of Common Prayer.* We use the Revised Common Lectionary for Sundays and holy days. Observe major feasts and holy days; we do not normally observe lesser feasts and fasts. Your heading, below the date, should quote your biblical text, generally taken from the NRSV; if a particular wording is required, you may also use the RSV, KJV, TEV, NEB, Jerusalem Bible, or NIV; identify the translation. All Psalm texts, however, must be taken from the Psalter in the Prayer Book. Remember that *Forward Day by Day* is intended to be read without a Bible or Prayer Book at hand.

Techniques: Use concrete images, illustrations, analogies, and parables when possible. First person stories are very effective. Do not assume your readers are Episcopalians or Anglicans. Be sensitive to readers from other churches, non-Christian readers, and readers with limited education. Use inclusive language when possible. Many writers find it helpful to write a day at a time a full year in advance so that they live through the same season of the church year they write about.

Controversial topics: *Forward Day by Day* is not the place to score points on controversial topics. Occasionally, when the Scripture passage pertains to it, an author chooses to say something about such a topic. If you write about a hot-button issue, do so with humility and make certain your comment shows respect for persons who hold a different view.

Computers: We accept manuscripts in MS Word in MAC or PC format. . . . *Always* (1) tell us the software program version used, (2) include a printout, and (3) send a back-up copy of your text via e-mail attachment.

Editing: All *Forward Day by Day* meditations are subject to editing for length, grammar, spelling, clarity, theology, and style. That is one reason authors are not identified by name. (The other reason is that some of our authors are well-known figures and we want the meditations to be judged on their merits, not because the reader likes or dislikes the author.)

Due date: Completed meditations are due in our office one year in advance of the day of your first meditation. Earlier than this date is acceptable; later is not.

> **Send submissions to:**
> The Editor, Forward Movement,
> 300 West Fourth Street, Cincinnati, OH 45202-2666
> *OR send by e-mail to:*
> rschmidt@forwarddaybyday.com
> *Questions? Call us at* 800-543-1813

The Word in Season

Audience: *The Word in Season* is primarily directed to an adult audience that is new to the Christian faith and Lutheran understandings. This market focus has a bearing on your writing in that content needs to be appropriate for people who may not have been raised in the church and therefore they are just beginning their Christian faith journey.

Purpose: *The Word in Season* is designed for the many seasons and cycles of adult faith experience. It is meant to help readers grow in their relationship with God; strengthen their faith journey in its earlier stages; hear the Word of God, a word of grace.

Content:

The Texts: The daily meditations are based on a Bible passage. The Bible texts are predetermined and have been selected from the RCL Daily Readings. This year the texts will parallel the texts in *Bread for the Day* (Augsburg Fortress). The texts are selected thematically and wrap around the Sunday theme. Usually, the cycle begins on Thursday and ends on the following Wednesday.

Developing Your Ideas: The meditations are based on a Bible verse in its context. As you approach each text, take time to read the entire passage as well as the Scripture surrounding it. Check cross references, too, for a wider perspective. After you have studied the passage assigned for the day, select one idea on which to base the meditation. The text is not a jumping-off point for topics you want to write about; it's the heart of the meditation. Select a key Bible verse, or a portion of a verse, from the entire passage and place this before the meditation.

The Word in Season readers want devotions that are true to the Bible. Therefore, when preparing to write your devotions, make use of Bible commentaries, Bible dictionaries, and other resources that will add to your understanding of the text for the day.

Developing Content

1. Choose one idea for your meditation. Make sure that each meditation connects the Bible text with the daily life of the reader.
2. Use short sentences and simple, familiar words. Do not use church language that won't be familiar to unchurched people.
3. One effective way of reaching readers is through a storytelling style. A well-written story may touch people of different ages and experiences in ways that a didactic approach cannot.
4. Use your own experience *if* it genuinely relates to the text and will be of help to others. Tell about times when you have seen or felt God at work or when you have witnessed the truth of Scripture. The third person or a fictitious name may be used, but the story should be true. Remember, the biblical text is primary, and the purpose of the meditation is to draw the reader to God in Christ, not to learn about the writer's personal life. Do not make the story the main focus of the meditation. The Bible text is the focus. The story is only a means to illuminate the text. Be sure you tie your story to the Bible text in a way that it helps the reader apply it to his or her daily life. Do not make the story more than half of the meditation.

5. Avoid the use of terms only church "insiders" understand. Use simple language that will be understood by the person who has not spent a lifetime within the church. Draw on everyday experience and link that with the text. Avoid specific Lutheran references, such as references to the Augsburg Confession, the Small Catechism, or the Book of Concord. Steer away from theological issues that divide Christians from different denominations. Keep your message gospel-centered, and bring encouraging and comforting words to the reader. Do not dwell on the negative or end your meditation on a negative note.

6. If you use Bible references that are not a part of your assigned text, give the complete citation (book, chapter, and verse). Try to avoid quoting other Bible texts if possible—you don't have much space.

7. Avoid quoting any outside source. It is best that you do your own writing, instead of relying on someone else's words. However, if you use quotations, please give us complete information on the source: title, page, date of publication, publisher. It is necessary that you make a photocopy of the quotation, including a photocopy of the title page of the book from which the quote is taken. Avoid quoting poetry. Copyrighted material, including hymn stanzas, should not be used unless you are confident that reprint permission will be granted.

8. Use a variety of names to address God in prayer. Try to use a name that relates to the theme of your devotion.

9. Please use the New Revised Standard Version (NRSV) of the Bible.

This may be the reader's only devotional experience of the day. You have the chance to emphasize the good news that God is with us, regardless of what happens during the day. Ask yourself how your meditation will help the reader experience the Living Word, God's presence.

Some Words of Caution: *The Word in Season* is a devotional booklet and should, as much as possible, be kept free from ideological pronouncements about controversial subjects, lest it lose its devotional value. If your words alienate a reader, he or she is likely to stop reading, or at least to stop hearing your message. Be aware of biases in your writing. Biases may be sexual, racial, socioeconomic, and other. They suggest that one group is by nature inferior to or an adversary of another.

The Word in Season is read throughout the world, so avoid slanting your writing to U.S. residents. Avoid use of masculine pronouns and metaphors when you write about human beings or God. Balance the use of male and female examples in your stories. Ask yourself if the meditation will be helpful to both men and women, married and single, old and young, able and disabled.

You are writing meditations that will be read in about a year, so do not retell (or write commentaries about) movies or stories from television. (Not all of your readers will have seen them, anyway!)

THE SECRET PLACE

Guidelines for Writers

Information about THE SECRET PLACE

THE SECRET PLACE was begun over seventy years ago by a woman who wanted to provide a way to draw Christians closer to Christ and one another. It's now a quarterly devotional magazine with a worldwide readership of over 150,000 and editions in regular print, large print, and Braille. Produced by Judson Press, National Ministries of the American Baptist Churches in the U.S.A., THE SECRET PLACE is published jointly by the American Baptist Churches in the U.S.A. and the Christian Church (Disciples of Christ), Christian Board of Publication. To order THE SECRET PLACE, call 1-800-458-3766 (ABC/USA).

How to Submit Devotions and Poems

THE SECRET PLACE is written solely by freelance writers, and anyone may submit original, unpublished meditations for consideration. Each submission should be typed (if possible), double-spaced, and contain:

- your name, address, and phone number in the upper left-hand corner of each devotion
- a title
- a suggested Scripture passage to be read
- a "Thought for Today," usually a Scripture verse (cite full reference and Bible version) but may also be a pertinent thought. We use the New Revised Standard Version unless you specify otherwise.
- an original meditation of 100 to 200 words that relates to your Scripture reading and "Thought for Today." (Do not quote other sources at length unless you include written permission to do so.)

- a brief concluding prayer.
- your name, city, and state as you would like them to appear in print.

We are especially interested in devotional meditations that:

- are original, creative, and spiritually insightful.
- are concise and focused on one theme.
- explore less familiar biblical passages and themes.
- address urban/suburban as well as rural/nature experiences.
- appeal to young adults as well as older adults.
- encourage outreach, mission, and service.
- are written by men as well as women, young adults as well as older adults.
- reflect racial and cultural diversity and use inclusive language.

We retain the right to edit submissions as necessary for clarity, brevity, and inclusivity of language. Original poems (thirty lines maximum) are also welcome. We work nine to twelve months ahead of schedule, so please plan any seasonal submissions accordingly. We pay $20 for each submission published and purchase first print rights to the use of original, unpublished material in THE SECRET PLACE and unlimited rights for use in related electronic material (www.judsonpress.com). Include a stamped, self-addressed envelope with your submissions (maximum six at a time) for their return if not accepted. E-mail devotions will be responded to via e-mail. Due to the volume of material we receive, we are unable to give updates on the status of individual submissions. Allow six to eight months for notification. Thank you for contributing to this ministry through your support, submissions, and prayers.

Mail your submissions to Kathleen Hayes, Senior Editor, THE SECRET PLACE, P.O. Box 851, Valley Forge, PA 19482-0851 or e-mail them as individual attachments to TheSecretPlace@abc-usa.org.

THE UPPER ROOM

Introduction

The meditations in each issue are written by people just like you, people who are listening to God and trying to live by what they hear. *The Upper Room* is built on a worldwide community of Christians who share their faith with one another.

The Upper Room is meant for an international, interdenominational audience. We want to encourage Christians in their personal life of prayer and discipleship. We seek to build on what unites us as believers and to link believers together in prayer around the world.

Literally millions of people use the magazine each day. Your meditation will be sent around the world, to be translated into more than forty languages and printed in over seventy-seven editions. Those who read the day's meditation and pray the prayer join with others in over one hundred countries around the world, reading the same passage of Scripture and bringing the same concerns before God.

Have God's care and presence become real for you in your interaction with others? Has the Bible given you guidance and helped you see God at work? Has the meaning of Scripture become personal for you as you reflected on it? Then you have something to share in a meditation.

Where do I begin?

You begin in your own relationship with God. Christians believe God speaks to us and guides us as we study the Bible and pray. Good meditations are closely tied to Scripture and show how it has shed light on a specific situation. Good meditations make the message of the Bible come alive.

Good devotional writing is first of all authentic. It connects real events of daily life with the ongoing activity of God. It comes across as the direct, honest statement of personal faith in Christ and how that faith grows. It is one believer sharing with another an insight or struggle about what it means to live faithfully.

Second, good devotional writing uses sensory details—what color it was, how high it bounced, what it smelled like. The more sensory details the writing includes, the better. Though the events of daily life may seem mundane, actually they provide the richest store of sensory details. And when we connect God's activity to common things, each encounter with them can serve as a reminder of God's work.

Finally, good devotional writing is exploratory. It searches and considers and asks questions. It examines the faith without knowing in advance what all the answers will be. It is open to God's continuing self-revelation through Scripture, people, and events. Good writing chronicles growth and change, seeing God behind both.

How do I get started writing a meditation?

When you find yourself in the middle of some situation thinking, "Why—that's how God is, too!" or, "That's like that story in the Bible . . . ," that can become a meditation.

Excellent ideas come from reading and meditating on Scripture, looking for connections between it and daily life. When you see such a helpful connection, here's a simple formula for getting it on paper:

Retell the Bible teaching or summarize the passage briefly.

Describe the situation that you link to the Bible passage, using a specific incident. Write down as many details of the real-life situation as you can. For example, if you write about an incident when people were talking, write down what each person said.

Tell how you can apply this spiritual truth in days to come.

After a few days, look carefully at what you have written. Decide which details best convey your message, and delete the others. Ask yourself whether this insight will be helpful to believers in other countries and other situations. If you feel that it will, add any elements that are necessary to *The Upper Room's* format. Then you are ready to submit your meditation for consideration for possible use in *The Upper Room*.

Tips to keep in mind

Begin with studying and meditating on the Bible so its power supports your words.

Connect Scripture with your own life. Your experience is unique.

Each day's meditation includes a title, suggested Bible reading, quoted Scripture verse, personal witness or reflection on Scripture, prayer, a "thought for the day" (a pithy, summarizing statement), and a "prayer focus" (suggested subject for further prayer).

Meditations should be about 250 words long.

Remember that what you write will be translated for use around the world, so use clear, direct language. Hymns, poems, and word plays such as acrostics or homonyms ("God's presence/presents," "the light of the sun/Son") make meditations unusable.

Poetry and quoted lines from poems cannot be used.
Previously published material cannot be used. Use of material that cannot be verified (such as quotes) will hinder publication.
Very familiar illustrations have little impact and should not be used.

Appendix I: Guidelines for Devotional Periodicals

Avoid preaching ("you should . . . ," "you need to . . . ," "we must . . . ," etc.)

Use language and examples that appeal to the five senses. Tell what you heard, saw, touched, smelled, tasted. When appropriate, use dialogue to tell your story.

Make only one point. Think snapshot, not movie.

Focus on how you can deepen the Christian commitment of readers and nurture their spiritual growth.

Indicate the version of the Bible quoted in the text, and give references for any Scripture passages mentioned.

Seek always to encourage readers to deeper engagement with the Bible.

Include your name and address on each page you submit. Please include a guide for pronouncing your name as our meditations are recorded for an audio edition. If possible, please type your meditation, double-spaced.

Always give the original source of any materials you quote. Meditations containing quotes or other secondary material that cannot be verified will not be used.

When are the deadlines?

We continually need meditations, and you can submit a meditation at any time. However, seasonal material should reach us fifteen months before use date. Below are the due dates and special emphases for the various issues.

January - February Issue

Deadline: August 1 of second year preceding. (For example, 2009 should reach us by Aug. 1, 2007) Special emphases: New Year, Epiphany, Ash Wednesday

March - April Issue

Deadline: October 1 of second year preceding. Special emphases: Lent, Palm Sunday, Maundy Thursday, Good Friday, Easter, World Day of Prayer

May - June Issue

Deadline: December 1 of second year preceding. Special emphases: Mother's Day, Father's Day, Ascension Day, Pentecost, Trinity Sunday

July - August Issue

Deadline: February 1 of preceding year. Special emphases: Creative uses of leisure

September - October Issue

Deadline: April 1 of preceding year. Special emphases: World Communion Sunday, God and our daily work

November - December Issue

Deadline: June 1 of preceding year. Special emphases: Bible Sunday, All Saints' Day, Thanksgiving, Advent, Christmas

Special emphases

January-February issue:

New Year, Epiphany, Ash Wednesday

March-April issue:

Lent, Palm Sunday, Maundy Thursday, Good Friday, Easter, World Day of Prayer

May-June issue:

Festival of the Christian home, Ascension Day, Pentecost, Trinity Sunday

July-August issue:

Creative uses of leisure

September-October issue:

World Communion Sunday, God and our daily work. Tithing/Stewardship

November-December issue:

Bible Sunday, All Saints' Day, Day of Prayer for Persecuted Christians, Thanksgiving, Advent, Christmas

Our response to your work

If your work is being considered for publication, we will send you a postcard, usually within six weeks. Later, if your meditation is chosen for publication, you will receive a copyright release form to return to us. It may be as much as a year before a final decision is made. If you wish to be notified if your work is eliminated from consideration, include a stamped, self-addressed postcard for each meditation.

We buy the right to translate meditations for one-time use in our editions around the world, including electronic and software-driven formats, and to include them in future anthologies of Upper Room material should we choose. We pay $25 for each meditation, on publication.

We are unable to give updates on the status of submitted material or to offer critiques. All published meditations are edited.

Please be sure to include your postal address with each meditation, since we must send a form to be signed if your work is chosen for publication. If you submit by e-mail, send your meditation as the body of the message, not as an attachment.

Meditations cannot be returned, so keep copies of what you submit. Please send no more than three meditations at a time. If you wish to know we have received your work, include a stamped, self-addressed postcard in addition to the one(s) previously mentioned. We will use the postcard to notify you that your work has reached us.

We look forward to receiving meditations from you to be considered for possible use in future editions of *The Upper Room.*

Where do I send my meditation?

Meditations should be mailed to:

Editorial Office
THE UPPER ROOM MAGAZINE
P.O. Box 340004
Nashville, TN 37203-0004
E-Mail: TheUpperRoomMagazine@upperroom.org

(This material is reprinted from *The Upper Room* Web site, www.upperroom.org, copyright 1996-2008 by The Upper Room, Inc. P.O. Box 340004, Nashville, TN 37203-0004, and is used by permission of the publisher.)

Devotions Writer's Guidelines

About *Devotions*. *Devotions* is the adult-level quarterly devotional booklet published by Standard Publishing. It is based on the Daily Bible Readings of the International Sunday School Lessons and is used in many countries throughout the world. Our goal is to encourage, uplift, and inspire Christians to walk triumphantly with God and grow toward Christlikeness.

Remember that a devotional time is an act of prayer or *private worship*. It is a religious exercise or practice other than the regular corporate worship. In our quiet time, worship means an act of expressing respect and reverence toward the divine being. The devotions in the quarterly *Devotions*, the 365 *Devotions*, and the *Companion Devotions* will *direct us to the worship of God rather than the instructions and information for people.*

Use. Most often, *Devotions* is used at home, either in the morning or evening, as part of a devotional time. It may be used by individuals, couples, or families. For those studying with our Standard curriculum, it also helps them prepare for the Sunday school lesson.

Reading Level. Gear your writing to about *an eighth-grade reading level*, which is the same as in many newspapers and newsmagazines. You can achieve ease of understanding by using familiar words and writing mostly short sentences and paragraphs.

Inclusive Language and Tone. Use no sexist language, such as the generic use of man, mankind, and he. But always refer to the persons of the Trinity as masculine. Capitalize the pronouns for deity ("He" "Him" "You" "Your," etc.) Most important: *avoid a tone of preachiness, legalism, and "super-spirituality."* Speak to people where they really live. Be real, not phony. *Avoid Christian clichés.* Also, keep in mind that, because of the short nature of these pieces, they'll tend to have a certain "poetic" feel. Pay attention to the rhythm of your words and sentences as you read them aloud. Does everything flow smoothly?

Theology and Psychology. Be sensitive to issues of theology and biblical interpretation. Since our readers belong to many denominations and theological traditions, they will differ on such things as communion, women in leadership, or eschatology. Try to confine your theological or Bible-interpretation statements to matters on which most or all Christians agree. Also: *Don't forget that human beings have a psychological life, too. Pay attention to psychological issues, and try not to super-spiritualize by glossing over those issues with trite Christianese.*

Submissions. E-mail your devotionals to gwilde1@cfl.rr.com. (Author's note: check *Christian Writers' Market Guide* or Web site for up-to-date submission information.)

Please put your devotionals *within the email* message itself. Do NOT send them as attachments.

We now ask you to send a credit line for the songs you choose. Tell us where you found them: a hymnal/cyber hymnal.

Your manuscript's contents:

Devotions format

Date (Do *not* include year. Example: January 1)

Title of the Devotion

Verse (Type the words of the verse you've chosen from the Scripture passage assigned to this day. If you use a translation other than the *New International Version*, please identify the version, spelled out in full. Do not put the verse in quotation marks.) Example:

Whoever belittles another lacks sense, but an intelligent person remains silent. (Proverbs 11:12, *New American Standard Bible*).

Scripture reference (type Bible book and verse numbers of assigned passage for the day.)

Song (Title of hymn, chorus, worship song—include source credit line)

Devotional paragraphs (Should contain about 165-185 words)

Here is the centerpiece of your devotional, the body. Become familiar with the day's Bible passage and its context. Pick one of the verses in that passage and then construct a devotional to present one main thought to the readers. The usual elements of the body of a devotional are—(1) a "lead" or opening; (2) a tie-in to the day's Scripture passage; and (3) an application to the life of the reader. *The devotional is to be anecdotal and applicational, not an exposition of the passage! Personal or historical story, rather than exegesis.*

One of the best kinds of leads is an anecdote. This can either be something that you have experienced personally or an actual incident that you have heard or read about, whether recent or in the past. Include specific names, dates, and other facts, if possible. Anecdotes can be either serious or humorous. The best anecdotes are those that readers can relate to and that are picture-oriented, producing an image in the reader's mind. Other good leads include striking statements, questions, descriptions, quotations, a re-telling of an historical event, etc.

Of course, the lead should "hook" into the point you are making from the day's Scripture passage, and you may wish to make that relationship explicit. Mentioning the tie-in is especially advisable if there's any danger your readers might not immediately sense what your lead has to do with the Scripture.

Somehow you must make it clear to the readers how your devotional thought *applies to them, personally.* Possibly the lead and/or the tie-in will make the application clear. Or possibly you could write the prayer in such a way that it implies the application. But most likely you'll want to draw out the application explicitly within the body of the devotional.

Note: Do assume the reader is intelligent enough to get your point if you close by simply raising a question or making a subtle, invitational suggestion. The devotional is a gentle, humble invitation to take the next small step of commitment; or to pause a moment to lift our hearts in praise; or to take a moment to become more aware of God's presence. Sometimes it's good just to leave a question in the reader's mind and let him or her struggle a bit with personal application. Isn't that how the Lord so often works with us in daily life?

Bottom line: You are not expected to have "all the answers" all neatly tied up in one devotional. Simply come alongside your reader as a fellow traveler along the pathway of spiritual growth. Take the reader's hand, be willing to admit your own struggles, move forward with the next small step, together . . . . A gentle, humble tone goes far toward influencing others.

A Prayer (about fifty words and in FIRST PERSON only—"I . . . " not "We . . . ".

Biographical information (Give us a brief statement of your "occupation" and/or hobbies—or whatever you'd like to say about you! About thirty words.)

Appendix J
Income Taxes for Writers

Because tax laws change so rapidly, I won't give a lot of technical advice in this chapter. However, you need to know that the Internal Revenue Service considers you, a writer, a self-employed person, which means you have to file a Schedule C. This also means accurate record keeping and saving receipts.

The secret: Whenever you open your checkbook or get into your car, think taxes!

It's easy to remember purchases, such as computers, printer, toner, envelopes, and paper. However, you may forget smaller items such as postage for manuscripts and query letters and requests for sample magazines (if you don't do this via e-mail). Or you may remember the postage, but forget to count the mileage.

Schedule C

On pages 340 and 341 I've included pages 1 and 2 of a Schedule C. Following are instructions for the lines you will use most.

On line A you'll put your name as the owner/proprietor of the business and your Social Security number. (If you are filing jointly with your spouse, use *your* Social Security number here as you are the owner.)

Line B asks for your business code (for a writer it's 812990).

Line C asks for your principal business. (I include three here: freelance writer, editor, proofreader.)

Line D is for an employer ID number (EIN). This is not only for employers. I use this as identification when preparing tax returns for others, and it can also be used to give editors and publishers instead of your Social Security number. This EIN can be used

SCHEDULE C
(Form 1040)

Department of the Treasury
Internal Revenue Service   (99)

Profit or Loss From Business

(Sole Proprietorship)

▶ Partnerships, joint ventures, etc., generally must file Form 1065 or 1065-B.

▶ **Attach to Form 1040, 1040NR, or 1041.**   ▶ **See Instructions for Schedule C (Form 1040).**

OMB No. 1545-0074

2008

Attachment
Sequence No. **09**

Name of proprietor

Social security number (SSN)

A Principal business or profession, including product or service (see page C-3 of the instructions)	**B** Enter code from pages C-9, 10, & 11 ▶
C Business name. If no separate business name, leave blank.	**D** Employer ID number (EIN), if any

E Business address (including suite or room no.) ▶
City, town or post office, state, and ZIP code

F Accounting method: **(1)** ☐ Cash   **(2)** ☐ Accrual   **(3)** ☐ Other (specify) ▶

G Did you "materially participate" in the operation of this business during 2008? If "No," see page C-4 for limit on losses   ☐ Yes   ☐ No

H If you started or acquired this business during 2008, check here   ▶ ☐

Part I   Income

1	Gross receipts or sales. **Caution.** See page C-4 and check the box if:	
	• This income was reported to you on Form W-2 and the "Statutory employee" box on that form was checked, or	
	• You are a member of a qualified joint venture reporting only rental real estate income not subject to self-employment tax. Also see page C-4 for limit on losses. ▶ ☐	**1**
2	Returns and allowances	**2**
3	Subtract line 2 from line 1	**3**
4	Cost of goods sold (from line 42 on page 2)	**4**
5	**Gross profit.** Subtract line 4 from line 3.	**5**
6	Other income, including federal and state gasoline or fuel tax credit or refund (see page C-4).	**6**
7	**Gross income.** Add lines 5 and 6 ▶	**7**

Part II   Expenses. Enter expenses for business use of your home **only** on line 30.

8	Advertising	**8**	**18**	Office expense	**18**
9	Car and truck expenses (see page C-5)	**9**	**19**	Pension and profit-sharing plans	**19**
10	Commissions and fees	**10**	**20**	Rent or lease (see page C-6):	
11	Contract labor (see page C-5)	**11**		**a** Vehicles, machinery, and equipment	**20a**
12	Depletion	**12**		**b** Other business property	**20b**
13	Depreciation and section 179 expense deduction (not included in Part III) (see page C-5)	**13**	**21**	Repairs and maintenance	**21**
			22	Supplies (not included in Part III)	**22**
			23	Taxes and licenses	**23**
			24	Travel, meals, and entertainment:	
				a Travel	**24a**
14	Employee benefit programs (other than on line 19)	**14**		**b** Deductible meals and entertainment (see page C-7)	**24b**
15	Insurance (other than health)	**15**	**25**	Utilities	**25**
16	Interest:		**26**	Wages (less employment credits)	**26**
a	Mortgage (paid to banks, etc.)	**16a**	**27**	Other expenses (from line 48 on page 2)	**27**
b	Other	**16b**			
17	Legal and professional services	**17**			

28	**Total expenses** before expenses for business use of home. Add lines 8 through 27	▶	**28**
29	Tentative profit or (loss). Subtract line 28 from line 7		**29**
30	Expenses for business use of your home. Attach **Form 8829**		**30**
31	**Net profit or (loss).** Subtract line 30 from line 29.		
	• If a profit, enter on both **Form 1040, line 12,** and **Schedule SE, line 2,** or on **Form 1040NR, line 13** (if you checked the box on line 1, see page C-7). Estates and trusts, enter on **Form 1041, line 3.**		**31**
	• If a loss, you **must** go to line 32.		
32	If you have a loss, check the box that describes your investment in this activity (see page C-8).		
	• If you checked 32a, enter the loss on both **Form 1040, line 12,** and **Schedule SE, line 2,** or on **Form 1040NR, line 13** (if you checked the box on line 1, see the line 31 instructions on page C-7). Estates and trusts, enter on **Form 1041, line 3.**	**32a** ☐ All investment is at risk. **32b** ☐ Some investment is not at risk.	
	• If you checked 32b, you **must** attach **Form 6198.** Your loss may be limited.		

For Paperwork Reduction Act Notice, see page C-9 of the instructions.   Cat. No. 11334P   Schedule C (Form 1040) 2008

Schedule C (Form 1040) 2008   Page **2**

Part III   **Cost of Goods Sold** (see page C-8)

33   Method(s) used to
value closing inventory: **a** ☐ Cost   **b** ☐ Lower of cost or market   **c** ☐ Other (attach explanation)

34   Was there any change in determining quantities, costs, or valuations between opening and closing inventory?
If "Yes," attach explanation   . . . . ☐ **Yes**   ☐ **No**

35   Inventory at beginning of year. If different from last year's closing inventory, attach explanation . . | **35** |

36   Purchases less cost of items withdrawn for personal use   . . . . | **36** |

37   Cost of labor. Do not include any amounts paid to yourself . . . . | **37** |

38   Materials and supplies . . . . | **38** |

39   Other costs   . . . . | **39** |

40   Add lines 35 through 39   . . . . | **40** |

41   Inventory at end of year   . . . . | **41** |

42   **Cost of goods sold.** Subtract line 41 from line 40. Enter the result here and on page 1, line 4 . . | **42** |

Part IV   **Information on Your Vehicle.** Complete this part **only** if you are claiming car or truck expenses on line 9 and are not required to file Form 4562 for this business. See the instructions for line 13 on page C-5 to find out if you must file Form 4562.

43   When did you place your vehicle in service for business purposes? (month, day, year) ▶ ...... / ...... / ......

44   Of the total number of miles you drove your vehicle during 2008, enter the number of miles you used your vehicle for:

   a   Business ....   **b**   Commuting (see instructions) ....   **c**   Other ....

45   Was your vehicle available for personal use during off-duty hours?   . . . . ☐ **Yes**   ☐ **No**

46   Do you (or your spouse) have another vehicle available for personal use?.   . . . . ☐ **Yes**   ☐ **No**

47a   Do you have evidence to support your deduction?   . . . . ☐ **Yes**   ☐ **No**

   b   If "Yes," is the evidence written? .   . . . ☐ **Yes**   ☐ **No**

Part V   **Other Expenses.** List below business expenses not included on lines 8–26 or line 30.

....

....

....

....

....

....

....

....

48   **Total other expenses.** Enter here and on page 1, line 27   . . . . | **48** |

Schedule C (Form 1040) 2008

for opening a bank account, applying for business licenses, and filing a tax return. (See http://www.irs.gov/businesses/small/article/0,,id=102767,00html.)

Line E is your business address—either your home or a rented office.

Line F is your accounting method—which will normally be cash (this means you count your income as you receive it).

Line G—yes, you did "materially participate" in the operation of this business.

Check Line H if this is the first year you're filing a business return.

On lines 1, 3, 5, and 7, show your total income for the year. (Ask your accountant about returns and allowances if you keep an inventory.) This income will include checks from any manuscripts you sell, book royalties, and money you earn speaking.

Deductions

Below is a list of deductions allowed on the Schedule C, with a few hints on each one. (Line numbers refer to the 2008 form on page 340.)

Line 8, Advertising. This includes such things as business cards, and ads placed in newspapers or magazines offering your services as a writer, to buy or sell business equipment, or to publicize a workshop. Also include on this line books given away for advertising purposes.

Line 9, Car and truck expenses. There are two ways you can deduct your car expenses, either by deducting your mileage or using actual expenses. If the former, keep track of mileage to the post office, the office supply store, your writers' club or workshop, attending a business luncheon or dinner, or other business-related activities. Keep a list of places you frequent often so you don't have to keep track each time. (MapQuest is a great help on this.) Multiply the total miles by the per mile amount allowed by IRS, and add to this any cash amounts you paid someone to drive you to a business event. (Note: The amount IRS allows changes every year, so you need to determine the current amount for your tax year.)

If you take actual expenses, first determine the percentage you used your car for business, and multiply this percentage by what you spent on gas, oil, repairs, tags, insurance, loan interest, and so on. If you choose this method (and most people don't unless they use their auto more than 50 percent for business), you must keep *all* receipts.

Line 10, Commissions and fees. The only time you might use this is if you pay a percentage of your royalties to an agent for helping you sell your book, or if you pay someone a commission for helping you with a conference.

Line 11, Contract labor. Did you pay someone to type your manuscript, to do research, to transcribe tapes? The amount goes on this line. Be careful, however. If this person works on your property, uses your equipment, and has assigned hours, he or she is considered an employee, subject to withholding, not an independent contractor.

Line 13, Depreciation. This is too complicated a subject to cover in this chapter, but basically if an item has a useful life of over a year, it can be depreciated over a period of time or, if you choose, in the first year of purchase. You will complete Form 4562 for this. (See www.irs.gov for a list of booklets concerning depreciation.)

Line 15, Insurance (other than health). This line covers insurance for a rented office space. (The prorated portion of insurance, mortgage interest, and real estate taxes for a home office is shown on Form 8829.)

Line 16, Interest. Because you can no longer take interest on personal credit cards on Schedule A, you may want to keep one credit card solely for business purchases and deduct the interest on this line. For example, if you have an airlines credit card for business travel, or an account with an office supply store, you can deduct the interest here. These cards can be in your own name or issued under the name of your business.

Line 17, Legal and professional services. Did you pay someone to prepare your taxes last year because of your writing? Did you ask someone to look over a contract? Did you need legal help to collect money due you for a writing project? Deduct this here.

Line 18, Office expense. This is not the same as office supplies. This line is for expenses for your home office or rented office and includes such things as drapes, ceiling fans, and redecorating.

Line 20, Rent or lease. This includes renting an office or business machine. However, if you rent an item and later purchase it, you need to amend this year's return and show depreciation. You also show on this line if you rented a post office box or a safety deposit box for your business papers.

Line 21, Repairs and maintenance. This covers any repairs to your machines, as well as a maintenance agreement you purchase for a computer, copier, or printer.

Line 22, Supplies. The list is endless here: stapler/staples, paper clips, paper, envelopes, toner, pens/pencils, day planners, business card holders, software—anything you buy *specifically* for use in your business. I find it helps to keep two sets of these supplies—one for the family and one for your office.

Line 23, Taxes and licenses. Some states have a personal property tax for items purchased for a business. Others require a license to operate a business out of the home. Check your city's zoning laws.

Line 24, Travel, meals, and entertainment. This line covers such things as airline tickets, rental cars, taxi fares, shuttles, and curbside baggage fees. Meals include out-of-town and overnight stays, as well as taking someone out for a business luncheon or dinner. Entertainment can include taking a client to a play, a sporting event, a concert, or another activity. Only a certain percentage of the cost for meals and entertainment is deductible, however. Any cleaning or laundry expenses while on a business trip will also be included here.

Line 25, Utilities. This is for a rented office space only. (Utilities for a home office are included on Form 8829.)

Line 27, Other expenses. These expenses are covered in Part V, page 2, of your Schedule C and include such things as:

Conferences/courses. Note: These conferences or courses must be to "improve your skills in your present occupation," not to learn a new one. In other words, you must show in some way—submission records, rejection letters, assignments, and so on—that you've been working at writing for a while and want to improve your skills. You're not taking a course or attending a conference just to *learn* how to become a writer.

Permissions. Did you pay to use a quotation in a book or article? Deduct this here.

Contest fees. Any fee to enter a manuscript in a contest.

Critiquing/editing. Did you pay someone to edit your manuscript? That cost is deductible.

Postage. Until editors began accepting queries and manuscripts via e-mail, this was a writer's biggest expense. You can buy a roll of stamps strictly for business, keep track of the expense as it happens, or invest in a postage meter.

Books/publications/tapes/CDs. As a writer, you are fortunate that almost every periodical you buy can be deducted as it is a possible market. Be honest, however, and don't count a magazine you buy purely for entertainment without any thought of ever submitting anything to that editor. Books on writing or reference materials can be counted here, as well as tapes and CDs bought at writers' conferences.

Printing/copies. This includes letterhead stationery (or that could also go under advertising or supplies), photocopies of manuscripts, copies of handouts for conferences, and any books/booklets you self-publish.

Gifts/cards. Keep track of gifts and cards you buy for other writers, or for someone who helped you with a project or a workshop. (Right now the deductible limit for gifts per person is $25.)

Camera/film/developing. A camera you buy strictly for business can be deducted 100 percent here, or prorated if you only use it partly in your writing. Film and developing for writing-related photographs are also deducted here, along with professional photos you have taken at a studio.

Tape recorder/tapes/digital recorders. Used for interviewing purposes.

Hotel/motel. This can also go under travel, and includes any overnight trips for a conference or writing project. If you stayed extra nights for personal reasons, deduct only the nights required for business. If you took your spouse along, determine what the cost would be for *one person only* and deduct only that amount, unless it's necessary for him or her to accompany you to help with your business.

Dues. This relates to dues for a writers' association, not a club for entertainment purposes only.

Phone/Internet. At one time IRS allowed you to prorate your personal phone and take a percentage for business. Now, in order to deduct telephone expenses, you need a separate line. If you have only one line, however, you still can deduct any long-distance business calls, along with such things as Call Waiting or Conference Calling installed specifically for business. Your monthly Internet cost can also be deducted here, as well as a cell phone used mainly for business.

Bank charges. If you have a separate business account, you can deduct any monthly charges and the cost of your checks.

Office in home. This can be complicated, so I will just touch on the subject here, but suffice it to say that it must be a room or a portion of a room used *only* for business. The IRS can get particular on this, especially if you also have W-2 income from an outside job. Be ready to show proof if you take this deduction.

If you choose to take it, keep records on such things as real estate taxes; mortgage interest; home insurance; repairs such as roof, air conditioning, heating, and plumbing; landscaping; exterminating; carpet cleaning; and so on. Figure the percentage of square feet you use for business and multiply these expenses by this percentage.

You can also depreciate the business portion of your home but that's a little too much to get into in this chapter. Talk to your accountant about this.

When you've added up all your expenses, subtract them from your income. This is the amount you not only pay income taxes on, but also your self-employment tax. (This is shown on Schedule SE.) If you work for an employer, he takes Social Security out of your paycheck, matches it, and sends it in quarterly to the government. As a self-employed person, you pay the total amount based on your net income after expenses.

One word here: You do not have to wait until you have writing income to subtract your expenses. You only have to *prove* that your goal is to make a profit. You do this by keeping good records—of query letters, submissions, conferences, and so on. Your Schedule C will then show a loss, which you transfer over to page 1, line 12, of Form 1040 (or whichever line reads "Business Income or Loss").

If you are not sure whether you are running a business or simply enjoying a hobby, here are some of the factors you should consider:

- Does the time and effort put into the activity indicate an intention to make a profit?
- Do you depend on income from the activity?
- If there are losses, are they due to circumstances beyond your control or did they occur in the start-up phase of the business?
- Have you changed methods of operation to improve profitability?
- Do you have the knowledge needed to carry on the activity as a successful business?
- Have you made a profit in similar activities in the past?
- Does the activity make a profit in some years?
- Do you expect to make a profit in the future from the appreciation of assets used in the activity?

An activity is presumed carried on for profit if it makes a profit in at least three of the last five tax years, including the current year. If your activity is not carried on for profit, allowable deductions cannot exceed the gross receipts for the activity.

(For more information see IRS Publication 535 Business Expenses.)

Record Keeping

Whether using a computer program such as Quicken or keeping handwritten records, write down your income and expenses every day. Total them up at the end of each month, with a running year-to-date total, and at the end of December you have your total for the year.

Summary

If you prepare your own taxes, a program such as Turbo Tax walks you through each line. If you use an accountant, find one who has worked with writers. Either way, you must keep good records. The best CPA or tax software can't help you if you don't know how much you made or how much you spent on business-related items.

Give to Caesar what is Caesar's.

—Matt. 22:21 NIV

Endnotes

Writing Is a Calling

1. Victor Frankl, *The Cumberland Presbyterian,* March 1, 1981, p. 3.
2. Sherwood Eliot Wirt, with Ruth McKinney. *You Can Tell the World* (Minneapolis, MN: Augsburg Publishing House, 1975), pp. 12, 23, 66.

Introduction

1. "Carving Bars Behind Bars," *Mesa* (AZ) *Tribune,* December 18, 1986.
2. Published by Vocatio Publishers, www.vocatio.us. English version may be ordered on Kitty Chappell's Web site: www.kittychappell.com

Chapter 2—Fiction

1. Colleen Reece, "The Greatest Short-Short," *The Christian Writer,* June 1986, p. 27.
2. Bea Carlton is the author of fourteen mystery novels, two young adult novels, and three puppetry books. Visit her Web site at www.beacarlton.com
3. Katherine Paterson, "People I Have Known," *The Writer,* April 1987, pp. 22-24.
4. Nancy Jane Sharp, "Hire Real Characters," *The Writer,* September 1987.
5. Adapted from Carole Gift Page, "Fiction Facts—Similarities and Differences: The Novel and the Short Story," *Christian Communicator,* April 1992, pp. 7-8. Carole is the author of forty-seven books, including *Becoming a Woman of Passion* and *The House on Honeysuckle Lane.*
6. Customline Wordware www.customline.com. Used by permission.

Chapter 3—Nonfiction

1. www.aacap.org/cs/root/fcts_forfamilies/teen_suicide. Accessed 5/23/09.
2. Paul Thornton, "Coming Full Circle," *Lutheran Standard,* May 3, 1985, p. 15.
3. Larry Mowrey, *Come Ye Apart*, Nazarene Publishing House, Kansas City, Missouri, November 30, 1996.

Chapter 4—Writing Devotionals and Fillers

1. Marlene Bagnull. Expanded from "Contest Criteria," printed in the May-June 1985 issue of *Cross & Quill.* Copyright 1985 Christian Writers Fellowship. Used by permission of author.

Chapter 5—Writing and Selling Your Poetry

1. Peter Finch. *How to Publish Your Poetry* (London, England: Allison & Busby Writers' Guides, 1998).
2. "In God's Own Time," by Dave Clark and Danny Bunnelle, © 1984 Emmanuel Music (ASCAP); all rights reserved. Reprinted by special permission of Integrated Copyright Group, Inc., Nashville, Tennessee.
3. E. Ruth Glover, *Standard*, December 20, 1992.
4. Sherri Langton, "Handyman," *Standard*, November 13, 1994. Used by permission of author.
5. Barbara Steiner, "Writing Poetry for Children," *Writer's Digest,* February 1986, p. 35.
6. http://en.wikipedia.org/wiki/Print_on_Demand
7. www.ahajokes.com/eng003.html

Chapter 7—Conducting An Effective Interview

1. Dennis Hensley, talk at American Christian Writers' conference, Phoenix, Arizona, November 1999. Used by permission.
2. Hope Clark, editor, FundsforWriters, www.fundsforwriters.com/Writer's Digest 101 Best Web Sites for Writers—2001 through 2008.

Chapter 8—Travel

1. Bob Brooke, "Travel Article Types," www.WritersCrossing.com. Used by permission of Pennsylvania-based writer Bob Brooke; visit his Web site at www.bobbrooke.com
2. See www.sirlinkslot.net/travel.html for names, addresses, phone, and fax numbers of every tourism office in the United States. Information on other countries is also available.

3. Kayleen J. Reusser, "Travel That Pays," *Christian Communicator*, July 2005, pp. 5-6.
4. "Around Oslo, Indoors and Out," Perri Glass. *New York Times,* February 3, 2002, section 5, p. 8.

Chapter 9—Writing for Children

1. Writer of poetry and fiction, Hannah Gomez also works as an associate editor for Kiwibox.com and as a book reviewer for TeenReads.com
2. © Joëlle Anthony, 2007. Originally published in the Society of Children's Book Writers and Illustrators Bulletin, July/Aug. 2007. Used by permission.
3. Jean Conder Soule, "Children's Markets: Three Things to Know," *Christian Writers Newsletter*, February 1989, p. 3.

Chapter 10—Writing the Personal Experience Story

1. Jeanette Littleton, "Editor's Corner" column, *Christian Communicator,* April 1999, p. 3.
2. Tim Riter, author and educator, writer of *Not a Safe God* and the Twelve Lies series.

Chapter 11—Other Types of Writing

1. Donna Clark Goodrich, *Through the Bible Puzzles* (Cincinnati, OH: Standard Publishing, out of print).
2. www.citehr.com/24361-some-dumb-ads-free-classifieds.html
3. http://www.religioustolerance.org/chr_kid.htm
4. http://www.homeschooloasis.com/storehs_obituary_of_pillsbury.htm

Chapter 13—Writing and Selling Your First Book

1. Lolly Gasaway, University of North Carolina. http:/www.unc.edu/~unclng/public-d. htm. Used by permission.
2. Thanks to Cecil Murphey for his permission to use this letter.
3. Terri Pilcher, "Fast Facts: Top Online Research Sites for Writers," *Christian Communicator,* May 2006, pp. 3-4.

Chapter 15—Editing Hints

1. Judith Ross Enderle and Stephanie Gordon Tessler, "The Fiction-writer's Polish Kit," *Writer's Digest*, May 1986, pp. 29-30.

2. Max Lucado, *No Wonder They Call Him the Savior* (Portland: Multnomah Press, 1986), pp. 105-6.
3. H. V. Morton, *In the Steps of the Master* (London: Methuen & Co.), p. 1943.
4. June Masters Bacher, *The Heart Remembers* (Eugene, OR: Harvest House Publishers, 1991).
5. Michael Hemmes, "The Terrible 20," *Writer's Digest*, June 1986.
6. William G. Tapply, "Don't Be a Showoff," *The Writer,* 2005, p. 23.
7. Source unknown. Received in conference handout.

Chapter 17—Other Sources of Income

1. *Chicago Manual of Style, 15th ed., rev.* (Chicago, IL: University of Chicago Press, 2003). Used by permission.
2. Bruce O. Boston, ed., *STET! Tricks of the Trade for Writers and Editors* (Alexandria, VA: Editorial Experts, Inc., 1986), p. 8.
3. Used by permission of Dr. Mary Ann Diorio. All rights reserved. Dr. Diorio is a widely published author, speaker, and writing coach, who may be reached at maryann@maryanndiorio.com
4. Kathy Collard Miller is the author of 49 books and over 190 magazine articles. She is a popular women's conference speaker. Visit her at www.KathyCollardMiller.com
5. Read his story in *Healing in God's Time* by Donna Clark Goodrich (Washington, DC: Believe Books, 2009).

Chapter 18—Writer's Block

1. Lisa R. Cohen, "Is It Really Writer's Block?" http://www.sff.net/People/LisaRC/isit.htm

Chapter 19—Time Management: 12 Ways to Add More Hours to Your Writing Day

1. Suzanne Eller. http://tsuzanneeller.com/ Used by permission.
2. Charlotte Hale Allen, "Just 15 Minutes a Day," *Guideposts*, December 1978, p. 9. Taken from *Full-Time Living* (Old Tappan, NJ: Fleming H. Revell, 1978). Italics added in #7.
3. Emilie Barnes, *15 Minutes Alone with God* (Eugene, OR: Harvest House Publishers, 2003), p. 25.
4. Bob Phillips, *42 Days to Feeling Great* (Eugene, OR: Harvest House Publishers, 2001), p. 163.
5. Tim Hansel, *When I Relax I Feel Guilty* (Elgin, IL: David C. Cook Publishing Co., 1979), p. 22.

6. Kim Thomas, *Living in the Sacred Now* (Eugene, OR: Harvest House Publishers, 2001), p. 109.
7. Brandt Dodson, author of the Colton Parker Mystery Series.
8. Elizabeth George, *Life Management for Busy Women* (Eugene, OR: Harvest House Publishers, 2002), p. 146.

Chapter 20—How to Handle Rejection

1. http://woddaze.blogspot.com/2008/08/september-1-author-rejection-day.html
2. Shirley Pope Waite, "You're in Good Company," *Christian Communicator*, January 2002, p. 20.
3. James C. Magruder, *Christian Communicator*, January 1990, p. 9.

Chapter 21—Social Networking and Online Promotions

1. I want to thank Joy Moore for writing most of this chapter, and also Kathi Macias for sharing her experiences in social networking. This chapter would not have been included in this book without their expertise.
2. There are currently two main types of electronic book readers, the Kindle and the Sony Reader. Each uses a different electronic format for uploading books. In addition, many other electronic devices, including the Blackberry, the Palm, and the iPhone, can upload electronic books. It is important to discuss with your publisher which electronic book formats are right for your book. The cost to produce these electronic copies is small, therefore using as many as possible will benefit book sales. For more information on Kindle, go to <http://en.wikipedia.org/wiki/Amazon_Kindle>.

Conclusion

1. http://en.wikipedia.org/wiki/Hank_Aaron
2. Stan Toler and Martha Bolton. *God Has Never Failed Me, But He Sure Has Scared Me to Death a Few Times!* (Tulsa, OK: Honor Books, 1998), p. 107.
3. *Facts on File* (New York: Rand McNally & Co., October 7, 1993), p. 759B1.

Appendix D—Creative Collaboration

1. Jennifer Brown Banks of Corporate and Creative Communications is a veteran freelance writer, editor, consultant, and popular relationship columnist residing in Illinois. Used by permission. http://www.writergazette.com/jenniferbrownbanks.shtml

CPSIA information can be obtained at www.ICGtesting.com
Printed in the USA
BVOW062248311011

274959BV00003B/1/P